SOCIAL MEASUREMENT
SOCIAL SURVEY

To Sir Roger Jowell

Social Measurement through Social Surveys

An Applied Approach

Edited by

MARTIN BULMER
University of Surrey, UK

JULIE GIBBS
City University, London, UK

LAURA HYMAN
University of Surrey, UK

ASHGATE

Published by
Ashgate Publishing Limited
Wey Court East
Union Road
Farnham
Surrey, GU9 7PT
England

Ashgate Publishing Company
Suite 420
101 Cherry Street
Burlington
VT 05401-4405
USA

www.ashgate.com

British Library Cataloguing in Publication Data
Social measurement through social surveys : an applied
  approach.
  1. Social sciences--Research--Methodology.
  I. Bulmer, Martin. II. Gibbs, Julie. III. Hyman, Laura.
  300.7'2-dc22

Library of Congress Cataloging-in-Publication Data
Bulmer, Martin.
  Social measurement through social surveys : an applied approach / by Martin Bulmer,
Julie Gibbs and Laura Hyman.
      p. cm.
  Includes bibliographical references and index.
  ISBN 978-0-7546-7487-0 (hbk) -- ISBN 978-0-7546-7488-7 (pbk)
  1. Social surveys. 2. Sociology--Statistical methods. 3. Sociometry. I.
Gibbs, Julie, 1977- II. Hyman, Laura. III. Title.
  HM538.B85 2009
  302.01'5195--dc22
                                                                        2009041396
  ISBN 9780754674870 (hbk)
  ISBN 9780754674887 (pbk)

Mixed Sources
Product group from well-managed
forests and other controlled sources
www.fsc.org Cert no. SA-COC-1565
© 1996 Forest Stewardship Council
FSC

Printed and bound in Great Britain by
MPG Books Group, UK

Contents

List of Figures

List of Tables

Notes on Contributors

Jonathan Allen is currently a Senior Research Officer at the Ministry of Justice. He has an MSc in Social Research Methods and a BSc in Sociology, both from the University of Surrey, UK, where he also tutored. Upon graduation he took up a position at the Home Office working on the British Crime Survey (BCS), where he worked for a number of years with responsibilities including research into fear of crime, confidence in the criminal justice system, policing issues and violent crime. With the latter he re-designed the Inter-personal Violence module, which remains the leading national indicator for the measurement of the extent of domestic and sexual violence in England and Wales.

Peter Brierley is a statistician, originally working as a teacher in Southampton, then joining the government's Statistical Service, serving in both the Ministry of Defence and the Cabinet Office. Moving to the charitable sector, he became a director of the Bible Society and in 1983 began MARC Europe which after ten years became Christian Research, of which he was Executive Director for 14 years. In these later capacities he undertook eight national church censuses in England, Wales and Scotland, the most recent results being published in *Religious Trends* and *Pulling Out of the Nosedive.* He has also undertaken much leadership training with the clergy and written up vision building in *Coming Up Trumps!*, a theme continued in *God's Questions*, due for publication in 2010.

Ian Brunton-Smith is a Lecturer in Criminology and Survey Methodology in the Department of Sociology at the University of Surrey. He has also worked as a criminologist in the Crime Surveys team at the Home Office. His recent research has examined the effect of neighbourhood level characteristics on individual's levels of fear of crime, combining census and administrative data with information from the British Crime Survey. He has also been assessing the competing influences of interviewer and clustering effects on survey outcomes, and has previously looked at panel attrition effects in longitudinal surveys.

Martin Bulmer is Emeritus Professor of Sociology at the University of Surrey. From 2000 to 2008 he was director of the ESRC Question Bank, an online resource of social survey questionnaires which is now part of the Survey Resources Network (SRN) <URL:http://surveynet.ac.uk/>. From 2002 to 2008 he also directed the ESRC Survey Link Scheme, now also part of the SRN. He is editor of the academic journal *Ethnic and Racial Studies*. His academic research and publications have been in the fields of the methodology of social research, the history of sociology and social research, and the application of social science to policy making. His most recent collection is *Secondary Analysis of Survey Data* (edited with P. Sturgis and N. Allum), four volumes published by Sage in 2009.

Bob Erens is Director of the Survey Methods Unit at the National Centre for Social Research (NatCen), having previously directed the Health Research Group at NatCen. Bob has over 20 years' experience of designing and running large and complex surveys. He was one of the investigators on the second National Survey of Sexual Attitudes and Lifestyles (Natsal) in 2000 and is an investigator on the third Natsal taking place in 2010. He has co-authored a number of journal articles arising from Natsal 2000, as well as on methodological issues including surveying ethnic minorities and designing questions on sensitive topics.

Julie Gibbs is a Senior Research and Information Officer for the Information Centre about Asylum and Refugees (ICAR) at City University, London. ICAR provides information and research on asylum and refugee issues and is an independent research centre. Julie is currently managing two research projects as well as the information work of the centre. Julie was previously the manager of the ESRC Question Bank project for three years, having worked on the project for nearly eight years in total. She has a Masters degree in Social Research from the University of Surrey. Julie has previously published on social survey resources available to researchers in the UK and has a wide experience of teaching and presenting on this subject.

Eric Harrison is Senior Research Fellow in the Centre for Comparative Social Surveys at City University, where he manages a programme of methodological research supporting the European Social Survey. Between 2004 and 2006 he was the assistant Academic Convenor of a project to develop a European Socio-economic Classification (ESeC). He has research interests in the areas of social stratification, social inequality and research methodology. He is the co-editor (with David Rose) of *Social Class in Europe: An Introduction to the European Socio-economic Classification*.

John Haskey holds a Visiting Senior Research Fellowship at the University of Oxford, and was formerly President of the British Society for Population Studies. He has analysed survey data on a wide variety of social and demographic subjects, principally marriage, divorce, cohabitation, families and households – including one-parent families, stepfamilies, living alone, and Living Apart Together relationships – and ethnicity. He has devised special modules of survey questions to test out the feasibility of asking new questions and collecting fresh data to advance analyses on family demography. He has recently analysed surveys on aspects of family life and on unfaithfulness in partnerships, and is currently exploring data from the British Household Panel Survey.

Oliver Heath is Lecturer in Politics at Royal Holloway, University of London. His research interests include political participation, electoral behaviour and civic engagement in Britain. He has published articles in *Political Behavior*, *Electoral Studies*, and the *European Journal of Political Research*.

Laura Hyman is studying for a doctorate in Sociology at the University of Surrey, and, between 2005 and 2007, was Research Officer at the ESRC Question Bank, which is now part of the Survey Resources Network (SRN) <URL: http://surveynet. ac.uk/>. Her research interests include survey measurement and the sociology of happiness and wellbeing. She developed the Topics area of the Question Bank resource, which focused particularly upon survey questions and the measurement of concepts within a wide range of substantive areas, including health, social attitudes, crime, social class, religion and political behaviour.

Robert Johns is Lecturer in Politics at the University of Strathclyde. He teaches, researches and has published in the fields of political psychology, electoral behaviour and questionnaire design.

Yaojun Li is Professor of Sociology at the Institute for Social Change, Manchester University. His research interests are in social mobility and social stratification, social capital, labour market, ethnicity and cross-national comparisons. He has published widely in these areas. He also has many book chapters and consultation papers for government organizations, such as the Economic and Social Research Council, the Department of Trade and Industry, the Equality and Human Rights Commission, the National Employment Panel, and the National Assembly of Wales. He is a frequent reviewer for top sociology journals in the world and for government and other research agencies.

Sally McManus is a Research Director in the Health Research Group at the National Centre for Social Research (NatCen). She has worked on the National Survey of Sexual Attitudes and Lifestyles 2000, the Health Protection Agency's Gay Bars survey series, and a study of ethnicity and sexual behaviour. She has written on methodological aspects of researching sensitive issues, including *Sexual Orientation Research: A Review of Methodological Approaches* and *Life on the Scene: Ten Years of HIV Prevention Research in Gay Bars*. She authored a chapter with Bob Erens on conducting surveys among ethnic minorities, published in *Health and Social Research in Multiethnic Societies*.

Catherine H. Mercer is a Senior Lecturer in the Centre for Sexual Health and HIV Research at University College London. She led the statistical analyses for Britain's second national sex survey, the National Survey of Sexual Attitudes and Lifestyles (Natsal), and will do so again for the third Natsal study due to take place in 2010. She has published over 50 journal articles and reports from the Natsal studies covering a wide range of topics including same-sex behaviour, young people's sexual behaviour, sexual mixing and sexual function problems.

Jennifer Mindell is a public health physician in the Department of Epidemiology and Public Health, University College London (UCL). Jennifer leads the UCL team of the Joint Health Surveys Unit, working on the annual Health Survey for England, as well as the UK-wide National Diet and Nutrition Survey and the Low Income Diet and Nutrition Survey, and contributing to the Scottish Health Survey and work on a pan-European Health Examination Survey.

Caroline Roberts is a post-doctoral fellow in the Research Centre for Methodology, Inequalities and Social Change (MISC) at the University of Lausanne. She has a PhD in Social Psychology from the London School of Economics and Political Science. Her thesis investigated the challenges involved in measuring British public attitudes towards the euro. She has worked on the questionnaire design teams of the American National Election Studies (at Stanford University) and the European Social Survey (at City University, London). She is co-editor of two books on measuring social attitudes: *Attitude Measurement* (2008) and *Measuring Attitudes Cross-nationally* (2007).

Nicola Shelton is a health and population geographer and the Head of the Health Surveys Research Group in the Department of Epidemiology and Public Health, University College London. Dr Shelton's interests lie in health and wellbeing inequalities particularly from a geographical perspective; she is currently working on comparative analysis of the Scottish Health Survey and Health Survey for England and has published research using data from both surveys. She has also worked on parental survival, geographical proximity and contact in contemporary Britain using social survey data and geographic inequalities in mortality in contemporary and Victorian England.

Preface

This book tackles the challenge of social measurement, aiming to provide a bridge between theory and empirical research. The relationship between theory and research is an important and challenging one. This collection is a product of the collaborative work of the three editors and others in running the ESRC Question Bank over a period of more than a decade. The Question Bank tackled the challenge of trying to make the social science community more aware of UK social survey research. This book is one product of that endeavour and of the continuing challenge which improving social measurement represents.

The Question Bank (Qb) was established in 1995 as part of the Centre for Applied Social Surveys, located jointly at the University of Southampton and at Social and Community Planning Research (SCPR) in London (now the National Centre for Social Research), directed by Roger Thomas of SCPR, with Martin Bulmer from the University of Surrey as Academic Director. From the outset, Qb attempted to provide not only the questionnaires of major UK social surveys, but also commentary upon the measurement of key social variables. In 2000, SCPR ceased to be involved in Qb and it moved to the University of Surrey, with Martin Bulmer as Director. Julie Gibbs worked for Qb from 2001 to 2005 as Content Manager, and from 2005 to 2008 as Qb Manager. Laura Hyman worked for Qb from 2005 to 2007 as Research Officer with special responsibility for content. With the retirement of Martin Bulmer in 2008 and the end of the current grant, Qb became part of the wider ESRC Survey Resources Network, and is now based in the UK Data Archive at the University of Essex. It may be consulted via URL: <http://surveynet.ac.uk/sqb/introduction.asp>.

The editors would particularly like to thank those involved in Qb in the period 2005 to 2008, Graham Hughes as Content Manager, Zoe Tenger as Administrator, Jenny Rains as Documentation Assistant and Suzanne Barbalet as Web Assistant. The work of Tom Daly on the linked ESRC Survey Link Scheme, running in parallel, was complementary. The teamwork involved proved particularly congenial. The Department of Sociology at the University of Surrey, a centre of expertise in research methods, proved a particularly happy home for Qb. Jo Moran Ellis as Head of Department, and Patrick Sturgis and Nick Allum as the department's specialists in advanced survey methods, provided important support. Looking further back, Harshad Keval was Qb Manager from 2002 to 2005 and a congenial colleague to work with. The orignal CASS bid in 1994–95 was encouraged by Sir Roger Jowell, then Director of SCPR, without whose belief in the importance of methodological work on survey methods, Qb would never have seen the light of day. We should like to pay tribute to the contribution of Roger

Thomas, the first director of CASS and of Qb, and Chris Skinner, co-director of CASS, and to previous Qb staff members Teresa McGarry (who first set up the Qb web site), Paul Donagher (now with Market Strategies International in Little Rock, Arkansas) and Adam Guy (now of the BBC web service) who helped to establish Qb between 1995 and 2001. Jean Martin, then of the Office for National Statistics, chaired the CASS Advisory Committee throughout its existence, and provided important support for Qb in its CASS period and beyond, throughout the vagaries of dealing with the ESRC as a complex organization. We would also like to thank international correspondents such as Mick P Couper at Michigan and David DeVaus at LaTrobe.

The challenges of social measurement using surveys, as Chapter 1 and Chapter 12 of this collection suggest, are still with us, and will not be easily resolved. As Anthony Heath and Jean Martin have pointed out (1997), social measurement is in a much less well-developed state than either economic measurement or psychological measurement, and there are many fewer standardized measures available than there are in these fields. Creating the ESRC Question Bank over a period of 13 years was a pioneering work, still without precise parallels in other countries, and pioneering too in making use of the World Wide Web as a means of disseminating an information resource about a professional activity, survey research. By the end of its existence as Qb in 2008, about 80,000 pages of questionnaires from major UK surveys had been assembled. Qb was somewhat less successful in accumulating a large amount of material about the measurement process itself, partly due to its concentration outside the academic world in organizations like the Office for National Statistics and NatCen, partly due to the shortage of survey methodologists in the UK, and the time limitations upon those working professionally in survey organizations. This book has been produced in recognition of the continuing need to address measurement issues, and to take up the challenges which the large-scale measurement of social phenomena present.

Martin Bulmer
Julie Gibbs
Laura Hyman

References

Bishop, C.F. (2005), *The Illusion of Public Opinion: Fact and Artifact in American Public Opinion Polls* (Lanham, MD: Rowman & Littlefield).

Burgess, R.G. (ed.) (1986), *Key Variables in Social Investigation* (London: Routledge).

DeVaus, D. (2002), *Surveys in Social Research* (5th edition) (London: Routledge).

Gittus, E. (ed.) (1972), *Key Variables in Social Research*, Vol. 1: Religion, Housing, Locality (London: Heinemann Educational Books).

Heath, A. and Martin, J. (1997), 'Why Are There So Few Formal Measuring Instruments in Social and Political Research?' in L. Lyberg, P. Biemer, M. Collins, E. De Leeuw, C. Dippo, N. Schwartz and D. Trewin (eds), *Survey Measurement and Process Quality* (New York: John Wiley), 71–86.

Stacey, M. (ed.) (1969), *Comparability in Social Research* (London: Heinemann Educational Books).

Chapter 1

Introduction

Martin Bulmer, Julie Gibbs and Laura Hyman

This book is about social measurement through social surveys and the ways in which social surveys can be used to improve the quantitative measurement of key aspects of social and economic life. This is a continuing challenge to the social scientist, despite the proliferation of social surveys of all kinds in the contemporary world. These range from public opinion polls through social attitude surveys to major studies of social and economic life such as the Labour Force Survey. All attempt to use social measurement to illuminate contemporary society. What does such measurement involve?

Measurement is any process by which a value is assigned to the level or state of some quality of an object of study. This value is given numerical form, and measurement therefore involves the expression of information in quantities rather than by verbal statement. It provides a powerful means of reducing qualitative data to a more condensed form for summarization, manipulation and analysis. Classical measurement theory argues that numbers may perform at least three purposes in representing values: (1) as tags, identification marks or labels; (2) as signs to indicate the position of a degree of a quality in a series of degrees; and (3) as signs indicating the quantitative relations between qualities. On some occasions, numbers may fulfil all three functions at once (Cohen and Nagel, 1934).

A common distinction drawn in social and economic measurement is in terms of the 'hardness' or 'softness' of data. Economists pride themselves on their access to significant quantities of 'hard' data, and have devoted considerable efforts to creating such data to serve their purposes. Demographers limit themselves to a restricted number of variables in the analysis of population, but pride themselves that many of the variables with which they are concerned – such as age and sex – are relatively 'hard' and derived from a limited range of sources, particularly the Census of Population and from registration data. Sociologists deal much more frequently with data that is 'softer' in character, drawn from a wider range of official sources, and poses more intractable measurement problems. One example of this is the concept of race and ethnicity (Bulmer, 1996). Even straightforward variables like marital status can give rise to difficult problems of classifying persons whose union is not legally sanctioned, or where a marriage has been dissolved but not succeeded by a second marriage. More complex constructs, such as the 'dark figure' of crime – referring to offences not recorded in official statistics – require a series of presuppositions: about a definition of crime, of its formal measurement, of the occurrence of events that for one reason or another are not recorded as crime, and of the measurement of these events (cf. Sparks, Genn and Dodd, 1977: chapter 1). 'Before counting persons with characteristics associated with soft data, one must set certain conventions to define each such attribute, which is thus moved partway from the population to statisticians' concept of it' (Petersen, 1987: 187–8).

Social measurement differs from economic measurement not only in relative 'hardness' or 'softness' of data, but in terms of conceptual underpinnings. A sustained effort has been made in the field of economics to tie economic measurement and economic theory together in a much more direct way than is characteristic of other social sciences in relation to social and public policy (cf Morgenstern, 1963). This dates back to the creation in the United States after World War I of the National Bureau of Economic Research, and to the influence of Keynes and the formation of the Statistical Section in the British Cabinet Office under Lord Cherwell during World War II, and much elaboration since. In a work such as Robin Marris's *Economic Arithmetic* (1958), one can follow how the economist builds up by statistical means what Marris calls 'a coherent anatomical description' of the economic system. The aim, moreover, has been to construct a picture of the economic system as a whole:

> [W]e may use the same analogy – that of a system of connected pipes and tanks – as a basis for a general statistical picture of the economy. Further, the specific pattern of the imaginary system will be basically similar whether we are thinking exclusively of quantities or exclusively of money or of prices. The actual painting of the picture is done by collecting statistical data which measure the rates of flow past selected points in the imaginary pipes, the selection of the points to be made in such a way that the totality of measurements effectively describes all the important economic characteristics of the system. The measurements will be of three types – rates of flow of quantities of goods and services, rates of flow of money payments and average level of prices (Marris, 1958: 4).

Nothing comparable exists or has existed for society as a whole or for social processes in the way that economists have sought systemic data about the working of the economy. Richard Stone's system of social and demographic accounts aspired to that goal, but it has not been adopted as a model for the compilation of official statistics. Much social data compiled by government is produced according to what might not unfairly be described as pragmatic criteria, definitions and measures, reflecting a sustained failure to develop the integrating theoretical model underpinning the data collection process characteristic of economics.

The social sciences themselves must bear a good deal of responsibility for the present state of affairs. Although some disciplines such as psychology have devoted considerable attention to questions of systematic definition of concepts, in several disciplines the area has been relatively neglected. Unlike psychology, sociology and political science are not disciplines with large numbers of abstract concepts embedded in formal theories. In survey research, many items have at best an ad hoc rationale, and have no underlying concepts. Moreover, there are few opportunities for rigorous validation, and hence 'anything goes'. Most measures can satisfy the rather weak criteria of face and construct validity, which is usually all that is expected (Heath and Martin, 1997: 82).

Although concepts are one of the central features that differentiate the social sciences from ideographic intellectual pursuits such as the study of history or literature, the process of concept formation and verification tends to have received relatively little attention in sociology and social research, whether quantitative or qualitative (cf. Bulmer, 1979; Hox, 1997). How is it then, political scientist Giovanni Sartori has asked, that the route of concept analysis has been pursued as lightly as it has? One answer is the dead-end offered by logicians and linguistic analysts, particularly in philosophy, who have offered microanalysis of the meaning of words without dealing with their usefulness in substantive analysis (cf. Gellner, 1959). Sartori himself pursued within the International Political Science Association an ambitious programme to achieve conceptual synthesis and agreement across the discipline that seems to have ended in failure. But he recognized that the work of conceptual foundation laying was systematically neglected.

> At the other end or extreme, much of what is currently labelled social science 'methodology' actually deals with research techniques and statistical processing. In moving from the qualitative to the quantitative science, concepts have been hastily resolved and dissolved into variables .... [C]oncept formation is one thing and the construction of variables is another; and the better the concepts, the better the variables that can be derived from them. Conversely, the more the variable swallows the concept, the poorer our conceiving (Sartori, 1984: 9–10).

A few leading social science researchers, such as Paul Lazarsfeld, paid systematic attention to these issues of improving social measurement, but in general the dialogue has been somewhat fitful (for three British sociological exceptions, see Stacey, 1969; Gittus, 1972; Burgess, 1986). The development and justification of concepts belongs to the context of discovery rather than the context of justification. Consequently, it tends to have received much less systematic attention from methodologists (Hox, 1997). The present collection attempts to take some steps to rectify this situation by discussing the improvement of social measurement in relation to a number of key social topics.

Why is this Book Necessary?

Each chapter in this collection focuses on a key substantive topic area of social investigation, authored by experts in their respective fields – who are themselves involved in empirical research – who highlight ways of measuring concepts within each topic area, as well as potential caveats and problems that researchers may encounter in doing so.

The book aims to provide a bridge between theory and empirical research, so that we can think about such sociological concepts as family, crime, health, religion and social class (to name but a few) not just as theoretical constructs but as measurable phenomena. The relationship between theory and research is an important one in sociology; the empirical collection of data must be informed by relevant theoretical categories, and such concepts should also form the framework upon which such data collection rests. The relationship between survey measures and social 'reality' is also touched on: as Bishop (2005) notes, both the nature of survey data and the 'picture' that they paint can be affected by the wording, presentation, order and context of questions.

Elizabeth Gittus's *Key Variables in Social Research* (1972), Margaret Stacey's *Comparability in Social Research* (1969) and Robert Burgess's *Key Variables in Social Investigation* (1986) all provide similar examinations of survey measurement issues in a range of substantive areas such as race and ethnicity, health and illness, social class and employment; however, as these volumes are now all between two and four decades old, we hope that this new collection will be able to account both for the advances made in survey research over the last 20 years, and for some of the challenges that may have accompanied these, by extending and further developing many of the ideas put forward by these social science researchers.

The book is also an indispensable tool for researchers and students of sociology and survey methods who wish to learn – from examples of 'best practice' – how to measure concepts and collect data on a variety of key sociological topics. It helps readers to gain an understanding of the convergence between concepts, variables and their indicators, and the way in which appropriate indicators, via the use of variables, can be developed from concepts in order to measure them (DeVaus, 2002). The reader is able to acquaint him or herself with the ways in which concepts are created and used, and the extent to which particular indicators are 'good' indicators of the concepts they are measuring.

Each chapter in this collection is written by author/s who are experts in measuring the variable they are discussing in a social survey setting. The topics were chosen as they are either difficult to measure, such as sexual behaviour, or so common that social scientists sometimes neglect their importance when collecting survey data, such as family, religion or race.

Chapter 2 is concerned with 'Measuring Family and Household Variables', and shows how the concepts of the 'family' and the 'household' relate to other topics within sociology. Often when we set out to quantify the social world, it is concepts such as these which we will consider last, even though they are often a key part of the phenomena being studied. Haskey shows how surveys have incorporated measurement of the family and household and demonstrates how variables have been altered or added in to key surveys as thoughts and opinions on family and household structure have changed over time.

In Chapter 3, 'Measuring Crime', the focus is on how crime has been measured over time up to the present day. There are two main ways that crime is measured in official surveys: victim surveys and self-report offender surveys. Each main crime survey is discussed with regard to the way in which the variables are measured and the strengths and weaknesses of the approach. The chapter also discusses a subject which is often neglected in social crime surveys, that of crime against businesses, often called 'white collar crime', and how this can be measured.

In 'Measuring Political Behaviour and Attitudes', which is the focus of Chapter 4, Heath and Johns describe the many pitfalls that can render social measurement in this area particularly problematic. By focusing on the ways in which political behaviour has been successfully measured, with particular attention paid to question wording and the known problems associated with the instruments, this chapter gives readers interested in the measurement of political behaviour a valuable starting point.

Chapter 5, 'Measuring Religious Behaviour', reviews the most frequently used groupings of religions before going on to explain how three aspects of religion can be measured using survey instruments: affiliation, practice and belief. The chapter describes the various Church Censuses and the variables that they have measured by the regions of the UK and points to where the questionnaires for these can be obtained. The chapter concludes be asking why researching religion is important for social scientists and lists some of the key areas of life that religion touches upon, but where little research has been undertaken on the effect that religion has on them.

Chapter 6 is about 'Measuring Social Class' and explores why social class continues to be a key variable in social survey work, and a key predictor for a wide-ranging series of other variables such as health and education. Questions on social class are often added to surveys with little thought given to them, despite the existence of a number of survey instruments that measure class that could be thus incorporated. The chapter also looks at the concepts behind the measurement of social class and the requirements of data needed to fully measure it. The chapter also examines the pitfalls of re-analysing existing survey data for social class and provides practical suggestions for those who wish to do so.

Chapter 7, on the measurement of ethnicity and race in surveys, starts with a discussion of the different terms used to distinguish between groups on the basis of ethnicity or race. Emphasis is placed upon the idea of self-identification, and upon questions in which respondents are asked to assign themselves to a group among a range of alternatives offered. Thus the definition of ethnicity turns upon membership which is subjectively meaningful to the individual, and is not something which is established on the basis of objective characteristics. The chapter then proceeds to consider a variety of indicators which have been used historically as a way of measuring ethnic membership, such as country of birth, parents' country of birth, nationality, skin colour, national or geographic origin, or racial group (such as 'Chinese' or 'Arab'). The development and current prevalence of questions which invite the respondent to identify an ethnic group from a list is discussed. Other issues covered include the number of groups which are identified, the treatment of persons of mixed descent, and the reliability of such questions in social surveys.

The measurement of sexual behaviour, as discussed in Chapter 8, is clearly a sensitive and highly emotive topic. Yet, sexual behaviour has important health connotations and, particularly since the advent of the Aids epidemic, social scientists have been researching sexual behaviour in a number of ways, both qualitatively and quantitatively, in the form of the National Surveys of Sexual Attitudes and Lifestyles (Natsal) which the authors of this chapter have a long involvement with. The survey measurement of sexual behaviour is examined in this chapter, which begins by looking at some of the key considerations that researchers need to take into account when designing survey instruments, samples and so on, and then ends by looking at five key variables within this topic commonly used in sexual attitudes and behaviour surveys.

Chapter 9 is concerned with the measurement of health, and focuses particularly on the way in which a typical health survey is carried out. After providing a short history of health surveillance in Britain, the authors highlight a number of UK survey examples, whilst also considering the feasibility of running internationally comparable health surveys.

The measurement of social capital is the focus of Chapter 10, in which Yaojun Li takes a theoretically informed and methodologically rigorous approach to measuring both formal and informal social capital. The chapter begins with a review of the social capital debate, focusing on the implications of the key traditions for measurement using survey data, before going on to present analysis and findings of some empirical research that draws particularly on the Home Office Citizenship Survey of 2003.

Chapter 11 explores a number of complex issues surrounding the measurement of social attitudes. Caroline Roberts discusses a range of methods that can be used for measuring attitudes, before going on to examine their survey measurement specifically; she focuses upon potential sources of variability in attitude measurements, including cognitive processes, questionnaire design and factors affecting the response behaviour of survey respondents, such as possible 'social desirability' bias.

The book concludes with Chapter 12, in which Martin Bulmer considers a number of obstacles that are met in social measurement, as well as some ways of circumventing these. He highlights the issue of the lack of measuring instruments in social surveys, before proceeding to delineate an approach to social measurement that has been adopted in many major UK government surveys, known as question 'harmonization'. The chapter emphasizes a need for theoretical integration between social scientific concepts – like those explored in this book – and their empirical measurement, before concluding with a look at how progress could be made in social and socio-economic measurement.

References

Alonso, W. and Starr, P. (eds) (1987), *The Politics Of Numbers* (New York: Russell Sage Foundation [For the National Committee for Research on the 1980 Census]).

Bishop, G.F. (2005), *The Illusion of Public Opinion: Fact and Artefact in American Public Opinion Polls* (Lanham: Rowman & Littlefield).

Bulmer, M. (1979), 'Concepts in the Analysis of Qualitative Data', *The Sociological Review* 27, 4 (November): 653–77.

Bulmer, M. (1996), 'The Ethnic Group Question in the 1991 Census of Population', in D. Coleman and J. Salt (eds), *Ethnicity in the 1991 Census*, Vol. 1: Demographic Characteristics of Ethnic Minority Populations (London: HMSO), 33–62.

Bulmer, M. and Burgess, R.G. (1986), 'Do Concepts, Variables And Indicators Interrelate?' in Burgess (ed.), 246–55.

Burgess, R.G. (ed.) (1986), *Key Variables in Social Investigation* (London: Routledge).

Cohen, M. and Nagel, E. (1934), *An Introduction to Logic and Scientific Method* (New York: Harcourt Brace).

DeVaus, D. (2002), *Surveys in Social Research* (5th edition) (London: Routledge).

Gellner, E. (1959), *Words And Things* (London: Penguin).

Gittus, E. (ed.) (1972), *Key Variables in Social Research*, Vol. 1: Religion, Housing, Locality (London: Heinemann Educational Books).

Heath, A. and Martin, J. (1997), 'Why Are There So Few Formal Measuring Instruments in Social and Political Research?' in Lyberg et al. (eds), 71–86.

Hox, J.J. (1997), 'From Theoretical Concept to Survey Question', in Lyberg et al. (eds), 47–69.

Lazarsfeld, P.F. (1961), 'Notes on the History of Quantification in Sociology – Trends, Sources, and Problems', in H. Woolf (ed.), *Quantification: A History of the Meaning of Measurement in the Natural and Social Sciences* (Indianapolis: Bobbs-Merrill), 147–203.

Lyberg, L., Biemer, P., Collins, M., De Leeuw, E., Dippo, C., Schwartz, N. and Trewin D. (eds) (1997), *Survey Measurement and Process Quality* (New York: Wiley).

Marris, R. (1958), *Economic Arithmetic* (London: Macmillan).

Moore, P.G. (1995), 'Editorial', *Journal of the Royal Statistical Society, Series A*, 158, 3: 359–61.

Morgenstern, O. (1963), *On the Accuracy of Economic Observations* (2nd edition) (Princeton: Princeton University Press).

Petersen, W. (1987), 'Politics and the Measurement of Ethnicity', in Alonso and Starr (eds), 187–233.

Sartori, G. (1984), 'Foreword', in G. Sartori (ed.), *Social Science Concepts: A Systematic Analysis* (Beverly Hills: Sage), 9–12.

Sparks, R.F., Genn, H.G. and Dodd, D.J. (1977), *Surveying Victims: A Study of the Measurement of Criminal Victimization* (Chichester, Sussex: Wiley).

Stacey, M. (ed.) (1969), *Comparability in Social Research* (London: Heinemann Educational Books).

Chapter 2
Measuring Family and Household Variables

John Haskey

Introduction

Purposes of Social Surveys Involving Family and Household Variables

In general, the aim of social surveys is to monitor trends, or to allow new conclusions to be drawn. Historically, sociologists have been slow to recognize the power of surveys to do more than describe situations; inferences are also possible with the correct planning, design, fielding – and, not least, with the appropriate and best formulation of questions (Marsh, 1982).

Conceptualization, research design and survey data collection have received perfunctory treatment in the literature (Bulmer, 2004). Social scientists carrying out or making use of social surveys ideally seek to identify *causative* factors for observed phenomena or variations in key variables. Whilst this goal can never be achieved with absolute confidence, much can be learned from the inter-relationship between factors. Likely causative mechanisms can be postulated – and supportive evidence accumulated.

The aim of social surveys is usually the collection of information for descriptive purposes – to illuminate and quantify existing situations and conditions, and to document areas of concern. Some surveys are specifically designed to investigate one particular phenomenon, and to determine the factors influencing it. Others are tailored to study differentials and to derive explanatory mechanisms for their existence. Yet others are specially constructed to probe the underlying dynamics behind trends in order to gain a better understanding of the processes involved. Some surveys are designed to be multi-purposed, not only to establish a body of descriptive information on a variety of subjects, but also to provide a dataset to test for possible causative factors and to explore hitherto unsuspected associations and correlations.

There are many fields of study in which information on families and households is required – ranging from social, legal, economic and health policy and practice subjects, to those in which considerable detail and history are needed in order to analyse families and households in their own right. Information is also needed to examine the relationship and interactions between these fields. For example, employment and housing – and its availability and affordability – clearly impact upon household formation and composition. Studies on poverty, deprivation and social exclusion are frequently focused on families and children, for example, to identify 'target groups' for policy action purposes. More generally, the effects of a variety of influences on individuals are mediated through the relationships, families and households in which they live.

Statistical information on families and households is also required for official purposes, the main one being for planning and financial forecasts. The various population projections which are published – including those by marital status, and household projections – are the best examples. Unpublished projections of the number of one-parent families are used to estimate the extent of likely future State Benefit payments. An important, though easily overlooked, role of official statistics is to ensure that data are collected on emerging topics; recognizing and starting their collection at the earliest possible stage is crucial to charting and understanding their growth in the future. Last, but not least, data on families and households are needed for demographic, social and health research.

Family researchers have borrowed methods and techniques developed in other disciplines, leading to a wide variety of approaches and findings. This diversity brings both strengths and weaknesses, but the possibility of new insights from applying fresh analytic tools needs to be set against the potential for a lack of uniformity in definitions and scope (Marcos and Draper, 1990).

Whilst some studies need only basic, background, information on families and households, other specialized studies on the family require questions whose number and complexity are considerable – and which usually form a unique set each time. In the former case, there is a strong case for identifying and adhering to a standard set of basic questions which can be added to, or elaborated, as required; in the latter case, the specialized questions are likely to comprise most of the survey. However, basic, contextual, information is still needed, and is usefully obtained using the same standard set of basic questions, to ensure comparability of results between surveys of all kinds.

This chapter focuses on the issues and practicalities of asking a basic set of appropriate questions on families and households in national surveys.

Background

Types of Families

It is a truism that there are as many *types* of families as there are families, since each family is unique in some way, if not in many ways. Because everyone is familiar with the *concept* of a family, it is exceedingly easy to take the *definition* of a family for granted. In practice there can be many definitions, each of which can be further elaborated.

At first sight, it may seem obvious who 'belongs' to a family. However, it is not immediately clear what the essential conditions are for membership of a family. Family members certainly need to be related to one another, either by blood, marriage or partnership (however defined). Certain combinations of these relationship factors may also qualify individuals to be treated as being in the same family; for example, the spouse of one's cousin, or, more remotely, the cohabiting partner of one's stepson. Clearly the allowable 'distance' of the relationship needs to be circumscribed. For example, the term 'distant cousin' carries the implication that, although the person is a cousin (and so part of one's family), he or she is scarcely part of one's *immediate* family. Whilst it might be difficult to draw boundaries in general, in a given instance, it will depend upon the particular interpersonal relationship of, and degree of contact between, the two people concerned. Because women tend to value, invest in, and nurture links more than men, relationships mediated through mothers/wives/daughters/female partners tend to be stronger, and more likely to be regarded as *family* relationships than those mediated through the corresponding male relatives. However, it would be anachronistic to entertain a non-symmetrical definition of a family based on the sex of the relatives concerned. Adopted children are, of course, legally accepted as part of the family, but foster children, being cared for by a family on a temporary basis, are not treated as family members.

Individuals can belong to more than one family – especially where there has been relationship breakdown and ex-partners have re-partnered. The most obvious examples are stepchildren and half-brothers and half-sisters. Each individual does not necessarily have sole membership of just one family – and this needs to be reflected in survey planning and definitions. Usually, a family member belongs to a basic or '*nuclear*' family, and also simultaneously belongs to various kinds of '*extended*' family. Consequently, at the simplest level, a family is perhaps best understood as either a very small group, or as one of several larger configurations.

In contrast to family members, household members need not be related to one another – although they can be, and frequently are. In national surveys, the important distinction between a family and a household is that a household is a group of people living together in a fixed, tangible, *building*, sharing the living accommodation of that building (or sharing a daily meal together), whereas the key feature of a family is their members' mutual *inter-relationship* (and *support*). In household-based surveys, families tend to be confined to those usually living together at the household address.

Some researchers regard the distinction between families and households as pedantic, since, in the majority of cases, a family, and the corresponding household, are identical in their membership (Marsh and Arber, 1992). To some extent this stance may be justified, since there has been an increasing trend over several decades for 'nuclear' families to acquire their own homes, rather than share with other families or individuals. Nevertheless, there are some circumstances in which a household contains several independent and self-contained 'family units'.

One attribute of a family is that of being a self-contained *economic* unit, and, in surveys on family expenditure, families are termed 'economic units'. Originally, a family unit was defined, in official surveys, as the unit potentially eligible to receive State Welfare Benefits. This definition – which is still used in official surveys and the census – reflects this origin and purpose, and coincides with the 'nuclear' family. An important corollary is that a dependent child, usually part of a 'nuclear' family, has been defined similarly to accord with State Benefit eligibility.

Families and Households in Surveys –
Some Practical Considerations Concerning Membership

Practical considerations are very important in determining who is 'captured' in a survey or census. To obtain information on families and households, surveys and censuses usually ask questions only of residents of private households. Most people live in private households, but some reside in establishments, such as boarding schools, universities, the Armed Services, hospitals, prisons, care homes, and so on. Some reside in these establishments temporarily, others permanently. Some alternate between home and other addresses, with regular or irregular spells of residence in each, for example, children away from home during term time, invalids receiving respite care, and men and women on spells of active duty in the Armed Forces. Some residents in private households have a family member living in a communal establishment, whilst many of the population living in communal establishments have family members living elsewhere, mostly in private households.

A key decision for the social scientist is whether a particular person should be treated as a family or household member, despite being elsewhere when the household was interviewed, or being elsewhere at other times on a periodic basis. The decision to include or exclude them as a household member depends crucially on the questions asked – and how the answers to them are used, following suitable rules. If there are reasons for including certain types of family or household members, appropriate arrangements must be made either to collect information from the individuals themselves, or, if not possible, then from others. Proxy responses, though, are often of poorer quality or incomplete through lack of knowledge by the proxy respondent. In panel or longitudinal surveys, some or all of the family might move before the survey is completed, and it is desirable to continue obtaining information on the original members of the family.

In general terms, despite some variation, the rules on absent members have been fairly consistent, although vigilance is needed where there have been changes. For example, in the 2001 Census, students and schoolchildren in full-time education studying away from the family home were treated as usually resident at their term-time addresses; in contrast, in the 1991 Census, such students and schoolchildren were treated as usually resident at their home address.

These considerations indicate the importance of systematic and, if need be, arbitrary, decision rules on family and household membership. This is particularly important in large-scale data collection operations, such as the census, where the processing of the statistical information has to be completely automated.

As a unit of analysis, households may have enjoyed the attention they have received by virtue of their ease of identification. As mentioned, the unit of data collection is usually the residential address, and sampling frames of all addresses are readily available. In contrast, there are relatively few sampling frames enumerating all families; families tend to be identified after household surveys – and censuses based on households – have identified household membership and assigned their members to families. Viewed in this way, identifying households may be considered as a preliminary – and necessary – step to identifying families. Viewed in another light, though, households may be seen as needlessly introducing the extra factor of geographical location, which may be an irrelevance – or even a hindrance – to considering some kinds of family membership, based on relationship only. An example concerns stepparents and stepchildren. It is not uncommon for one stepparent in a stepfamily to have a natural child who is living in another household. For this reason, it cannot be assumed that *all* the children of the stepparents are usually resident in the stepfamily household (Haskey, 1994).

A Basic Set of Questions on Families and Households

Context

The basic set of information collected on families and households has to fulfil many functions. It is often used to make comparisons between surveys, with the national picture, or with the situation in earlier years, when considering trends, for example. For all these reasons, there is a strong case for adopting a standard set of definitions. Even if a study is a 'one-off' exercise, it is often desirable to be able to compare certain results – for example, prevalence rates – with national estimates to confirm that no biases or inadvertent errors are present.

Harmonization of a number of variables connected with families – and other subjects – was introduced into official surveys some years ago. This harmonization has formalized the trend towards consistency of definitions and – equally important – of question wording (Office for National Statistics, 2003). It should be noted, though, that, despite some minor differences, the definition of a family in official statistics has remained essentially unchanged since 1961, when families were first properly distinguished from households. Similarly, the definition of a household (which has always included one in which a person is living on their own) has remained basically unchanged since 1971. The key element of the definition is that the household consists of those members who share common housekeeping (although the rules for interpreting this feature did change in 1981). Consideration is being given to updating this definition in the 2011 Census.

The 'common housekeeping' definition of a household has implications for household composition. For example, consider a grandmother living by herself in a 'granny flat', which adjoins her daughter's home. Because her accommodation is self-contained and as she looks after herself, she will usually be treated as living in a separate household to her daughter – and hence not in her family. As a result, a three-generational 'enclave' cannot routinely be detected statistically. Similarly, if relatives live in adjacent houses, so forming an 'extended family community', they cannot be discerned from censuses and surveys. Of course, if extended families or particular kinds of family are of interest, relevant questions need to be devised and asked.

Family and Household Variables –
Some Theoretical and Analytical Considerations

As with measurement variables in other subjects, those concerned with families and households can be considered as belonging to one of three kinds (Moser and Kalton, 1971). The first two are those where the variable is categorical; in the first type, the variable takes *nominal values*, that is, the categories have no intrinsic ranking, for example, legal marital status. In the second type, the variable takes *ordinal values*, that is, its values represent categories with some intrinsic ranking, for example, attitude score on degree of contentment with family life. The third kind of variable takes *scale values* which have been measured using an appropriate metric. The measured 'distances', which can, in theory, be measured as finely as required, may be validly compared, for example, duration of marriage.

In general, the type of family or household variable will determine the kind of variable to be measured, although occasionally there is a choice – though it may not always be recognized. An example concerns measuring age. If, as so often happens, a survey question asks the respondent to identify the age-group into which they fall, the resulting age variable takes *ordinal values*. If, however, the question asks for age in years, the variable can be treated as having a *scale value*. Strictly speaking, as age is taken as 'age last birthday', it is really a 'rounded down integer'. The best option is not to request the respondent's age at all, but to ask their date of birth. Age at any given date can then be calculated, to the nearest day if necessary.

Wherever possible, *scale value* variables are to be preferred to *ordinal value* variables, since they contain more information. A scale value variable can be converted into an ordinal value variable, but not vice versa. In general, the more information that can be collected the better – whether for distinguishing the true extent of differentials, or improving the chances of more definitive conclusions on employing more elaborate statistical methods to analyse the survey data. In practice, more information means either finer detail or a greater degree of categorization.

However, it must be recognized that there are practical constraints on choosing the precise form of questions. A balance has to be struck and compromises made. Such considerations include: the length of the questionnaire; the mode of collection; resources for coding and questionnaire design. All these factors affect response rates. Taking 'age', for example; the questionnaire can be completed more quickly if respondents are asked to tick an age group box, rather than writing or keying their age.

Of course, analytical considerations are also important. For example, if the age *difference* between partners/spouses is required, asking for their respective age-groups will not allow age differences to be derived. It is also not advisable to ask *directly* about differences. It is better to ask more 'elemental' questions – for example, each partner's age or date of birth – for the increased flexibility they provide. By the same token, to establish durations or time intervals, it is usually preferable to ask the appropriate start and end dates.

Some caution is needed in using or interpreting the basic variable 'age'. Often attitudes concerning relationships, family behaviour and responsibility are found to be highly dependent upon age, but, on closer examination, there is a more direct correlation with stage in the life cycle or 'demographic history' – both of which will tend to be associated with age, which would be an 'intervening' variable. The moral is to keep an open mind on seemingly fundamental variables when investigating potentially causative factors – they may be intermediate ones for more fundamental determinants (Marsh, 1982).

Perhaps the most important principle in conducting surveys on families, relationships and households is to identify the fundamental issues first, breaking them down into their most 'elemental' form, and then constructing clear, straightforward, questions on them. As an example, when cohabitation became more prevalent, an additional response category was added to the question on marital status – that of 'living together'. The purpose was to discover whether the respondent was part of a couple – and not just whether he or she was married. Unfortunately, though, by so doing, information on the marital status of those cohabiting was no longer collected and so was not available for analysis. There was also scope for confusion on how to answer the question. For example, if you were divorced and cohabiting, should you answer 'divorced' or 'cohabiting'? The guidance given was that 'living together' should take precedence over all other possible responses – and, for this reason, 'living together' was placed second in the list after 'married'. However, doubts remained over how faithfully this precedence rule was followed.

The underlying fault with this formulation of the fundamental question was that 'legal marital status' and 'whether living together or not' are two independent variables, rather than mutually exclusive values of the same, single, variable. As there was a need to document the growing prevalence of cohabitation and the characteristics of those cohabiting, the General Household Survey, GHS, was persuaded by the author to break down this composite question into two separate questions – one on legal marital status, and the other on cohabitation. The separation out of this latter question has proved particularly beneficial in that it subsequently allowed 'same-sex cohabitation' to be simply added as another category. More recently, same-sex civil partnership was also easily added as yet another category. 'Living Apart Together', being another form of non-married cohabitation, might yet form a further category at some future date (Haskey, 2005).

Key Demographic Variables for Identifying Families within Households

The statistical information derived from questions in national surveys on families and households has increased considerably over the years, both in coverage and in detail. This expansion was generated by an increased demand and growing need to monitor social and societal change. Consequently, some questions have evolved, whilst others have remained virtually unchanged. The current basic set of variables collected in all national surveys to ensure that families and relationships within households can be properly identified are listed below. Others, often found useful, are given in italics:

Date of birth
Sex
Current legal marital status
Living arrangements (for example, whether or not currently partnered/living with spouse, and so on)
Relationship between each pair of household members
Household Reference Person*/head of household
Family Reference Person**/head of family
Economic relative position***
Absent members of family/household – circumstances/reasons for absence

Date and duration of current marriage/partnership
Partnership (cohabitational) history and marital history
Child-bearing/paternity history
Kin and extended family living elsewhere
Details of adoption/stepparenthood/stepchildhood

Other important variables contextualizing the situation of family and household members are:

Occupation   ⎫   *from which both social class and*
Whether full-time or part-time, and so on   ⎬   *socio-economic group*
Employment status   ⎭   *are derived*
Industry
Age left full-time education
Highest educational level attained
Tenure of accommodation
Time lived at present address
Income – or proxy variable
Ethnic group
Nationality
Country of birth
National identity
Religion
Postcode of usual residence)

* the Household Reference Person (HRP) usually coincides with the Family Reference Person (FRP) ** in the household – or one of them if there is more than one family in the household

*** the HRP/FRP is the person with the highest income in the household/family, or, if equal incomes, the older/oldest person of the two (or more). The HRP in a one-person household is taken as that sole household member, and the FRP in a one-parent family is taken as the lone parent

The usual strategy is to use the key variables to undertake the following actions:

1. Identify each household
2. Identify and enumerate all household members
3. Obtain the age, sex, marital status and living arrangements of each household member
4. Establish the relationship between each possible pair of household members
5. Using those relationships, plus age, sex and legal marital status of each household member, group household members into families (or a single family – or none at all) and distinguish any remaining household members *not* belonging to families
6. Identify the Family Reference Person for each family, and the Household Reference Person

Stage 1 involves applying the definition of a household:

A single person or a group of people who have the address as their only or main residence and who either share one meal a day or share the living accommodation. (Sharing a kitchen or a bathroom does not count.)

Stage 2 requires the interviewer – or person filling in the form or census schedule – to list everyone usually resident at the address.

Stages 3 and 4 rely on the answers to the appropriate questions being recorded – with the information on those absent being provided by one or more of those present.

Stage 5 occurs after all the information has been collected, consistency checks performed, and data editing completed.

Stage 6 employs the definitions for the FRP and HRP (see *** above) which permit comparisons between families, and between households, based on the characteristics of the individuals so taken to represent them.

As mentioned, the definition of a family in official surveys has varied slightly. It has also developed, partly reflecting the collection of fuller and new information, for example, to cover cohabitation and, more recently, civil partnerships. In the latest General Household Survey, in its Family Information Section, a family is defined as:

1. *A married or opposite sex cohabiting couple on their own; or*
2. *A married or opposite sex cohabiting couple, or a lone parent, and their never-married children (who may be adult), provided these children have no children of their own; or*
3. *A same-sex couple in a legally recognized civil partnership*

The definition of a family, a 'nuclear' family, relates to the smallest feasible group of parents and their children. For children to be included in their parental family, they must never have been married nor had any children of their own. Other children are not included in their parental family. For this reason, the first category of families – couples on their own – includes those with children who are either excluded by this definition or who live elsewhere.

By using this definition, households comprise one or more 'nuclear' families, plus other household members who are not included in any of these families. These remaining household members may be related to someone in one of these families, for example, cousins, aunts, brothers and sisters, and, as described above, some children. By the same token, the members of one family may well be related to those of another family in the same household. A common example is a lone divorced mother living with her child and her own parents. In this case, the lone mother and her child would constitute one family – and her parents another. All the household members would be related to one another – as an extended family.

This convention of using 'nuclear' families as 'building bricks' has stood the test of time. The framework within which this information is collected has proved flexible and accommodating, able to incorporate developments and improvements to the questions. The statistical information on families has served most basic and general purposes – partly because a large majority of households containing inter-related people are single-(nuclear)family households.

The Key Role of the Relationship Question

Occasionally, information on nuclear families is not sufficient or relevant for the task required. This was the case, for example, in a study on the variations in family composition of the different minority ethnic populations (Haskey, 1989). The study examined the variation in the prevalence of *extended* families – that is, the extent to which a variety of relatives, not just those of parent and child, live together in the same household. The study was undertaken using data from the Labour Force Survey, LFS. It was necessary to determine whether members of one nuclear family were related either to members of *other* nuclear families in the household, or to any remaining household members. Information on the relationship of each household member to the 'head of household' had to be used. (It was the only relationship information collected then.) The relationship of each 'head of family' and of each person not in a family to the 'head of household' was examined. The exercise was involved and indirect, and could not guarantee to identify all extended family members.

Based on this experience, the author requested the GHS to record *all* the information on relationships in the household, not just each household member's relationship to the 'head of household', which had hitherto been the norm. Interviewers had previously established all the relationships in the household in order to allocate individuals to nuclear families, without *recording* all those relationships. As a result of this request, the 'relationship matrix' was introduced into the GHS, a matrix in which everyone's relationship to everyone else in the household is recorded. It was subsequently introduced into the LFS, and other surveys, as a 'harmonized variable'. In addition, a new variable indicating the presence of an extended family was included in the LFS set of derived variables.

There was another important beneficial outcome of the introduction of the relationship matrix. In a number of survey situations, there is no interviewer, so that information on families has to be derived solely from the recorded answers to the survey question – which included the relationship of each household member to the 'head of household'. In most household situations, this information was sufficient to establish the family composition of the household, but, in some cases, the presence of one of the families in the household was not apparent, or could not be unambiguously identified or detected – the so-called 'concealed' families.

The census is the best example of an 'interviewer-less' survey, and up to the 2001 Census, the only question on relationship was that to the 'head of household'. In these earlier censuses, therefore, in the example quoted above of a divorced lone mother and her child living with her parents, the mother's father would usually complete the first column of the census form, and all other household members would have to state their relationship to him. Whilst there would be no ambiguity of his wife's or his daughter's relationship to him, his grandchild would not necessarily be the child of his daughter *who was living in the household*. It could be that the child was that of *another* daughter, or son. Only by knowing the *direct* relationship between the daughter and grandchild can it be confidently concluded that the household contains two (nuclear) families – the lone mother family, and the family comprising the parents of the lone mother. The relationship matrix was introduced into the 2001 Census and enabled these direct relationships to be identified and the 'concealed' families revealed.

More generally, if two household members are related to each other, but neither is related to the 'head of household', it is impossible to deduce the two household members' relationship *to each other* from what is recorded about their separate relationships to the 'head of household'. (For clarity, the term 'head of household' has been used up to this point. In recent years it has been replaced by a different concept, the Household Reference Person. Similarly, the 'head of family' has been replaced by the 'Family Reference Person'.) Only by collecting information on the relationship between each pair of household members can all families – 'nuclear' and 'extended' – be distinguished with certainty; and individuals who do not belong to any.

Analysing relationships within large households can, however, prove particularly challenging analytically, through the large number of pairs of relationships to consider and categorize (Blackwell et al., 2005). In addition, there is a case for not editing answers to the relationship question to accord with standard family types; some data on same-sex couples have been 'corrected' – and other forms of genuine relationship combinations may similarly have been lost to analysis.

Purpose and Scope of Questions, and Acceptability Requirements

Often in surveys, questions designed for a specific purpose later become relevant to another group of respondents, or of more general interest. An example is the subject of cohabitation. Initially, questions were asked only of women of childbearing ages, because of its relevance to family building. Later, when cohabitation became more prevalent as a form of partnership, questions were asked of both men and women, in a wider age range.

In national surveys, particularly in the GHS since 1979, the actual term 'cohabitation' has never been used in questions (Haskey, 2001a – see the Appendix to that paper). Instead, different phrases have been used in different periods, reflecting not only the prevailing social mores, but also a changing approach and acceptability of question wording. Hence in the Family Information Section of the GHS, the earliest form of question addressed to women was very much an 'end-piece'. After introducing the subject by saying: 'Thinking of your present marriage, did you get married in a church, a registry (sic) office, or *are you just living together as man and wife*?' The same general introduction was retained when the question was extended to men and the age range widened in the late 1980s. The final part of the question was: '*Are you simply living together as husband and wife*?' Subsequently, in the early 1990s, the topic was brought more to the fore, with an introductory statement: 'As you know, some couples live together without actually getting married', followed by: 'thinking of your present marriage, did you marry in … or *are you simply living together as a couple*?' Since the mid-1990s, the key question, in another part of the GHS, has been even more direct: '*May I just check, are you living with someone as a couple*?'

There are several aspects of this development worth noting. In earlier decades, cohabitation was stigmatized, and the question had to be framed in terms of the respondent pretending to be living 'as if married'. This device was gradually dropped as the stigma faded. Even so, on the way, the inclusion in the preface: 'As you know, some couples live together without actually getting married' still provided reassurance that respondents did not need to feel that they belonged to an aberrant minority. Only in more recent times, when cohabitation has become widely accepted as a partnership and family form, can a simple, direct, question be employed.

One consequence of using different wording at different times concerns the validity of comparisons over time in measuring prevalence. However, the *trends* in the prevalence of cohabitation from different surveys are highly consistent, even if the estimated level of cohabitation depends on the particular type of question asked at any one time (Murphy, 2000). More generally, questions on certain family and relationship topics need particular attention and development to maintain usable and dependable results.

Sensitivity of Subject Matter

One form of relationship which can prove particularly sensitive is that of stepchildren and stepparents. The subject of stepfamilies has always tended to evoke negative images and possibly some stigma. Often, stepfamilies consciously or sub-consciously avoid the explicit recognition of the step-relationships within their family, although part of the reason may be society failing to provide unambiguous terms for the different kinds of relationships. There is also uncertainty about whether the term 'stepfamily' applies to both married *and cohabiting* couple families with stepchildren.

The relationship matrix includes the categories 'stepchild' and 'stepparent', but in an earlier study on stepfamilies, a specially devised set of questions was asked avoiding the mention of step-relationships. Instead, the couple were each asked whether each child in their family was their natural child, or the natural child of their partner, or the natural child of both of them (Haskey, 1994). In addition, the same set of questions was asked for any children living elsewhere. This device, though possibly raising sensitivities over 'true parenthood', did overcome the reluctance of some respondents to recognize their step-relationships. It also allowed *cohabiting couple* stepfamilies to be identified and distinguished, and proved an acceptable approach.

Clarity of Meaning of Questions

In general, questions in the census and self-completion questionnaires have to be self-contained and simple, whilst in interview surveys, they can be more sophisticated and probe aspects more thoroughly. Information on some topics is relatively straightforward to collect; questions can be readily framed to be direct and unambiguous. Questions on date of birth, date of marriage, sex, relationship, and so on are factual; there is little room for uncertainty – beyond ensuring that a full list of possible answers is available to choose from. In some circumstances, it can be advantageous *not* to give a definition because of its potential complexity; for example, cohabitation, and 'ethnic group' in the 1991 Census. Instead, reliance is placed on respondents' understanding of what is required through an example, a simple phrase, or just a list of possible alternatives. (An 'Other – please specify' category can be added, if necessary.)

In other situations, it is helpful to indicate exactly what *is* required. For example, with legal marital status, it is important to clarify that 'single' means 'never-married'; 'divorced' means 'having obtained a decree absolute'; and 'separated' means 'still married, but not living with one's spouse'. (In practice, it has never been stipulated that 'separated' means having obtained a Judicial Separation.) If the respondents do not appreciate that it is their *legal* marital status which is being requested, there can be ambiguity. 'Single' can be interpreted as: 'not currently *partnered*'; and 'separated' interpreted as: 'parted from one's previous *informal partner*'. In both cases, the respondent could be of *any legal* marital status.

Questions on other topics may need more attention to be formulated and worded so that they strive for objectivity, specifically countering the tendency to answer in a 'socially or politically correct' way, irrespective of the circumstances. When the precise meaning of a question is mistaken, or there is a mismatch between the questions of a survey and the intended subject for investigation, incorrect conclusions can be drawn. This phenomenon has been referred to as solving the wrong problem and sometimes called a 'Type III error' (accepting or rejecting the null hypothesis on inappropriate data) (Ransom et al., 1990; Tukey, 1977). With retrospective questions, knowledge or recall can be difficult, with forgetting and distortion increasing with elapsed time (Bradburn et al., 1978).

An example of retrospective questions involved asking about the durations of past spells of cohabitation. The importance of collecting complete histories of both marriages *and* cohabitations in surveys was demonstrated in a study – which led to a subsequent pilot survey testing some questions on spells of cohabitation which had ended in the past (Haskey, 2001b). Respondents who had previously cohabited were first asked how long they had lived together as a couple in that relationship. They were then asked whether they had stopped living with their partner either because they had stopped living in the same accommodation, or because it was the end of the relationship. These questions were designed to discover how respondents interpreted the question on the duration of their relationship. About one half of respondents who had had only one past cohabitation said that both reasons applied, with roughly equal proportions, about one quarter each, giving one or other of the two reasons.

The lesson is that it is insufficient to ask about duration alone, or indeed the beginning and end dates, without also specifying the event which is to define it. (After testing the pilot questions described above, they were subsequently included as a revised and extended set of questions on cohabitation in the GHS, starting with the 2000 GHS.) It has since been possible to measure such durations on either a 'shared accommodation' basis (of interest to those studying housing subjects), or on a 'duration of relationship' basis (which is of greater relevance for demographic purposes, such as fertility). Another challenge to measuring cohabitation is that specialized surveys (Wellings et al., 1994) indicate that a small proportion of respondents have *concurrent* relationships; most surveys assume any cohabitation – or marriage – to be monogamous.

Questions may be asked on subject matters at different levels – the individual, the couple, the family, the household. It is then important to keep clearly in mind the level at which information is being measured and collected – and to analyse it only at that level. In particular, some questions are only applicable to specific levels; for example, it is possible to consider the age of an individual, but not of a couple, a family or of a household. Similarly, it is possible to consider the length of partnership of a couple, but not of a family or a household. More generally, it is essential to distinguish between, and avoid confounding, the unit or level of *interest*, the unit or level of *analysis*, and the unit or level of *measurement* (Ransom et al., 1990).

If all the individuals within a household are asked about their household, members about their family, or partners about their marriage or relationship, posing the same question to different individuals may yield different responses. The only way in which comparisons may be made is if a comparable individual is identified to represent the couple, family or the household. As mentioned earlier, this is the role of the Family Reference Person and the Household Reference Person. These devices can be very useful, especially for economic analyses and comparisons of families and households. For example, they allow comparisons between single family households and one-person households. However, they do have disadvantages; in particular, the numbers and characteristics of other members of the family and household may not be taken into account.

Researchers need to be prepared for discrepancies in responses, and to decide what action to take, such as trying to reconcile the differences within the interview. Whilst small discrepancies are usually due to random measurement error, larger discrepancies tend to be due to genuine differences in respondents' perceptions which have been recorded accurately (Larsen and Olson, 1990). In some surveys, on cohabitation, men and women partners in the same relationship evidently have different ideas about what constitutes 'living together as a couple' – with varying emphases on commitment, having sexual relations, the intention to marry, the wish to have children, and so on. Their ideas can translate into their view of how long the relationship has lasted.

The recognition of potential discrepancies raises two important points about the interpretation of answers to questions. First, findings depend upon who answers the questions. Second, questions need to be framed as factually and objectively as possible. Indeed, care in formulating questions is crucial not only to addressing the key objectives of a study, but also to obtaining dependable and reproducible results.

Open-ended questions have the advantage of allowing respondents some scope to interpret the meaning and purpose of questions themselves – which may be more useful for identifying interviewer difficulties than respondent comprehension difficulties. Once within an interview, respondents are invariably keen to answer questions – and occasionally conceptualize them slightly differently to try to provide an answer (Foddy, 1993). The received wisdom is that open-ended questions are most suitable for pilot surveys and other situations where the range and type of responses is largely unknown (Converse and Presser, 1986), whilst fixed choice questions are more appropriate for major and final stage surveys where such preliminary work has already been undertaken. In large-scale surveys, coding costs are significant, so fixed choice questions are indispensable, although they are based on the results of previously trialled open-ended questions in pilot surveys.

Attitudinal Questions on the Family and Relationships

Some of the issues in asking questions on cohabitation – such as the phraseology of question wording, acceptability of subject matter, and the reproducibility of results – also apply to other questions about the family and relationships; for example, to belief and attitudinal questions. Such questions have been asked in the British Household Panel Survey, BHPS, and in the series of British Social Attitudes surveys, BSA. For example, in the BHPS, a question was asked on whether respondents agreed or disagreed that living together outside marriage was always wrong. In the BSA, respondents were similarly asked whether they agreed or disagreed that it is all right for a couple to live together without intending to get married.

In other surveys, questions have been asked such as: 'How important or not is family life to you?'; 'How happy or unhappy are you with your family life?'; and 'How often does your family argue?' Whilst these are areas of legitimate enquiry, it is difficult to ask such direct questions without respondents giving 'respectable', 'socially conforming' or 'politically correct' answers – or ones which they feel will receive the interviewer's approval. There are a few devices which can be utilized to obtain as accurate an answer as possible, and avoid this difficulty. Vignettes can be provided (which depersonalize the answer) – and long questions can be used (which give the respondent time to think and appear to answer less starkly) (Bradburn et al., 1978).

It has been noted that respondents seem to act as though information and facts can be *surrendered*, while attitudes, feelings and emotions can be *shared* (Schuman and Presser, 1979). These tendencies are usefully recognized and accepted, and questions tailored to take them into account, building on their potential benefits. At the same time, steps need to be taken to avoid their inherent hazards, to ensure as accurate a response as possible.

With questions on a person's family, spouse or partner, and other relationships, it is obviously important to choose effective words and language which resonate with the person being interviewed and do not require them to give a socially unacceptable or embarrassing answer. Phrasing the questions using vocabulary with which the respondents are familiar conveys empathy – which engenders trust and reinforces cooperation.

Prospects for the Future

There are several factors which are favourable to conducting surveys on families, relationships and households in the future. Others could prove more challenging. In general, respondents have proved willing to answer questions on family matters – and evidence has shown that they are well received, even enjoyed. Anecdotally, the last taboo about revealing personal details is reserved for disclosing income rather than, say, relationships. This frankness is expected to continue, facilitating the conducting of family surveys.

Other recent trends may be problematic. There has been a long-term decline in survey response rates, as well as a growing resistance to full-scale compulsory censuses. Public concern has grown about the ways in which personal data may be used; whether unease over marketing the data to the private sector, or disquiet on the possibility of officialdom making use of the personal details of the entire population for unknown or unspecified purposes. Such apprehension is undoubtedly exacerbated by recent reports of large datafiles containing personal information being mislaid or lost by government, or contractors working for them. A further concern is that much of the information collected in a census has already been collected before in a variety of administrative records. Some respondents see no reason to provide it again, whilst others are wary of the record linkage potential.

Probably the greatest, increasing challenge will be logistic, to locate people within households – or elsewhere – successfully. For a minority of people, there is a trend towards more temporary relationships and more transitory lives. As a result, they have multiple or indefinite patterns of residence – which in turn jeopardize response rates. People have become increasingly mobile – not only within the country, but also internationally. In most couple families, both parents work, and often one works away during the week. Many either work regularly in different locations, or are away from home for training or other related work experience. The family is only together at weekends, or even less frequently. In addition, the use or ownership of more than one home has grown considerably.

Of importance, too, is the likely extent of Living Apart Together, LAT, relationships, in which both (unmarried) partners each maintain their own home. There is evidence that, for every two cohabiting couples, there is at least one LAT couple (Haskey, 2005). These relationships bring into question each partner's 'usual residence' – and, in particular, where they may be found on the day of the survey. More specifically, the LAT phenomenon has challenged the interpretation of the previously accepted dramatic growth in the proportion of men and women supposedly living alone. Undoubtedly, some have a partner, but maintain their own home in which no-one else is resident. Also, some lone parents might not be quite as alone as they might otherwise appear.

Such trends indicate that, to understand couples and families fully, it will be increasingly necessary to ask about relationships with any others who maintain a home elsewhere, but who have some attachment to a member of the sampled household. Such individuals would include those who periodically reside or play an economic role in the sampled household. Indeed, it may be necessary to regard these individuals as having a 'degree' of household residence such as 'half-resident' – which might also be applicable to certain second homeowners. More radically, since the concept of 'usual residence' is becoming increasingly problematic, there will be a growing need to find alternative ways of relating people together, other than through 'households' and 'residence', thereby challenging what some might view as the 'hegemony of the household'.

Acknowledgements

Thanks are due to Dr Peter Goldblatt who kindly coordinated Office for National Statistics colleagues' comments on an earlier draft, and who provided helpful comments and recommendations for drafting improvements.

References

Blackwell, L., Akinwale, B., Antonatos, A. and Haskey, J. (2005), 'Opportunities for New Research Using the Post-2001 Longitudinal Study', *Population Trends* 57: 8–16.

Bradburn, N., Sudman, S., Blair, E. and Stocking, C. (1978), 'Question Threat and Response Bias', *Public Opinion Quarterly* 42: 221–34.

Bulmer, M. (ed.) (2004), Editor's preface, in *Questionnaires – An Overview, Vol. 1* (London: Sage Publications).

Converse, J. and Presser, S. (1986), *Survey Questions: Handcrafting the Standardised Questionnaire* (Beverley Hills, CA: Sage Publications).

Foddy, W. (1993), *Constructing Questions for Interviews and Questionnaires: Theory and Practice in Social Research* (London: Cambridge University Press).

Haskey, J. (1989), 'Families and Households of the Ethnic Minority and White Populations of Great Britain', *Population Trends* 57: 8–19.

Haskey, J. (1994), 'Stepfamilies and Stepchildren in Great Britain', *Population Trends* 76: 1–12.

Haskey, J. (2001a), 'Cohabitation in Great Britain: Past, Present and Future Trends', *Population Trends* 103: 4–25.

Haskey, J. (2001b), 'Cohabiting Couples in Great Britain: Accommodation Sharing, Tenure and Property Ownership', *Population Trends* 103: 26–36.

Haskey, J. (2005), 'Living Arrangements in Contemporary Britain: Having a Partner Who Usually Lives Elsewhere or Living Apart Together (LAT)', *Population Trends* 122: 35–45.

Larsen, A. and Olson, D.H. (1990), 'Capturing the Complexity of Family Systems; Integrating Family Theory, Family Scores and Family Analysis', in T. Draper and A. Marcos (eds), *Family Variables: Conceptualisation, Measurement and Use* (London: Sage Publications).

Marcos, A. and Draper, T. (1990), 'Capturing Family Variables', in T. Draper and A. Marcos (eds), *Family Variables: Conceptualisation, Measurement and Use* (London: Sage Publications).

Marsh, C. (1982), *The Survey Method – The Contribution of Surveys to Sociological Explanation* (London: George Allen and Unwin).

Marsh, C. and Arber, S. (1992), 'Research on Families and Households in Modern Britain: An Introductory Essay', in C. Marsh and S. Arber (eds), *Families and Households – Divisions and Change* (London: Macmillan).

Moser, C. and Kalton, G. (1971), *Survey Methods in Social Investigation* (Great Yarmouth: Dartmouth).

Murphy, M. (2000), 'The Evolution of Cohabitation in Great Britain 1960–95', *Population Studies* 54.

Office for National Statistics, *Harmonised Concepts and Questions for Government Social Surveys (October 2003 Update)* <http://www.statistics. gov.uk/downloads/theme_social/HarmonisedConcepts_Oct03Update.pdf>.

Ransom, D., Fisher, L., Phillips, S., Kokes, R.F. and Weiss, R. (1990), 'The Logic of Measurement in Family Research', in T. Draper and A. Marcos (eds), *Family Variables: Conceptualisation, Measurement and Use* (London: Sage Publications).

Schuman, H. and Presser, S. (1979), 'The Open and Closed Question', *American Sociological Review* 44: 692–712.

Tukey, J.W. (1977), *Exploratory Data Analysis* (Reading, MA and London: Addison-Wesley).

Wellings, K., Field, J., Johnson, A.M. and Wadsworth, J. (1994), *Sexual Behaviour in Great Britain: The National Survey of Sexual Attitudes and Lifestyles* (London: Penguin).

Chapter 3

Measuring Crime

Ian Brunton-Smith and Jonathan Allen

Measures of the extent of crime provided by social surveys have become a central part of criminal statistics in the UK, offering an alternative picture of crime to police recorded crime figures and court statistics. These survey-based methods have painted a very different picture of crime, suggesting it is considerably more widespread than official measures would indicate, and have significantly advanced criminological theory and government policy. Yet despite the advances that have been made as a result of a crime survey approach, public confidence in these alternative sources of criminal statistics has recently begun to slide. Shifting definitions of different offences, and the proximity of those collecting data to the government, has led people to question their value as independent counts of crime, or the extent that they can provide consistent information over time. This loss of confidence prompted the commissioning of two independent review panels to assess the accuracy of existing survey measures, and how to improve them to raise public confidence (Smith, 2006; Statistics Commission, 2006). Since their completion, these independent reviews have heralded the extension of the British Crime Survey to under 16s, and led to renewed efforts to maximize comparability with recorded crime figures. Crime surveys, then, remain firmly in the public gaze, with their methods continuing to fall under intense scrutiny. This makes it essential for researchers to understand the methods employed and the rationale behind their introduction, but also the limitations with this type of approach and how these can impact on the types of measure produced.

In this chapter we provide an overview of the survey-based methods of counting crime, looking both at victimization surveys and self-reported offending surveys. These survey-based methods are discussed within the broader historical and social context of counting crime, helping to explain why they were introduced and what they offer to a fuller understanding of crime. Taking victimization and offending surveys in turn, we detail the rationale behind their introduction, the specific mechanisms employed to generate accurate counts of crime, and the limitations associated with each. Like all survey-based methods, measuring crime with social surveys comes with a number of health warnings, with non-response, coverage problems, and question-wording issues meaning that they can only present a partial picture of crime. As such, we present them here as a complement to official crime statistics, serving to further illuminate the extent of the crime problem in society.

The Advent of Survey Measures of Crime

Attempts to accurately measure crime have a long history, with recorded crime data collected in Britain as far back as 1857 (Beirne, 1993). In England and Wales this was based on annual returns to the Home Office from each of the 43 police forces, along with details of offending provided by the courts. Police-recorded crime figures were primarily composed of counts of the number of indictable offences recorded by the police (those triable in the crown courts), whilst court data was made up of the number of offenders processed through the courts, along with the number of cautions. These data sources provided the first detailed picture of how crime was distributed throughout society. Police-recorded crime statistics were also valuable for showing the number of arrests made by the police, and to help provide an indication of police workload.

This move towards the enumeration of crime was mirrored in many other domains of society, including health care, social services and employment, with statisticians attempting to present an accurate and objective picture of society and its inhabitants (Coleman and Moynihan, 1996). In the UK this wealth of new data was increasingly picked up by the government, who began to place emphasis on the benefits of crime statistics for monitoring the 'health' of the nation. This included the use of crime figures to help allocate resources, allowing the monitoring of police and court activity. These figures were later used as a way of charting the success of government initiatives implemented to reduce crime and raise public confidence in the criminal justice system.

In contrast to the current political climate, where each new release of crime data is accompanied by considerable media, public and political attention, estimates of the extent of crime throughout the nineteenth and early twentieth centuries generally went unnoticed by the majority of society (Maguire, 2007). Levels of crime appeared relatively stable over this time, and suggested that crime was not widespread. This relatively low profile meant that crime data was primarily collected as a record-keeping exercise, approached uncritically as a suitable measure of the extent of crime within society. As such, relatively little consideration was given to the development of a consistent, long-running measure, or how to provide a more detailed picture of crime (Coleman and Moynihan, 1996).

It was not until the early 1960s that alternative sources of data about the extent of crime, drawing on survey methodology, became more widespread. Originating in the United States, this was in part prompted by a sharply rising recorded crime level, and a growing public awareness of the problem of crime. Alongside this apparent escalation of the crime problem was a growing awareness that official figures were deficient in certain areas. Deficiencies centred on difficulties in counting offences consistently over time; the existence of a 'dark figure' of unmeasured crime; and a hypothesized 'justice gap' between the number of people convicted of a crime in the criminal justice system and the number of people that actually committed an offence.

The difficulty in consistently counting crime over time and across each police force has been well recognized, significantly limiting the ability of police-recorded crime figures to provide information on long-term trends and regional variations (Burrows et al., 2000). Police-recorded statistics are essentially administrative statistics, and as such, it is often argued that they are simply by-products of the administrative procedures involved in making out a crime record for those incidents that the police investigate. Inconsistencies over time resulting from legislative and definitional changes mean that the range of offences included in counts of recorded crime are also regularly subject to change. This makes comparisons over time problematic, as the composition of recorded crime figures also changes. The same is true of inconsistencies in the recording practices between police forces, with evidence suggesting that different police forces and officers have been prone to classify offences in different categories (Burrows et al., 2000). This is particularly true of crimes that are difficult to classify, for example, if there is no willing complainant.[1]

The 'dark figure' of crime refers to the amount of crime that is missing from official recorded crime figures (Pointing and Maguire, 1988). Focusing on the processes involved in the recording of crime, critics argued that there were a number of opportunities for considerable attrition in official counts of crime. The first of these was the requirement of an identifiable victim in most instances before a crime can be made known to the police, which in turn means that the 'victim' needs to identify the incident as a crime (Sparks, Genn and Dodd, 1977). Having defined the incident as a crime, victims also have to report it to the police. This is often less than guaranteed, with factors such as embarrassment, a lack of confidence in the police, and feelings that the offence is too trivial regularly highlighted as potential reasons for failing to report an incident to the police (Kershaw, Nicholas and Walker, 2008). Importantly, different crimes suffer from differential levels of non-reporting, with recent evidence indicating that vehicle crime and burglary are the most likely to be reported (93 per cent and 76 per cent respectively), whereas vandalism and assaults are much less likely to be reported (35 per cent and 34 per cent) (Kershaw, Nicholas and Walker, 2008). There is also some crime which is known to exist which is not well reported to the police, for example, forms of fraud against financial institutions (if commercially sensitive), intra-familial crimes, as well as those crimes that tend to be known to government, such as benefit or VAT fraud.

The justice gap refers to another source of attrition in official measures of crime, namely the disparity between the number of offenders that are processed through the courts and the number of offenders that actually committed crimes within a given time period. In 2007, the number of offenders processed through the courts was 518,000, while recorded crime figures placed the number of crimes

---

1   Significant advances have been made since to ensure consistency in recording practices, with the publication of the National Crime Recording Standards in 2002 providing detailed information for forces on how to accurately classify offences.

at around 4.95 million (Ministry of Justice, 2008). Even if it is assumed that some offenders commit more than one crime, and that recorded crime figures are missing a considerable amount of crime, this still points to a large number of offenders being missed from official records (using victimization surveys, the number of crimes is estimated at 10.1 million, suggesting a far larger disparity).

Drawing on the survey-based methods that were successfully being utilized by those involved in public opinion research, critics of official records advocated survey approaches as an alternative measure of the extent of crime. Two distinct approaches to measuring crime were introduced: victimization surveys and offending surveys. These proposed alternative methods to accurately capture the extent of crime, addressing many of the deficiencies with official figures. Victimization surveys presented an alternative picture to police-recorded crime figures, asking people about their own experiences of victimization rather than being restricted to those offences that people actually chose to report and that the police chose to record. These were instrumental in quantifying the dark figure of crime, and helped uncover the motivations behind reporting incidents to the police. In contrast, offending surveys provided a clearer picture than that given by offending statistics, asking people about their offending behaviour rather than relying on information about those processed by the criminal justice system.

Victimization Surveys

The origin of victim surveys has been tied directly to the rising profile of victimology, and a victim-centred approach to crime. Victimology can be traced to the 1940s, although it did not gain sufficient momentum to form its own distinct strand of criminology until the 1960s (Karmen, 1990; Mawby and Walklate, 1994). The development of victimology was itself fuelled by the complex socio-political forces of the time. These included the public recognition of the crime problem, the inability to accurately measure crime (considering both recording and reporting as discussed) and the need to address the extent of crime. This all cultivated a focus on prevention due to the failure to address crime through punishment, leading the spotlight away from the offender and onto the victim (Mawby and Gill, 1987; Pointing and Maguire, 1988; Zedner, 1996).

However, there was a lack of actual data on the victim, as highlighted by the victim movement itself, which specifically aimed for the victim's needs to be recognized and addressed (Maguire and Shapland, 1990). This then, in combination with the recognition of the shortcomings of the police-recorded statistics (not only as regards providing complete information on the extent of, and trends in, crime but also as a tool to help develop and inform *aetiological* criminological theories), lent an impetus to the development of victimology and victim surveys.

Consequently, in the 1960s American criminologists began developing and experimenting with the use of large-scale victimization surveys. Three studies were conducted in the United States as part of the 1967 President's Commission on Law

Enforcement and Administration of Justice (PCLEAJ) to elucidate the extent of the crime problem and give a measure unaffected by recording and reporting practises (Lee, 2001). These PCLEAJ surveys then led to the development of the first *national* victimization survey, the National Crime Victimization Survey (NCVS). This was established in the United States in 1972, designed to shed light on this dark figure. It was the NCVS which in turn pointed and paved the way for the rest of the world in their development of national, representative crime surveys (Lee, 2007).

By the 1970s the UK was also moving towards this victim-centric approach. The emergence and success of the NCVS had helped stimulate interest in and an appetite for a British version. The Home Office research unit of the time commissioned perhaps the first significant victim survey in the UK in the early 1970s, borrowing heavily from the American model (published as *Surveying Victims* – Sparks, Genn and Dodd, 1977). This was not a national survey, instead conducted in London on a comparatively small scale. However, it addressed some major methodological issues and became key in the development of the British Crime Survey (BCS).

Alongside police-recorded crime figures, the BCS has become the main source of data on levels of crime in England and Wales since 1981 (Mayhew and Hough, 1988). It is a nationally representative victimization survey, asking respondents directly about their experiences of crime. It interviews adults (aged 16 and over) living in private households and is conducted face-to-face in the respondent's house. From 1982 it was run approximately every two years until 2001; since then it has been run on a continuous basis, with the reference period for interviews becoming the last 12 months pre-interview. The current sample size for the BCS is around 47,000 (interviews per year) compared to around 11,000 in 1982, and as such it is one of the largest social research surveys in the country. Periodically, the survey has also included booster samples, whether for younger groups (for example, 16–24) or ethnic minorities, in order to help increase the accuracy of resulting crime estimates. Response rates to the survey have remained high during its lifetime, at around 75 per cent (ranging from 73 to 83 per cent).

Since 2002 the results of the survey have been published alongside the police-recorded statistics in the same volume (*Crime in England and Wales*) to paint a fuller picture of crime than either source can provide alone. Generally speaking the BCS and recorded crime have shown similar trends (if not numbers) over the years, taking into account reporting and recording changes and variation, and over the last few years this has been particularly apparent. The BCS has provided detailed and wide-ranging information about the crime experience in England and Wales, information which has helped inform criminological theory, debate and policy in a wide range of areas. With the ability to provide a guide to the nature of crime, as well as a crime trend and risk indicators, the survey has been central in formulating crime-prevention policy. It is now integral to the government's drug strategy, being used to monitor the target to reduce drug use among young people. It is also currently the main source of data on perceptions of crime, anti-social behaviour and attitudes to the criminal justice system for the government (Kershaw, Nicholas and Walker, 2008).

In contrast to the complete enumeration of crime offered by official crime statistics, victimization surveys ask a representative sample of the population whether or not they have experienced certain crimes in a specific period. If they have been a victim, it probes further, gathering detailed information on the incident(s). By directly asking people about their own experiences, rather than relying on them reaching the attention of the police, they provide an alternative measure of crime to police statistics, one unaffected by reporting and recording practices (Coleman and Moynihan, 1996; Jupp, 1989). By asking consistently about the same types of offence, defined in the same way, they can also provide a trend in the crime rate.

Considering the BCS, experiences of victimization are first identified using a screener questionnaire, where a range of questions is asked about different types of incident. These key questions are worded informally so they are clear to all respondents, and are intended to capture the widest range of possible offences. For each incident identified in the screener questionnaire, a 'victim form' is completed about the event (up to a maximum of six incidents). The victim form collects detailed information about incidents, using a series of questions that help elicit the characteristics of the incident including information about: when and where it occurred; whether any force was used; details about the offenders; reporting behaviour; contact with the police; and use of victim support. Each victim form also includes an open-ended description of the incident, whereby the respondent describes what happened, enabling the correct definition of each incident.

Having asked a detailed set of questions about each incident, the victim forms are coded to translate survey responses into legal offence categories that match recorded crime figures. The coding system applied to BCS data is such that only one code is given per victim form, therefore a hierarchy of offence seriousness is used, with more serious offences taking priority. The coding of offences is part automated and part manual, with trained coders ensuring each offence has been accurately classified. There is an automated element to the process, which is generated by computer through looking at the pre-coded answers given in the victim form. These offence classifications are then used to estimate crime figures for the entire population.

Victimization surveys also have the ability to provide information on the risks of victimization, and how they vary by socio-demographic characteristics, as well as the nature of crime, characteristics of offenders and also impacts of incidents upon victims (be they physical, emotional or financial). They can also illuminate public attitudes to crime and fear of crime, serve as a test-bed for various criminological theories, as well as provide insight into other crime-related issues. All this is not to say that they are without their limitations, however, which we outline below.

In common with other survey-based measures, victim surveys suffer from a number of limitations that need to be understood when judging their efficacy as estimates of crime. In their design, surveys have historically omitted various subsets of the population, namely those under the age of 16, the homeless, the institutionalized, the Armed Forces, those in residential care, prison, halls of residence, as well as commercial and public sector establishments. The BCS is no exception, meaning that counts of crime will necessarily fail to capture the full extent of crime. The BCS also omits certain types of crime, specifically victimless crimes and homicide. Victim surveys are also susceptible to item non-response, with the extent of more sensitive offences like domestic violence unlikely to be fully captured. Attempts have been made to limit this potential problem, with surveys like the BCS regularly incorporating self-completion sections, and discouraging respondents from completing the survey in the presence of other household members.

Victim surveys also suffer from recall problems, and the unwillingness (or indeed over-willingness) to report to the survey. Accuracy of estimates are highly dependent upon recall; the respondent must be able to decide whether an incident occurred within the requested recall period and faltering memory can be a factor (both in terms of remembering the incident and/or when it occurred). 'Telescoping' can occur, whereby victims may include incidents outside of the requested time-frame due to the incident's salience in their mind, which can lead to over-reporting. In an attempt to reduce the impact of telescoping and memory decay, the BCS uses a life event calendar. This attempts to contextualize events or incidents individually for each respondent by drawing upon memorable events in the last 12 month period (for example, birthdays).

The calculation of crime rates is complex and series victimization is capped at five incidents, placing a limit on the extent of victimization. Critics argue that this decision seriously underestimates the incidence of crime, suggesting that as many as three million offences are omitted as a result of this decision (Farrell and Pease, 2007). However, this is undertaken to prevent estimates being disproportionately affected by a small majority of respondents (typically somewhere in the region of 100–200) who suffer a very high number of offences, and to maximize consistency over time. Victim surveys are also not shielded against changes in the level of reporting to interviewers, which may be affected by changes in public sensibilities to crime, themselves influenced by changes in the law. So, increases in the count of a particular incident may not be 'real' ones, rather simply a reflection of an increase in the propensity to report (Aye Maung, 1995).

National victimization surveys have also been set up in many other countries, including Canada, Australia and the Netherlands (Aye Maung, 1995). In addition to separate surveys, researchers have also established the International Crime and Victimization Survey. This was started in 1989 as a result of the proliferation of the victim-survey format and a desire to index cross-nationally, providing broad estimates of victimization risk in approximately 70 countries (see Mayhew and White, 1997; Nieuwbeerta, 2002; Van Kesteren, Mayhew and Nieuwbeerta, 2000). The victim survey itself has also further fuelled victimology as a viable avenue of criminology, resulting today in the inextricable linkage of victimology and the victim survey. The methodological authority of the victim-survey format, commanded by meticulous attention to detail in conceptualization and implementation, has seen it emerge and become widely recognized as the leading alternative to police-recorded crime statistics, and in some countries, the key measure of crime.

Self-reported Offending Surveys

The other principal method of measuring the extent of crime with social surveys is the use of self-reported offending surveys. These take a complementary approach to the measurement of crime, asking people directly about their offending behaviours, and using this information to form a picture of the extent of offending in society. Offending surveys will also sometimes incorporate a panel design, enabling a more thorough examination of offending careers, and quantifying how prolific offenders contribute to the overall crime rate. As with the victimization-survey approach, there are several benefits to measuring offending using a survey-based strategy, and yet, inevitably, there are also a number of limitations that need to be understood in order to critically evaluate their utility. This includes some additional considerations that were not apparent with victimization surveys.

The first offending studies were conducted in the USA during the 1940s and 1950s (see, for example, Nye, 1958). These were largely unsystematic studies of offending behaviour, often relying on small-scale samples of male school pupils to gain a greater understanding of the distribution of offending in society. However, it was not until the 1960s and 1970s that self-reported offending surveys became increasingly used, adopting more carefully constructed and representative samples to accurately capture the extent of offending (see, amongst others, Gold 1970; Akers, 1964; McDonald, 1969; Chambliss and Nagasawa, 1969; Hindelang, Hirschi and Weiss, 1981). More recently in the UK, the Home Office commissioned the Youth Lifestyles Survey aimed particularly at young people's offending (Graham and Bowling, 1995; Flood-Page et al., 2000), and latterly the Offending, Crime and Justice Survey (OCJS) (Budd, Sharp and Mayhew, 2005; Roe and Ashe, 2008; Sharp, Aldridge and Medina, 2006). The OCJS was asked of a nationally representative sample of approximately 10,000 people from England and Wales, and implemented a number of innovative design features to enable significantly more accurate assessments of offending behaviour to be made. It was first conducted in 2003, with the sample of 10–25-year-olds re-interviewed on three separate occasions to form a four-wave panel survey.

Offending surveys were introduced to address a key gap in crime measurement, providing a count of the level of offending within the general population to contrast official court figures. In the same way that victimization surveys gave us an alternative picture of the extent of crime to that provided by recorded crime statistics, offending surveys give us additional information about the extent of offending. The rationale behind them is to provide an estimate of offending that is not influenced by the functioning of the criminal justice system or by whether someone was actually convicted of an offence. They also allow for a more detailed assessment of criminal careers (including age of onset and desistance), and the nature of offending behaviour, by including a range of questions about each offence. Importantly, by directly asking a sample of people about their offending behaviours, this also enables researchers to construct a picture of crime that incorporates information on offences that do not have an easily identifiable victim and hence are unlikely to ever come to the attention of the police or courts. This is an area that is inadequately captured by victimization surveys and official statistics alike, making offending surveys an essential resource.

Offending surveys have presented a somewhat different picture of offending to the official picture, challenging the traditional view that it was restricted to a small minority of people. Instead they have demonstrated a much broader population of offenders throughout society, suggesting that as many as four in ten people had committed an offence in their lifetime, and one in ten had committed an offence in the last year (Budd, Sharp and Mayhew, 2005). They have also been instrumental in highlighting the small minority of offenders that committed a disproportionate number of offences, later identified as prolific (or persistent) offenders. As such, and in conjunction with victimization surveys, they have presented many challenges to commonly held beliefs about crime and offending.

In contrast to official statistics, which rely on court data to construct a measure of offending, offending surveys ask people directly about the offences they have committed within a given time period (usually 12 months). This typically takes the form of a list of different offences, with each survey participant required to indicate how many times they have committed each offence. This is sometimes in the form of a direct count, and sometimes relies on more descriptive indicators of the frequency of offending (for example, 'a lot', 'not very often', 'not at all'). The decision to use more descriptive categories over a direct frequency is intended to account for the inaccuracies associated with correctly counting the number of offences someone has committed within a given time-frame. However, these more general descriptions have faced criticism for allowing for individual interpretations of the meaning of different categories; what one person may define as 'not very often' is unlikely to be the same as another person's (Coleman and Moynihan, 1996). Crucial to this method of uncovering offending behaviour is the construction of a full list of offences, and the ease with which offenders are able to classify incidents into discrete offence categories. Considerable attention is therefore spent on the development of a full list of offence categories, and the development of clearly delineated classifications.

Measuring offending using survey methods has meant that it has been possible to supplement basic offending counts with additional details about offenders and their progress through the criminal justice system. In this way estimates of the proportion of offenders that are caught can be obtained, and prolific offenders can be identified. Results from the Home Office offending survey suggest that only 6 per cent of people who had committed an offence in the last year were arrested, and only 3 per cent were charged, providing clear evidence of a large justice gap (Budd, Sharp and Mayhew, 2005). Importantly, offending-survey research has also estimated that only 2 per cent of people (25 per cent of offenders) would be classified as a persistent offender (defined as someone who had committed three or more offences within a year), but that this group were responsible for as many as 82 per cent of all offences (Budd, Sharp and Mayhew, 2005).

Offending surveys have been particularly useful for estimating the extent of victimless crimes, like drug offences and internet fraud. These are typically underestimated in official records and victimization surveys since they both largely rely on victims identifying the offences and offender. Since offending surveys ask people directly about whether they have committed these offences, it is possible to get clearer and more consistent estimates of the extent of these crimes. This has shown that drug use is considerably more widespread than other estimates would suggest, with much of this offending going unnoticed in official counts.

Offending surveys have also informed us about the nature of offending, including details on how many people were involved in a particular offence and whether they were under the influence of drugs or alcohol. Coupled with this, they also frequently collect information about the motivations of offenders, allowing researchers to explore in detail why people commit particular crimes. The recent Home Office offending study showed that approximately 24 per cent of offences are committed in groups, but that this figure differs widely by offence type, with vehicle-related theft and criminal damage the most likely to be committed with others. In contrast, they found that violent offences were far less likely to involve more than one offender (Budd, Sharp and Mayhew, 2005). They also identify a range of motivations behind offending behaviour, with vehicle-related thefts often the result of boredom or 'for the fun of the buzz', whereas assaults were more likely to be the result of being 'annoyed or upset with someone'.

In common with victimization surveys, and social surveys more generally, a number of limitations with self-report surveys have been highlighted that need to be understood when assessing existing evidence. Perhaps the greatest challenge to surveys that attempt to measure the extent of offending is non-response, both unit and item (Tarling, 1993). This is often a result of the inherently sensitive nature of offending, meaning that many people may be unwilling to admit to criminal behaviour (Coleman and Moynihan, 1996). This is particularly problematic because of the high likelihood that non-response is directly linked to the question of interest, with strong evidence to suggest that people are least likely to respond when thinking about more serious types of offence. Consequently, offending surveys tend to underestimate the extent of crime, with serious offending suffering most from underestimation. This often leads to an overemphasis on more trivial forms of offending, limiting their use as overall measures of crime (Maguire, 2007).

In an attempt to tackle this problem, offending surveys regularly incorporate a self-completion section to encourage respondents to report honestly about their level of offending without being influenced by the presence of interviewers or other household members. Whilst this cannot help the problem of unit non-response, these self-completion elements do tend to lead to significantly higher estimates of offending, particularly when considering more serious offences. The OCJS also incorporated an audio-assisted self-completion element, with the respondents given headphones, allowing them to listen to the questions privately, and record their own responses. This was thought to be particularly suitable because the study included young people and those whose native language was not English, where difficulties with reading may make straightforward self-completion elements unreliable (Phelps et al., 2007).

Offending surveys also require people to respond truthfully to questions asking about their offending behaviour, something that is difficult to verify during the interview. Like non-response, this is also expected to be the most problematic when considering more serious forms of offending. In an attempt to examine the extent to which people respond truthfully, Farrington (1989) linked respondents from the Cambridge study in delinquent development directly to official statistics, demonstrating that only 4 per cent of those who were involved in the criminal justice system had failed to identify the offence. However, this is clearly an imperfect test as it relies directly on those offending statistics that offender surveys intend to augment, and can tell us nothing about the accuracy of reporting of offences that do not get identified by the criminal justice system. It does, though, suggest that offending surveys may be getting us closer to the full extent of offending than if we were to rely solely on official records.

The coverage of offending surveys has faced considerable criticism, with many of the earlier studies using unrepresentative samples (typically school-age boys) to capture the extent of offending. This is particularly problematic when attempting to produce overall measures of offending, since it is well established that young people commit disproportionately higher numbers of less serious offences, but considerably fewer crimes like burglary (Coleman and Moynihan, 1996). The net result is that these early studies presented a distorted picture of the extent of crime, over-counting some types of offence, whilst failing to capture the true extent of other offences. This limited their use as general measures of the extent of crime. Early studies have also been criticized for focusing too heavily on more trivial offences like 'fighting', 'truancy' and 'petty theft', with considerably less information provided about more serious offence categories. The scope of offending surveys has since been greatly extended, with more recent examples using nationally representative surveys, and including more complete lists of offences. For example, the recent OCJS includes minor offences like truancy and anti-social behaviour, more serious offences like robbery, assault and burglary, and a range of less visible offences like fraud, hacking and handling stolen goods (Phelps et al., 2007). Yet like victimization surveys, there are still distinct groups that are missing from survey samples, for example, those in communal establishments, and those in institutions.

Offending surveys also rely on people being able to accurately self-classify their behaviour into particular offence categories, as well as requiring them to remember the extent of their own offending behaviour within a given time period. Research suggests that difficulties associated with self-classification typically lead to a certain degree of double counting, with people erroneously counting the same offence twice within different categories (Coleman and Moynihan, 1996). This further increases the risk that self-offending studies may be providing an inaccurate picture of the extent of offending. Like victimization surveys, offending surveys can also suffer from problems of recall, with a tendency for people to forget about incidents, or to incorrectly report an incident that occurred outside of the survey's time-frame.

Even with advances in the use of self-completion elements, extended sample designs and careful question design, it is still expected that offending surveys will underperform when considering the most serious types of offence. As a result, whilst these surveys have helped us to better understand offending, this has been restricted to less serious forms of offending. Consequently, we must still rely on official statistics for information about the most serious types of offence.

Crimes against Businesses

The measurement of white-collar crime has caused considerable debate, with recorded crime figures providing an inadequate picture of this group of crimes.[2] These crimes rarely have an easily identifiable victim, with offences often aimed at businesses rather than specific individuals. Consequently, the evidence from recorded crime figures is extremely limited, and largely restricted to counts of the extent of fraud and forgery (Kershaw, Nicholas and Walker, 2008). Instead, much of the information we rely on about this source of crime comes either from the Association for Payment Clearing Services (APACS), which deals with credit card fraud, or is restricted to large-scale incidents that feature heavily in the media (Slapper and Tombs, 1999). However, social surveys have also made a significant contribution to the measurement of white-collar crime, with the Commercial Victimisation Survey (CVS) fielded to businesses in England and Wales in 1994 and 2002 (Mirlees-Black and Ross, 1995; Shury et al., 2005), and the British Retail Consortium (BRC) annual survey of retailers forming a significant proportion of the evidence base (British Retail Consortium, 2008).

The CVS adopts the same logic and a similar methodology to victimization surveys, but differs by asking businesses directly about their experiences of white-collar crime. This is defined in a broad sense within the survey as crimes experienced by retail and manufacturing premises (Shury et al., 2005). In contrast,

---

2   The very definition of white-collar crime has also been the subject of considerable debate, and remains an under-researched area of criminology. For the purposes of this discussion, we use the term to refer to those crimes that are committed against businesses, either by the public, employees or other businesses, although we acknowledge that a range of other crime types can also be incorporated under this heading (for a recent review, see Nelken, 2007).

the BRC annual survey focuses specifically on the costs to retailers from all criminal activity.

The CVS, BRC retail survey and other private business surveys (Ernst and Young, 2003; PricewaterhouseCoopers, 2005) have helped our understanding of this relatively difficult to capture group of crimes. These have shown that a very high proportion of retailers experience one or more crimes within a given year (with theft the most common, but also including some incidents of major fraud), and that approximately half of manufacturers have experienced such crime (Shury et al., 2005). These types of finding have helped raise the profile of crimes against businesses, giving considerably more detail about the distribution of these crimes.

However, like the other survey methods outlined above, the use of business surveys has certain limitations that need to be addressed when assessing their validity as measures of the extent of crime. The first is the difficulty in assuring a complete sampling frame from which to select businesses to be included within the survey. This requires a complete list of all businesses that are operating within the population of interest, and also requires an all-inclusive definition of businesses to ensure full coverage. The CVS uses an electronic directory of businesses as its sampling frame, but restricts its scope to small and medium-sized businesses (no more than 250 employees). The BRC annual survey is administered to all members of the consortium, including larger businesses; however, it is not able to provide information on those businesses that are not members.

It is also often difficult to identify a suitable respondent within each industry, with a clear need to ensure consistency across businesses when completing the survey. Since many white-collar offences do not have a readily identifiable victim, finding a suitable representative can be problematic, as many employees may not be aware of any crimes occurring. The choice of representative may also be directly related to the type of organization, with a good representative in one business lacking adequate information in another.

Even if access can be obtained, these business surveys also face problems in defining what offences to include, and whether the respondents understand these incidents as a crime. The conceptual murkiness surrounding white-collar crime makes this particularly problematic, with many incidents proving difficult to classify. For example, small-scale theft from work by employees has been difficult to classify. Whilst this may fall within official definitions of crime, to an organization this may simply be classified as 'shrinkage', and hence not be referred to in a survey interview.

These specific limitations notwithstanding, the work of Mirlees-Black and Ross (1995) and of Shury et al. (2005) has produced valuable insights into white-collar crime, significantly extending the evidence base. It has also fed into the more detailed qualitative research that has been conducted, giving a clearer picture of these types of offence.

Summary

In this chapter we have presented a general overview of how social surveys have been used to provide a measure of the extent of crime in society. This has included details on the current state of the art in crime-survey design, but has also recognized the importance of the historical context of these approaches. The measurement of crime using surveys is a constantly evolving field, with increasing pressures from the public for transparency leading survey methodologists to introduce new techniques to ensure accuracy. This has included the introduction of audio self-completion methods, the extension of sample designs to capture ethnic minorities and young people, and the development of methods to uncover business crime. There is, however, still a way to go, with the limitations outlined here representing some of the challenges for the future. Following the recent expansion of the BCS to incorporate the under 16s, the number of people absent from these surveys is shrinking, but they still miss responses from people in institutions and communal establishments, along with homeless respondents, groups who potentially have very different experiences of crime and offending behaviour. Similarly, the dropping response rates facing many social surveys over the last 20 years, whilst yet to seriously affect crime surveys, will likely lead to more problems of coverage in the future that will need to be sufficiently addressed.

References

Akers, R.L. (1964), 'Socio-economic Status and Delinquent Behaviour', *Journal of Research in Crime and Delinquency* 1: 38–46.

Aye Maung, N. (1995), *Young People, Victimisation and the Police: British Crime Survey Findings on Experiences and Attitudes of 12 to 15 Year Olds*, Home Office Research Study 140 (London: Home Office Research Development and Statistics Directorate).

Beirne, P. (1993), *Inventing Criminology: Essays on the Rise of 'Homo Criminalis'* (Albany, New York: State University of New York Press).

British Retail Consortium (2008), *The Retail Crime Survey 2007–2008* (London: The Stationery Office).

Budd, T., Sharp, C. and Mayhew, P. (2005), *Offending in England and Wales: First Results from the 2003 Crime and Justice Survey*, Home Office Research Study 275 (London: Home Office Research Development and Statistics Directorate).

Burrows, J., Tarling, R., Mackie, A., Lewis, R. and Taylor, G. (2000), *Review of Police Forces' Crime Recording Practices* (London: Home Office Research Development and Statistics Directorate).

Chambliss, W.J. and Nagasawa, R.H. (1969), 'On the Validity of Official Statistics: A Comparison of White, Black and Japanese High School Boys', *Journal of Research in Crime and Delinquency* 6: 71–7.

Coleman, C. and Moynihan, J. (1996), *Understanding Crime Data: Haunted by the Dark Figure* (Buckingham: Open University Press).

Ernst and Young (2003), *Fraud – The Unmanaged Risk*, 8th Global Survey <www. ey.com>.

Farrell, G. and Pease, K. (2007), 'The Sting in the British Crime Survey Tail: Multiple Victimizations', in M. Maxfield and M. Hough (eds), *Surveying Crime in the Twenty First Century*, Vol. 22 of *Crime Prevention Studies* (Cullompton: Willan), 33–54.

Farrington, D.P. (1989), 'Self-reported and Official Offending from Adolescence to Adulthood', in M.W. Klein (ed.), *Cross-National Research in Self-Reported Crime and Delinquency* (Dordrecht, Netherlands: Kluwer), 399–423.

Flood-Page, C., Campbell, S., Harrington, V. and Miller, J. (2000), *Findings from the 1998/99 Youth Lifestyles Survey*, Home Office Research Study No. 209 (London: Home Office Research Development and Statistics Directorate).

Gold, M. (1970), *Delinquent Behaviour in an American City* (Belmont: Brooks/ Cole).

Graham, J. and Bowling, B. (1995), *Young People and Crime*, Home Office Research Study No. 145 (London: HMSO, Home Office Research Development and Statistics Directorate).

Hindelang, M., Hirschi, T. and Weiss, J.G. (1981), *Measuring Delinquency* (Beverly Hills: Sage).

Jupp, V. (1989), *Methods of Criminological Research* (London: Routledge).

Karmen, A. (1990), *Crime Victims: An Introduction to Victimology* (2nd edition) (Belmont: Wadsworth).

Kershaw, C., Nicholas, S. and Walker, A. (2008), *Crime in England and Wales 2007/08: Findings from the British Crime Survey and Police Recorded Crime* (London: Home Office Research Development and Statistics Directorate).

Lee, M. (2001), 'The Genesis of Fear of Crime', *Theoretical Criminology* 5: 467–85.

Lee, M. (2007), *Inventing Fear of Crime: Criminology and the Politics of Anxiety* (Portland, Oregon: Willan Publishing).

Maguire, M. (2007), 'Crime Data and Statistics', in M. Maguire, R. Morgan and R. Reiner (eds), *The Oxford Handbook of Criminology* (4th edition) (Oxford: Oxford University Press), 241–300.

Maguire, M. and Shapland, J. (1990), 'The "Victims Movement" in Europe', in A. Lurigio, W. Skogan and R. Davis (eds), *Victims of Crime: Problems, Policies and Programs* (Newbury Park: Sage), 205–25.

Mawby, R.I. and Gill, M.L. (1987), *Crime Victims: Needs, Services and the Voluntary Sector* (London: Tavistock).

Mawby, R.I. and Walklate, S. (1994), *Critical Victimology* (London: Sage).

Mayhew, P. and Hough, M. (1988), 'The British Crime Survey: Origins and Impact', in M. Maguire and J. Pointing (eds), *Victims of Crime: A New Deal?* (Milton Keynes: Open University Press), 156–63.

Mayhew, P. and White, P. (1997), *The 1996 International Crime Victimisation Survey*, Home Office Research Findings, 57 (London: Home Office Research Development and Statistics Directorate).

McDonald, L. (1969), *Social Class and Delinquency* (London: Faber).

Ministry of Justice (2008), *Criminal Statistics: England and Wales 2007. Statistics Bulletin* (London: Ministry of Justice).

Mirrlees-Black, C. and Ross, A. (1995), *Crime against Retail and Manufacturing Premises: Findings from the 1994 Commercial Victimisation Survey*, Home Office Research Study No. 146 (London: Home Office Research Development and Statistics Directorate).

Nelken, D. (2007), 'White-Collar and Corporate Crime', in M. Maguire, R. Morgan and R. Reiner (eds), *The Oxford Handbook of Criminology* (Oxford: Oxford University Press), 241–300.

Nieuwbeerta, P. (2002), *Crime Victimization in Comparative Perspective: Results from the International Crime Victims Survey, 1989–2000* (Cullompton, Devon: Willan Publishing).

Nye, F.I. (1958), *Family Relationships and Delinquent Behaviour* (New York: Wiley).

Phelps, A., Maxwell, C., Fong, B., McCracken, H., Nevill, C., Pickering, K. and Tait, C. (2007), *Offending Crime and Justice Survey 2006 (England and Wales) Technical Report*, Vol. 1 (London: Natcen and BMRB).

Pointing, J. and Maguire, M. (1988), 'The Rediscovery of the Crime Victim', in J. Pointing and M. Maguire (eds), *Victims of Crime: A New Deal?* (Milton Keynes: Open University Press), 11–16.

PricewaterhouseCoopers (2005), *Global Economic Crime Survey 2005* <www.pwcglobal.com>.

Roe, S. and Ashe, J. (2008), *Young People and Crime: Findings from the 2006 Offending, Crime and Justice Survey*, Home Office Statistical Bulletin 09/08 (London: Home Office Research Development and Statistics Directorate).

Sharp, C., Aldridge, J. and Medina, J. (2006), *Delinquent Youth Groups and Offending Behaviour: Findings from the 2004 Offending, Crime and Justice Survey*, Home Office Online Report 14/06 (London: Home Office Research Development and Statistics Directorate).

Shury, J., Speed, M., Vivian, D., Kechel, A. and Nicholas, S. (2005), *Crime against Retail and Manufacturing Premises: Findings from the 2002 Commercial Victimisation Survey*, Home Office Online Report 37/05 (London: Home Office Research Development and Statistics Directorate).

Slapper, G. and Tombs, S. (1999), *Corporate Crime* (Harlow: Longman).

Smith, A. (2006), *Crime Statistics: An Independent Review* (London: Home Office).

Sparks, R., Genn, H. and Dodd, D. (1977), *Surveying Victims* (Chichester: Wiley).

Statistics Commission (2006), *Crime Statistics: User Perspectives* (London: Statistics Commission).

Tarling, R. (1993), *Analysing Offending: Data Models and Interpretations* (London: HMSO).

Van Kesteren, J., Mayhew, P. and Nieuwbeerta, P. (2000), *Criminal Victimisation in Seventeen Countries: Key Findings from the 2000 International Crime Victims Survey* (The Hague: Ministry of Justice, WODC).

Zedner, L. (1996), 'Victims', in M. Maguire, R. Morgan and R. Reiner (eds), *The Oxford Handbook of Criminology* (Oxford: Oxford University Press), 577–612.

Chapter 4
Measuring Political Behaviour and Attitudes

Oliver Heath and Robert Johns

To the casual observer, measurement in political behaviour might look a decidedly ropey business. Opinion polls frequently get election outcomes wrong, sometimes spectacularly so, as we saw in 1992 when a Labour victory was widely predicted, only for the Tories to return to power with something to spare. Moreover, even after the event, the survey tally of votes cast for political parties rarely matches their actual vote share, and levels of turnout are seriously over-reported, almost to the tune of 20 percentage points in the 2005 British Election Study (BES). These large discrepancies between survey estimates of political behaviour and official tallies are undoubtedly a cause for concern; if surveys cannot be relied upon to get these basic objective facts of elections correct, or even close to the true mark, then they have little hope of accurately measuring the less tangible concepts in political science, such as party identification and political attitudes. These doubts are clearly not without foundation, but at the same time neither should they be overstated. In virtually no other field of survey research are the results faced with such immediate tests of their accuracy; as Jowell et al. (1993) note, most are never tested at all. These 'tests' have provided a fertile ground for examining the sources of the discrepancy between survey estimates of political phenomena and the official results, and in this way prior research has been able to shed light on the nature and magnitude of many of the factors that influence measurement problems in survey research. The findings from this research have relevance for a wide variety of measurement problems, and as we examine in this chapter, lessons can be taken on board to improve our understanding of other less easily verified phenomena.

Political Behaviour: Turnout and Vote Choice

Somewhat ironically, measurement issues in political behaviour have tended to focus more on attitudes, values and opinions than actual behaviour. However, despite the ostensibly objective nature of most political acts (which may be a reason why they have received comparatively little attention), survey measures of political behaviour are far from straightforward, and are beset with a variety of problems relating to memory, social desirability, sampling and non-response, to name a few. These problems potentially have two serious implications for our understanding of political behaviour. The first, more basic, problem is that surveys may not provide accurate measures of the 'true' level of political participation in the population. That is, they are not reliable or valid. The second and potentially more serious problem is that they may provide biased measures, which could distort our understanding of the explanatory factors associated with political behaviour. For example, if surveys tend to over-report turnout, they may not be very accurate. But if the sources of this over-report are randomly distributed, it may not bias our results.

Turnout

One example that illustrates many of these problems is the not so simple task of voting. The validity of self-reported turnout has been a cause for concern since the earliest election surveys. It is not uncommon to find that the proportion of respondents who report voting far exceeds the official estimates of actual voter turnout. For example, in the 2005 BES, self-reported turnout was measured at 79 per cent, well above the official turnout figure of 61 per cent. This substantial discrepancy between survey estimates of self-reported turnout and official estimates of turnout is not just limited to Britain, and is common to most surveys carried out around the world (and has been a particular source of concern in, for example, the United States). Discrepancies of this scale may have serious implications for our understanding of why people vote or not, which has become all the more pressing in recent years given the substantial decline in levels of turnout in many advanced democracies.

Over the last few years there has been a considerable amount of research on the sources of this discrepancy. Two main factors tend to be emphasized: problems to do with respondents misreporting what they have done (where some respondents say they have voted when in fact they have not); and problems to do with survey response bias (where turnout among non-respondents is substantially less than turnout among survey respondents). One popular and effective way of examining the sources of this over-report is through the use of voter validation studies. This involves getting access to the official electoral registers used by polling officials to mark off the names of people as they actually voted, and cross-checking what survey respondents tell interviewers they have done against what they actually have done. Using this approach, Swaddle and Heath (1989) highlight four main reasons for the discrepancy: response bias, failure to trace all movers, redundancy in the electoral register, and misreporting by survey respondents.

Non-response may introduce bias if those individuals who do not agree to be interviewed for the survey (or cannot be interviewed because they are away) are less likely to vote than those individuals who agree to be interviewed. Swaddle and Heath found that according to the official turnout register, turnout among the latter (83 per cent) was substantially higher than among the former (75 per cent). A substantial portion of the apparent over-report in turnout by surveys is thus attributable to issues of response and coverage. One obvious way in which survey measurement can be improved is therefore to ensure high response rates, which in recent years has fallen somewhat to around 60 per cent. But there is also the question of how accurately the survey instrument actually measures turnout. Swaddle and Heath attribute a quarter of the 11-point discrepancy to misreports, in which respondents said they had voted when in fact they had not (86 per cent claimed to have voted but 83 per cent actually did so).

Given the magnitude of the discrepancy between reported turnout and official turnout, it is now fairly standard practice in national election studies to validate turnout, but this is an expensive and time-consuming process, which ultimately would not be necessary with an improved survey instrument. Two factors are commonly emphasized: *memory failure* (Belli et al., 1999), and *social desirability bias*, in which respondents may claim to have voted so as to cast themselves in a favourable light, perhaps out of embarrassment at failing in their civic obligations (see, for example, Clausen, 1968; Silver, Anderson and Abramson, 1986; Traugott and Katosh, 1979).

Memory failure, or source monitoring errors (Belli et al., 1999), attributes over-reporting to a respondent confusing past voting behaviour with actual voting behaviour in the most recent election. In short some respondents may be unable to identify the source of the memory, causing them to confuse real participation with past thoughts or behaviour. While memory confusion implies an inability to distinguish a truthful from an untruthful response, social desirability bias leads either to respondents knowingly and falsely reporting voting out of a desire to appear a good citizen, or to memory errors regarding behaviours that the respondent intends or desires to do (Presser, 1990; Belli et al., 1999). One way to counter-act social desirability effects is to give respondents a ready-made excuse for not having voted. The standard BES question thus attempts to make non-voting appear like a normal and acceptable form of behaviour.

> **Question** (No. Bq12a) Talking with people about the general election on May 5th, we have found that a lot of people didn't manage to vote. How about you, did you manage to vote in the general election?

Yet experiments in revised question wording that have been based on these explanations have failed to reduce either the level of reported voting or the accuracy of reported vote (Abelson, Loftus and Greenwald, 1992; Presser, 1990). Belli et al. (1999) consider over-report to be a result of their combined influence. The wish to present oneself in a desirable light often affects what aspects of the past are remembered and the reconstructive inferences regarding what likely had happened (McDonald and Hirt, 1997; Sanitioso, Kunda and Fong, 1990). To tap into these joint pressures, Belli et al. (1999) conducted a question-wording experiment in which they devised a number of additional get-out clauses, such as: 'We also sometimes find that people who thought they had voted actually did not vote. Also, people who usually vote may have trouble saying for sure whether they voted in a particular election'; and also asked respondents to try and think about what the weather was like and who they saw on the way to the polling booth, amongst other things, to try and contextualize their memory. In addition to this somewhat lengthy question, they also introduced a number of additional response sets:

1. I did not vote in the November 5th election
2. I thought about voting this time but didn't
3. I usually vote but didn't this time
4. I am sure I voted in the November 5th election.

Perhaps unsurprisingly, given the overall tone of the question, they found that this format significantly reduced the level of reported turnout. However, it is unclear whether this was a consequence of the extended introduction to the question or the additional response sets. Whereas it is perhaps not desirable to have such a long, almost leading, question, if the addition of extra response categories reduces the level of misreport, this may be a more feasible way of improving the survey measure of turnout.

This may in turn have implications for analysis. Researchers on turnout generally seem to assume that the urge to give socially desirable responses, and in this case to over-report voting, affects all non-voters equally (Blais, 2000). However, studies of survey response long ago established that some types of people are much more likely to edit their answers for social acceptability (DeMaio, 1984; Paulhus, 2002). This has been addressed from a psychological perspective, with traits like self-deception strongly predictive of socially desirable response (Berinsky, 2004), or from a sociological angle, with speculation that working-class or less educated respondents might have less confidence in insisting on a potentially undesirable response. Yet both approaches neglect the importance of context. The respondents most susceptible to social desirability bias are those with a clear view that a particular answer is socially desirable, and evidence from turnout studies bears this out. Those most likely to over-report voting exhibit the characteristics of those most likely to vote: they are the highly educated, the old, strong party identifiers and those with a high sense of civic duty (Bernstein, Chadha and Montjoy, 2001; Silver, Anderson and Abramson, 1986; Swaddle and Heath, 1989). These biases thus serve to strengthen the association between key explanatory factors and turnout.

Vote Choice

While the problems of measuring turnout accurately are well documented, potential problems to do with measuring party choice are somewhat harder to quantify. Since we cannot match survey responses to official records of which party people voted for at the individual level, we must rely on aggregate comparisons with official vote tallies (which might disguise churning at the individual level). Broadly speaking, the measurement of vote choice is conducted from two temporal perspectives. The first aims to measure future, or predicted, vote choice, and in the run-up to a general election respondents are asked which party they are 'most likely' to vote for. The second measures past vote; and after the general election respondents are asked to report which party they did vote for. Each approach presents challenges, which survey researchers have attempted to meet in a variety of ways.

Intended Vote Choice   The practice of predicting election results using public opinion polls has a somewhat patchy record. Some of the criticism has been unfair, in that opinion polls conducted more than a few days before an election are an indication of how the parties stand at that point in the campaign rather than a prediction of the final outcome. Only last-minute polls can really be tested and hence criticized as inaccurate. However, even those eleventh-hour forecasts have sometimes been spectacularly wrong, such as in the 1992 British general election, when in the final week of the campaign opinion polls gave Labour a narrow average lead of around two percentage points, only for the Conservatives to run out comfortable winners by over seven percentage points. Although this was an extreme case, opinion polls of this type in Britain have consistently over-reported the Labour share of the vote, leading some commentators to speak of a pro-Labour bias (Crewe 2001).

The reasons for this bias are not well understood. And attempts to redress it have tended to focus on developing post-hoc weights to the data, rather than improved measurement instruments to address the underlying problem (at least in the commercial sector). Undoubtedly sample design has been a major contributing factor. Commercial opinion polls are most commonly based on quota sampling methods, and thus rely on the extensive use of weights to make them 'representative'. Incorrect weighting (assuming the working class population to be substantially larger than it actually is) was perhaps the single largest factor for the 1992 polls debacle (Jowell et al., 1993). But this is still only part of the story (though obviously an important part).

Another important factor concerns the relationship between intention and actual behaviour. Do people do what they say they will do? In 1992 there was a widespread belief that the under-recording of Conservative support reflected a 'spiral of silence' effect, in which people who believe that they hold unfashionable views refuse even to participate in opinion polls (Noelle-Neumann, 1993; Broughton, 1995), or refuse to reveal who they will vote for (perhaps opting instead for the undecided option, or to say they will not vote). Although this is a potentially plausible explanation for 1992, when the Conservative Party was viewed in a relatively unsympathetic light, it fails to explain why so many polls report a pro-Labour bias even when the Conservatives are relatively popular.

The relationship between intention and behaviour is not straightforward. Granberg and Holmberg (1990) report that the relationship between intended future vote and self-reported past vote tends to be stronger for strong party identifiers and people whose intended vote matches what they voted in previous elections, and is somewhat weaker for people who are planning to switch party allegiance. The implications of this are that vote intention is a more reliable instrument for predicting stability than it is for predicting change, and since most pre-election polls are primarily interested in whether or not a change will take place, this is a problem. More research is needed on how the relationship between intention and behaviour varies by different sub-groups, either with respect to demographics or political interest or political knowledge, for example. If the groups that are typically associated with weaker intention–behaviour relationships are also associated with greater support for one party, say the Labour Party, this might help to explain some of the pro-Labour bias that is frequently observed.

Recall of Past Vote   Now we turn to survey measures of past vote. Given the validity problems of self-reported turnout, political scientists have also been concerned that problems to do with misreporting past behaviour may infect survey measures of vote choice – one of the most prominent dependent variables in the field. Much of the research on this has been carried out in the United States, where a systematic over-report for the winning candidate has been observed, particularly for lower-level offices such as House, Senator and Governor (Wright, 1990, 1993; Eubank and Gow, 1984; Box-Steffensmeier, Jacobson and Grant, 2000; Atkeson, 1999). Wright, for example, reports that the average difference between the reported and actual vote for the winner was 7 per cent for the House of Representatives, and that the pro-winner bias increases with the time lag between the election and the interview. There has been much debate as to whether this actually refers to a *bandwagon effect*, in which survey respondents over-report having voted for the winning party or candidate; or whether it reflects a *pro-incumbent bias*, in which respondents over-report voting for the incumbent.

It is not so clear, however, whether these potential biases apply in the same way to the UK. As noted earlier, it is commonly thought that surveys tend to over-report Labour shares of the vote, and from Table 4.1 we can see that there is some evidence to support a pro-Labour bias in the BES surveys, which have never underestimated Labour support, and in some elections have substantially overestimated it, such as in 2001 when the self-reported Labour vote was nearly eight percentage points higher than their official share of the vote. By contrast, when the Conservatives lose an election, their vote has tended to be underestimated by the BES (on average by four percentage points), but when they win it is only slightly overestimated (on average by one percentage point). To be sure the magnitude of these differences is not great (although in close elections they would be far from trivial). But there may well be two competing factors at work here: a bandwagon effect and a pro-Labour bias. Although in many elections these two influences cancel each other out at the aggregate level (in particular when the Conservatives win), if the sources of these biases are not the same, then it may not be reasonable to assume that the biases cancel each other out at the individual level as well.

Table 4.1   Survey shares of the vote, and official shares of the vote, British general elections 1964–2005

	Party	1964	1966	1970	1974F	1974O	1979	1983	1987	1992	1997	2001	2005
BES	Con	40.1	37.8	45.3	38.0	36.0	47.0	44.7	43.9	42.0	26.4	25.3	28.7
	Labour	46.3	51.3	45.2	40.6	42.5	37.6	29.3	31.2	35.0	49.1	48.2	39.6
	Liberal	13.3	10.3	7.2	19.1	18.0	13.8	24.6	23.5	15.9	16.5	18.0	21.3
	Other	0.3	0.6	2.3	2.3	3.5	1.6	1.4	1.4	7.2	8.0	8.5	10.4
Official	Con	43.4	41.8	46	37.8	35.7	43.9	42.4	42.2	41.9	30.7	31.7	32.4
	Labour	44.1	47.6	42.7	37.2	39.3	36.9	27.6	30.8	34.4	43.2	40.7	35.2
	Liberal	11.1	8.6	7.5	19.3	18.3	13.8	25.4	22.5	17.8	16.8	18.3	22
	Other	1.3	2	3.8	5.7	6.7	5.4	4.6	4.5	5.9	9.3	9.3	10.4
Diff	Con	-3.3	-4.0	-0.7	0.2	0.3	3.1	2.3	1.7	0.1	-4.3	-6.4	-3.7
	Labour	2.2	3.7	2.5	3.4	3.2	0.7	1.7	0.4	0.6	5.9	7.5	4.4
	Liberal	2.2	1.7	-0.3	-0.2	-0.3	0.0	-0.8	1.0	-1.9	-0.3	-0.4	-0.7
	Other	-1.0	-1.4	-1.5	-3.4	-3.2	-3.8	-3.2	-3.1	1.3	-1.3	-0.8	-0.1

Source: BESIS: British Election Study <http://www.besis.org/Frameset_SplitThree.aspx?c ontrol=CCESDSeriesMenu&seriesid=17>. British Governments and Elections since 1945 <http://www.psr.keele.ac.uk/area/uk/uktable.htm>.

Various attempts have been made to try and understand the sources of error in past-vote recall. The most prominent explanations relate to the survey instrument, the non-voters who report voting, and social–psychological factors that may produce bandwagon effects or incumbency effects. Issues to do with the survey instrument have focused on question order and question-wording format. In Britain, the standard vote-choice question is open ended, without prompts and is asked to all self-reported voters: 'Which party did you vote for in the general election?' There is some debate as to whether it is better to ask an open question like this, or whether to ask respondents to mark a replica ballot (which would include information about the candidate's name). The rationale for this would appear sound, as it more closely reproduces the situation that voters face in the voting both, and could act as an *aide-memoire* to forgetful voters. However, experimental evidence from the US has shown that including candidate names tends to result in a substantial over-statement of the vote for incumbents, who tend to receive higher rates of name recognition (Box-Steffensmeier, Jacobson and Grant, 2000). The addition of the candidate's name provides an extra cue to voters, and since more people are able to recognize the name of the incumbent than the challenger, it acts as a 'prompt' for less informed voters to follow. A second factor related to the survey instrument is to do with question-order effects. Eubank and Gow (1984) have suggested that asking questions about incumbents before the vote item produces pro-incumbent bias. However, various question-wording experiments have not supported this assertion, and question placement does not appear to influence the high level of aggregate over-reporting for either the winning candidate (Wright, 1993) or the incumbent candidate (Box-Steffensmeier, Jacobson and Grant, 2000).

Another potentially important source of error in measuring vote choice may relate to the problems of self-reported turnout, which we highlighted earlier. It could be that non-voting voters (those who said that they voted when validated records show that they did not) are more likely to say that they voted for the winning party, since they are already influenced by social desirability biases (Atkeson, 1999). From the 2005 BES we can see that there is some evidence to support this, with non-voting voters much more likely to vote Labour (50 per cent) and less likely to vote Conservative (22 per cent) than recorded voters (39 per cent Labour versus 29 per cent Conservative respectively). However, even with these people excluded from the analysis, there is still a substantial over-report for Labour (although the magnitude of this effect is reduced by one percentage point).

The last set of factors that have been emphasized are more social–psychological (Wright, 1993; Atkeson, 1999). Wright argued that less politically engaged respondents are less likely to retain the information of who they voted for in their memory. Voters simply forget which party or candidate they voted for, and exposure to post-election media coverage of the winner tends to bias responses, creating a bandwagon effect. This suggests that the timing of the survey after the election is critical.

We can get an indication of how this matters by examining whether patterns of vote recall change over time. Fieldwork for the 2005 BES was carried out between 6 May (the day after the election) and 4 July, with most interviews conducted in May and June. From Table 4.2 we can see that over-report for Labour and under-report for Conservatives increased significantly over the course of these two months: in May there was a nine-point difference between the two parties, but by June there was a 17-point difference. Moreover, the effect of this time lag was much more pronounced in seats that Labour won (where there was a ten-point increase in the difference) than in seats which the Conservatives won (where there was just a three-point increase).

Table 4.2 Time of interview and reported vote choice, 2005

	Labour	Conservative	Liberal	Other	N
May	39	30	21	10	2168
June	42	25	21	12	815

This goes to show that even over a relatively short period of time the quality of data generated by measures of vote recall may decay quite quickly. More research is needed on the factors that affect this error, and what the implications are for analysis. But what seems clear is that when a question involves more effort – in this case of memory – then other biases are more likely to take effect. Respondents struggling to remember how they voted are probably more likely to infer that they voted for the winner (Wright, 1993; Atkeson, 1999), or more likely to infer that they voted for the party dominant in their particular social milieu (either in class terms or neighbourhood/area terms). This latter point is perhaps the most well equipped to explain persistent pro-Labour bias in the polls. If recall error is stronger for those with less political interest and less political knowledge, and these groups are disproportionately found in social milieus where Labour is the dominant party, then the respondents who misremember who they actually voted for may be most likely to report having voted for Labour.

Although the extent to which voters over-report for winning parties or incumbent parties is a matter of some debate in Britain, there is clear evidence that they tend to under-report voting for minor parties. On average the vote for parties other than the big three in BES surveys has been 42 per cent lower than the official share of the vote. One plausible explanation for this is simply to do with *salience*. Respondents who report voting for minor parties may forget having done so (Himmelweit, Biberian and Stockdale, 1978). However, there may also be other factors at work. In particular, the reported vote for extremist or far-right parties tends to be much lower than their actual vote share, and this may be a consequence of both *sampling bias* and *social desirability bias*. Votes for far-right parties such as the British National Party (BNP) tend to be concentrated in just a few areas, meaning that their supporters stand less chance of being picked up by a stratified national survey (which is the case with most surveys) than they would by simple random selection. This may introduce sampling bias, in which BNP supporters are simply not selected for interview. The other, potentially more serious, problem is to do with social desirability bias and whether or not respondents own up to voting for parties which may be regarded as socially unacceptable. Given the relatively small numbers of respondents that are typically involved, any bias may have a strong effect on the explanatory factors of vote choice. Closet supporters of extremist parties and declared supporters may be somewhat different (Coakley, 2008). Those who acknowledge their views to be socially unacceptable may be less extreme than those who do not, thereby extenuating the actual difference that exists between supporters of the far-right and other more mainstream parties.

Drivers of Political Behaviour: Party Identification and Issue Salience

Party Identification

Party identification, defined as an enduring commitment or attachment to a particular political party, has been at the heart of research in electoral behaviour for more than half a century. The concept was given detailed early exposition in the pioneering *American Voter* (Campbell et al., 1960), and here the key point is that the survey question used to measure party identification has proved every bit as durable. In its current formulation for British surveys (Clarke et al., 2004), the question asked was: 'Generally speaking, do you think of yourself as Labour, Conservative, Liberal Democrat, or what?' Probably the most striking feature is the abruptness of its 'or what?' ending. Arguably this contravenes even the basic requirement for politeness in survey question design. Certainly it turns this into an example of a *leading question*; that is, one in which the wording indicates to respondents that certain responses are more useful or acceptable to those asking the question. Here, attachment to one of the three major parties is presented as normal, with all other possibilities only grudgingly acknowledged and lumped together in a manner that suggests they are of marginal interest to the researchers. Some respondents are therefore likely to avoid the 'or what?' option and to opt for one of the major parties instead. One result is that such questions probably understate identification with smaller parties, such as the Green Party, that are omitted from the short list (and overstate attachment to a party like the Liberal Democrats, which is 'legitimized' by its inclusion).

Another group of respondents is badly served by that question, namely those lacking such an attachment to any particular party. The wording tends to presume identification: 'or what?' means that not to 'think of yourself as' a party supporter is more or less presented as deviant. Thus another consequence of this wording is that it is likely to overstate the extent of party identification. In other words, some people who do not really have an enduring partisan attachment are induced to report one by the leading question. These 'false positives' are a persistent problem in the measurement of political attitudes. They were first highlighted by Philip Converse in a famous essay in which he concluded that 'a large proportion of the electorate simply does not have meaningful beliefs, even on issues that have formed the basis for intense controversy among elites for substantial periods of time' (1964: 245). The problem for survey designers is that people are reluctant to admit as much. Converse suggested that respondents instead answer more or less at random, and coined the term *nonattitudes* for these responses, which reflect not real attitudes but the desire to oblige interviewers or to avoid appearing ignorant.

It is now widely agreed that few if any survey responses are delivered at random in this way. Instead, nonattitudes lie at one extreme of a continuum of attitude strength or 'crystallization' (Petty and Krosnick, 1995), and survey responses that appear largely random are thus because weaker attitudes are readily shifted by a variety of external influences, ranging from a story on the previous night's news to a nuance in the question wording (Zaller, 1992; Tourangeau, Rips and Rasinski, 2000). The potential influence of question wording leads us back to our party identification example. The concern now becomes whether respondents who lack enduring partisan attachments are deterred (by 'or what?') from admitting as much, and instead report weak and temporary party preferences. Since the whole point is to measure durable ties to parties, the question is less valid if it also elicits such ephemeral inclinations.

The arguments above led some researchers to advocate an alternative question which would make it easier for respondents to disclaim any partisan attachment (Bartle, 2001; Sanders, Burton and Kneeshaw, 2002). Thus, the original version was rephrased and split into two parts. Respondents were first asked: 'Some people think of themselves as being a supporter of one political party rather than another. Do you usually think of yourself as being a supporter of one particular party or not?' Only those who answered 'yes' were then asked: 'Which party is that?' The first part is an example of a *filter*, so called because it is designed to filter out those respondents who lack the attitude in question but might nonetheless answer the question unless non-response is thus legitimized. Filters are a common means of minimizing the nonattitude problem, and can sometimes have a dramatic impact on the proportions who acknowledge that they lack an opinion (Schuman and Presser, 1981: chapter 4).

To show the effect of changing the party identification wording, we draw on a split-half survey experiment incorporated into the 2005 BES. Such experiments, in which alternative versions of a question are tested simultaneously on random halves of the sample, are the standard method of gauging question-wording effects (Schuman and Presser, 1981). Random assignment ensures that a (statistically significant) difference in results can be attributed to differences in question wording rather than in the samples questioned. Table 4.3 shows first the proportion of respondents reporting a party identification, and second their distribution among the parties, for the traditional (unfiltered) and alternative (filtered) versions.

Table 4.3 Comparing unfiltered and filtered questions measuring party identification

	Without filter		With filter	
	%	%	%	%
Identify with a party				
No	24.1		56.6	
Yes	75.9		43.4	
Which party				
Labour		44.0		50.6
Conservative		34.3		35.1
Lib.Dem.		16.4		10.7
Others		5.4		3.6
N	*1698*	*1288*	*1819*	*787*

The lower panel of the table shows that even the partisan distribution of identification can be affected by wording. Contrary to earlier predictions, there is no evidence of small parties suffering with the traditional unfiltered version. However, as suggested, the Liberal Democrats do rather better with that version. In any case, the really conspicuous difference is in the upper panel of the table. When a filter makes explicit to non-respondents the possibility of non-identification, less than half claim a partisan attachment. However, on the unfiltered version, more than three-quarters report identification. Clearly these different questions lead to radically different conclusions about the extent of partisanship in the British electorate.

Such striking differences lead inevitably to the question of which is the 'right' wording. However, things are seldom so clear-cut. There is a strong argument for the filtered version, namely that the additional identification reported on the unfiltered version will resemble nonattitudes rather than real partisan attachments (Converse and Presser, 1986). However, others argue against filters on the grounds that they waste information (Krosnick et al., 2002). On this reading, that additional identification is not random noise but reflects genuine attitudes to the parties, albeit relatively weak 'leanings' rather than deeply held commitments. Rather than lose this information with a prior filter, these researchers would instead make use of a posterior measure of *intensity*. Such a measure has in fact typically followed the unfiltered question in British surveys: respondents reporting identification are then asked to say whether it is 'very strong', 'fairly strong', or 'not very strong'. In the example from Table 4.3, only just over half (52 per cent) of those who had named a party (76 per cent) then said that their attachment to that party was either 'very' or 'fairly' strong. Multiplying those two percentages together, we obtain a figure (40 per cent) similar to the proportion of identifiers (43 per cent) recorded by the filtered question. This suggests that the latter question does indeed tend to elicit only those stronger attachments. However, the advantage of using a measure of intensity rather than a filter is that we now have information about the leanings of 'not very strong' identifiers.

Whatever the pros and cons in using a filter, the striking differences in Table 4.3 are disquieting, especially given the centrality of partisanship – and hence this question – to so much political research. The results from a different split-half experiment are still more unsettling, because they show that far subtler alterations to *question wording* can also have dramatic effects. Burden (2008) investigates the gender gap in partisanship in the US, which sees women markedly more likely than men to report Democratic identification. He speculated that this was the result of media coverage of politics in which women and the Democratic Party were routinely associated, and hence women were inclined to 'think of themselves as' Democrats. To explore this possibility, Burden ran an experiment in which 'think of yourself as' from the traditional party identification question was replaced by the phrase 'feel that you are'. His hypothesis was that, by encouraging respondents to report deeper and more personal attachments, this 'feel' wording might narrow the gender gap. In Figure 4.1 we show, separately for women and men, the Democrat–Republican split recorded by the two versions ('think' and 'feel') of the question.

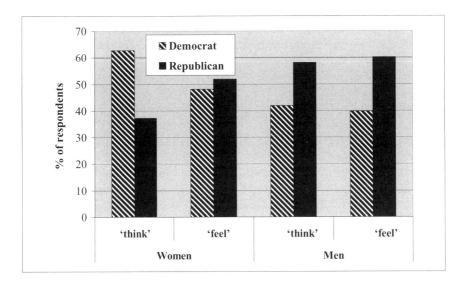

**Figure 4.1 Sex, question wording and party identification in Burden's
(2008) experiment**

Burden's expectations are resoundingly confirmed. With the usual 'think' question, women are clearly more likely to identify with the Democrats than the Republicans. Yet when asked the 'feel' question, women split more or less 50:50 between the two parties. Since men's responses are largely unaffected by question wording, the net effect is indeed that using the 'feel' question serves to narrow the gender gap. As before, we cannot simply declare either wording as superior. However, we must be aware that even small differences in question wording can have big impacts on results, and ideally we should undertake methodological research like this to explore how and why.

Issue Salience

Issues are the currency of political debate, and most researchers give them a prominent place in explanations of voting behaviour. Most also now take explicit account of the importance, or salience, of issues (for example, Hutchings, 2003; Whiteley et al., 2005). The basic premise is stated by Särlvik and Crewe: 'one would expect a stronger relationship between issue opinions and voting among those who consider a given issue important than among those who are less concerned' (1983: 222). Beyond electoral research, students of media and politics will be interested to observe whether broadcasters and the press tend to lead or to react to the public's agenda. As with party identification, then, there is good reason to measure issue salience. Unfortunately, again as with party identification, this measurement turns out to be anything but straightforward.

One very long-established measure of issue salience is the 'most important problem' (MIP) question, posed in Gallup polls since 1935 and also in many academic surveys. The wording is simple: 'What do you think is the *most* important problem facing this country at present?' For present purposes, three features of the question are worth highlighting. The first is the use of the word 'problem' rather than 'issue'. Wlezien (2005) argues that certain issues, like crime, are more readily seen as 'problems' than others, even if they are not necessarily more important to respondents and their voting decisions. Consider the well-established tendency for governing parties to be re-elected in good economic times. This implies that the economy is a highly salient election issue, even when the outlook is sunny. Yet few respondents are then likely to mention the economy when asked the MIP question, because that issue is not currently a problem. So, just as in the 'think'/'feel' party identification experiment, there is reason to suppose that an apparently minor feature of wording has a marked effect on responses.

The second key feature of MIP is that it is an *open* (or 'open-ended') question. That is, respondents answer the question without any further prompting, unlike in a *closed* version which would present respondents with a fixed list of issues from which they should choose. Both formats have their advantages. On practical grounds, closed questions are far preferable, being easier for interviewers, coders and those analysing the data. They can also remind respondents of answers that they might not otherwise have retrieved from memory (Schuman, Ludwig and Krosnick, 1986). However, this kind of prompting may be used by respondents to save themselves the mental effort of producing a valid answer themselves. Moreover, it is quite likely that the pre-determined list of alternatives will exclude some issues that are genuinely salient to many people. This is a problem given survey respondents' general reluctance to insist on a response that is not explicitly offered (and thus legitimized) by the question. These points are well illustrated by another split-half survey experiment comparing open and closed versions of MIP (Schuman and Presser, 1981: chapter 3). Eight alternatives were offered in the closed format, though respondents did have the option of 'Other'. The distribution of responses in the two versions is shown in Table 4.4.

The first point to note is that, when unprompted, 36.5 per cent of respondents named one of a bewildering variety of problems that were not included in the list of eight alternatives. In the closed version, hardly any respondents insisted on these 'other' issues; instead they chose from among the options explicitly offered. However, and this is the second key point, they did not choose between those eight issues in the same proportions as respondents to the open-ended version. Instead, they opted in disproportionately large numbers for 'crime and violence' and 'decreasing trust in government'. In contrast, the percentages for inflation and unemployment are barely different across the two versions. It seems that economic issues come to respondents' minds with or without prompting, but that crime is a problem of whose importance respondents need a reminder.

Table 4.4 Comparing open and closed versions of 'most important problem'

	% mentioning problem	
	Closed	Open
Food and energy shortages	6.2	1.7
Crime and violence	36.1	16.1
Inflation	13.0	13.6
Unemployment	20.4	19.6
Decreased trust in government	10.2	3.1
Busing	1.1	1.1
Breakdown of morals and religion	9.5	5.8
Racial problems	1.7	2.5
Other issues/problems	1.9	36.5
Total	100.0	100.0
N	*422*	*449*

As usual, our inclination is to ask which of the two columns of data in Table 4.4 gives a truer picture of issue salience. And, as usual, this is a difficult question to answer. Some might prefer the open-ended version, arguing that an issue cannot be particularly important to a respondent who cannot even recall it without assistance. On the other hand, the numerous 'other' issues mentioned in response to the open question may be akin to nonattitudes, answers delivered off the top of the head by respondents rather than genuine indications of issue salience. In that case, a more considered choice between the problems on the closed list is probably preferable. These conflicting arguments are reflected in conflicting evidence on the rival merits of open and closed questions – neither can be straightforwardly deemed superior (Schuman and Presser, 1981; Kessel and Weisberg, 1999). Hence most researchers opt for closed questions for the practical reasons noted above. However, expediency should not be the only criterion for choice. The argument for closed questions is stronger in those cases where survey designers are confident that their list would cover most if not all of the more common responses. The best route to such confidence is to use open questions in a pilot survey, and then to base the closed list on the results from that pre-testing.

The third feature of MIP is that it provides information about only one issue. That may be enough for some researchers' purposes; others will want to know about how respondents assess the importance of a range of issues. In those situations, one important decision facing the survey designer is whether to collect *rating* or *ranking* data. A typical ratings measure of issue salience would involve a scale running from something like 'extremely important' to 'not at all important', and respondents would be asked to rate each of a set of issues along that scale. The alternative is to ask respondents to rank that set of issues in order of importance, thus in effect extending the MIP question. A first point to note about these rival possibilities is that ranking tasks quite quickly become impractical once the number of items to be ordered goes beyond a certain point, say around seven or eight. Indeed, ranking is cognitively a more arduous task than rating, which is doubtless one reason why respondents tend to prefer rating scales. This problem can be eased, however, by asking respondents simply to rank the top three or four items. Such restriction incurs little cost, since researchers are unlikely to be particularly concerned with whether a given issue is seventh or eighth most important to a respondent – it is the higher rankings that tend to matter.

Unlike many of the design decisions considered so far, the advice for survey researchers here is clear-cut and backed up by plenty of evidence. Rankings outperform ratings on virtually every criterion (the exception being popularity with respondents), the data elicited being clearly more reliable and valid (Krosnick, 1999). To understand why, it is instructive to consider some of the biases that tend to affect rating scales. One such derives from a lack of respondent effort. For example, if a scale runs from '1 – not at all important' to '7 – extremely important' it is easier for respondents to fall into a pattern of choosing the same number rather than agonizing over whether, on that issue, they are closer to a '4' or a '5'. However, some response biases have a more substantive basis. One of the most persistent is *acquiescence*. In earlier research, this response bias was discussed largely in the context of agree–disagree attitude questions (for example, Rorer, 1965), and was defined as the 'tendency for respondents to agree with attitude statements' (Schuman and Presser, 1981: 203). However, more recently the interpretation of acquiescence has broadened to take in a range of what might be called 'positivity' biases.

In the context of issue salience, acquiescence would imply that at least some respondents systematically overstate the importance of issues. There are various reasons why we might expect such a bias, and they help to illustrate the factors that have been theorized to drive acquiescence. First, there may be a tendency to defer to the interviewer or the survey designers (a distinction probably lost on many respondents). Here, that could manifest itself in an assumption that any issues listed must be important – otherwise researchers would not be asking about them. Second, acquiescence is in some respects simply easier (in cognitive terms): respondents may agree that issues are important, not out of deference, but because it involves effort to come up with reasons why not. (These two points tally with evidence that acquiescence is more common among respondents with lower levels of education.)

A third reason for overstating the importance of at least some issues is *social desirability* (as already discussed in the sections on political behaviour). For instance, respondents may be particularly reluctant to dismiss the issue of unemployment as unimportant, in case they appear callous about the plight of the jobless. A parallel argument can be made about education and health, whereas the importance of issues like immigration or taxation may if anything be understated, as respondents bid to avoid appearing xenophobic or selfish. These points are much more than methodological niceties. The surprise Conservative victory in the 1992 general election was in some quarters attributed to voters' worries about tax rises under Labour, yet the salience of this issue seems to have been understated in pre-election polls which suggested that voters were primarily concerned with education and health (issues on which Labour enjoyed clear leads). Social desirability bias can explain why these polls tended to mislead, and thus why pre-election forecasts were so seriously awry.

Using ranking questions cannot eliminate social desirability, although it probably mitigates the bias by denying respondents an easy opportunity to designate lots of issues as important. In any case, the other arguments and evidence in favour of rankings are overwhelming. However, we should end by noting one different kind of bias that can affect rankings, and especially an abridged form of ranking question like MIP. This is *response-order bias*, in which choice between the options offered in a question depends at least in part on the order in which they are listed. While this notion is intuitively plausible, experimental research suggests that response-order effects are far from ubiquitous, and even simple generalizations – for example, that such bias is stronger with longer lists of options – are quite often confounded (Schuman and Presser, 1981: chapter 2). Complicating things further, early studies found evidence of both 'primacy' and 'recency' effects. In other words, in some studies respondents were drawn to options higher up the list, while in others the bias was in favour of options near the bottom of the list. Krosnick (1999) clarifies the picture considerably, noting that recency effects occur when respondents only *hear* the list of options – as in a telephone survey – while primacy effects are the norm when respondents read the list, as in self-completion surveys or when interviewers provide them with the list on a show-card. This makes sense: when hearing a list, the difficulty is in remembering what came earlier; when reading a list, the effort lies in maintaining effort all the way down. (Since voting is akin to a self-completion survey, it is not surprising that real elections show clear evidence of primacy effects benefiting candidates higher up the ballot paper (Ho and Imai, 2008).) One means of eliminating order effects is random rotation of the order in which options appear, and that is a good habit for survey designers (and electoral administrators), even if it carries non-trivial practical costs. Of course, this policy is only really applicable where there is no logical or natural order to the options offered.

Conclusions

In this chapter we have highlighted a wide range (though not all) of the difficulties that beset researchers trying to measure political behaviour and attitudes. Many of these can be seen to originate in the following chain of argument. The first point is that politics is at best peripheral to most people's lives. They vote largely out of habit and their choice of party may well involve little reflection. Few nowadays feel a close affinity with any particular political party. And strongly held political attitudes are the exception rather than the rule, most voters being preoccupied with just one or two issues most salient to them. All this contrasts starkly with those who conduct research in these fields, a highly atypical group so politically engaged that they struggle to empathize with those who lack strong views, and may simply not remember whether and how they voted. Hence surveys have tended to overestimate both the amount and the accuracy of political information that representative samples can provide.

This would matter less if respondents were reluctant to answer questions when unable to recall the answer or lacking an opinion on the issue at hand. However, the reverse is true – respondents are instead reluctant to leave questions unanswered. That is reasonable given the implicit pressures of the survey context. Merely by including a question, researchers are signalling to respondents that an answer can reasonably be expected, and respondents are understandably unwilling to confound those expectations. Hence much of the advice for survey designers in this chapter is about easing the pressures felt by respondents. Questions about turnout are best accompanied by concerted attempts to emphasize the normality of not voting, and questions about past vote should give due prominence to the possibility that respondents may not remember. Likewise, the filtered party identification question improves on the traditional version by offering encouragement (rather than borderline rudeness) to those who do not feel a partisan attachment. Finally, we should not be asking respondents to rate or rank the salience of far more issues than they can reasonably be expected to consider at election time – a simple ranking of two or three key issues is not only enough, but is more accurate.

This is not, however, an argument for a mass incitement to non-response. Our aim should be to maximize both quality and quantity of data. This involves convincing respondents to admit their uncertainty, lapses of memory, even lack of interest. Yet it also involves encouraging them to attempt questions. Thus a well-designed partisanship question will involve a follow-up, in which those who disclaim any identification are asked whether they lean towards a party. And a respondent unable readily to remember how they voted in the recent election can of course be asked to guess. Researchers need then to be mindful of the various biases – social desirability, bandwagons, order effects and so on – that are especially likely to affect these less certain attempts at response. In short, the difficulties inherent in measuring political behaviour and attitudes cannot be ignored, but are no argument for giving up.

References

Abelson, R., Loftus, E.F. and Greenwald, A.G. (1992), 'Attempts to Improve the Accuracy of Self-reports of Voting', in J.M. Tanur (ed.), *Questions about Questions* (New York: Russell Sage).

Atkeson, L. (1999), '"Sure, I voted for the winner!" Overreport of the Primary Vote for the Party Nominee in the NES', *Political Behavior* 21, 3: 197–215.

Bartle, J. (2001), 'The Measurement of Party Identification in Britain: Where Do We Stand Now?' *British Elections and Parties Review* 11: 1–14.

Belli, R., Traugott, M.W., Young, M. and McGonagle, K.A. (1999), 'Reducing Vote Overreporting in Surveys', *Public Opinion Quarterly* 63: 90–108.

Berinsky, A. (2004), 'Can We Talk? Self-presentation and the Survey Response', *Political Psychology* 25, 4: 643–59.

Bernstein, R., Chadha, A. and Montjoy, R. (2001), 'Overreporting Voting: Why It Happens and Why It Matters', *Public Opinion Quarterly* 65, 1: 22–44.

Blais, A. (2000), *To Vote or Not to Vote: The Merits and Limits of Rational Choice Theory* (Pittsburgh, PA: University of Pittsburgh Press).

Box-Steffensmeier, J., Jacobson, G. and Grant, J.T. (2000), 'Question Wording and the House Vote Choice: Some Experimental Evidence', *Public Opinion Quarterly* 64: 257–70.

Brady, H.E. (1999), 'Political Participation', in J.P. Robinson, P.R. Shaver and L.S. Wrightsman (eds), *Measures of Political Attitudes* (San Diego, CA: Academic Press).

Broughton, D. (1995), *Public Opinion, Polling and Politics in Britain* (London: Prentice Hall, Harvester Wheatsheaf).

Burden, B.F. (2008), 'The Social Roots of the Partisan Gender Gap', *Public Opinion Quarterly* 72: 55–75.

Campbell, A., Converse, P.E., Miller, W. and Stokes, D. (1960), *The American Voter* (New York: Wiley).

Clarke, H.D., Sanders, D., Stewart, M.C. and Whiteley, P. (2004), *Political Choice in Britain* (Oxford: Oxford University Press).

Clausen, A. (1968), 'Response Validity: Vote Report', *Public Opinion Quarterly* 32: 588–606.

Coakley, J. (2008), 'Militant Nationalist Electoral Support: A Measurement Dilemma', *International Journal of Public Opinion Research* 20, 2: 224–37.

Converse, J.M. and Presser, S. (1986), *Survey Questions* (Beverly Hills, CA: Sage).

Converse, P.E. (1964), 'The Nature of Belief Systems in Mass Publics', in D. Apter (ed.), *Ideology and Discontent* (New York: Free Press of Glencoe).

Crewe, I. (2001), 'The Opinion Polls: Still Biased to Labour', in P. Norris (ed.), *Britain Votes 2001* (Oxford: Oxford University Press), 86–101.

Crewe, I. (2005), 'The Opinion Polls: The Election They Got (Almost) Right', *Parliamentary Affairs* 58, 4: 684–98.

DeMaio, T. (1984), 'Social Desirability and Survey Measurement: A Review', in C.F. Turner and E. Martin (eds), *Surveying Subjective Phenomena* (New York: Russell Sage).

Eubank, R.B. and Gow, D.J. (1984), 'The Pro-incumbent Bias in the 1982 National Election Studies', *American Journal of Political Science* 28: 224–30.

Granberg, D. and Holmberg, S. (1990), 'The Intention–Behaviour Relationship among US and Swedish Voters', *Social Psychology Quarterly* 53, 1: 44–54.

Granberg, D. and Holmberg, S. (1991), 'Self-reported Turnout and Voter Validation', *American Journal of Political Science* 35, 2: 448–59.

Himmelweit, H. Biberian, M. and Stockdale, J. (1978), 'Memory for Past Vote: Implications of a Study of Bias in Recall', *British Journal of Political Science* 8, 3: 365–75.

Ho, D.E. and Imai, K. (2008), 'Estimating Causal Effects of Ballot Order from a Randomized Experiment: The California Alphabet Lottery, 1978–2002', *Public Opinion Quarterly* 72: 216–40.

Hutchings, V.L. (2003), Public Opinion and Democratic Accountability: How Citizens Learn About Politics (Princeton, NJ: Princeton University Press).

Jowell, R. Hedges, B., Lynn, P., Farrant, G. and Heath, A. (1993), 'The 1992 British Election: The Failure of the Polls', *Public Opinion Quarterly* 57, 2: 238–63.

Kessel, J.H. and Weisberg, H.F. (1999), 'Comparing Models of the Vote: The Answers Depend on the Questions', in H.F. Weisberg and J.M. Box-Steffensmeier (eds), *Re-election 1996* (New York: Chatham House).

Krosnick, J. (1999), 'Survey Research', *Annual Review of Psychology* 50: 537–67.

Krosnick, J., Holbrook, A.L., Berent, M.K., Carson, R.T., Hanemann, W.M., Kopp, R.J., Mitchell, R.C., Presser, S., Ruud, P.A., Smith, V.K., Moody, W.R., Green, M.C. and Conaway, M. (2002), 'The Impact of "No Opinion" Response Options on Data Quality', *Public Opinion Quarterly* 66, 3: 371–403.

McDonald, H.E. and Hirt, E.R. (1997), 'When Expectancy Meets Desire: Motivational Effects in Reconstructive Memory', *Journal of Personality and Social Psychology* 72, 1: 5–23.

Noelle-Neumann, E. (1993), *The Spiral of Silence: Public Opinion – Our Social Skin* (Chicago: University of Chicago Press).

Paulhus, D.K. (2002), 'Socially Desirable Responding: The Evolution of a Construct', in H.I. Brown, D.N. Jackson and D.E. Wiley (eds), *The Role of Constructs in Psychological and Educational Measurement* (Mahwah, NJ: Lawrence Erlbaum).

Petty, R.E. and Krosnick, J.A. (eds) (1995), *Attitude Strength: Antecedents and Consequences* (Hillsdale, NJ: Erlbaum).

Presser, S. (1990), 'Can Changes in Context Reduce Vote Overreporting in Surveys?' *Public Opinion Quarterly* 54: 586–93.

Rorer, L.G. (1965), 'The Great Response-style Myth', *Psychological Bulletin* 63: 129–56.

Sanders, D., Burton, J. and Kneeshaw, J. (2002), 'Identifying the True Identifiers: A Question Wording Experiment', *Party Politics* 8, 2: 193–205.

Sanitioso, R., Kunda, Z. and Fong, G.T. (1990), 'Motivated Recruitment of Autobiographical Memories', *Journal of Personality and Social Psychology* 59, 2: 229–41.

Särlvik, B. and Crewe, I. (1983), *Decade of Dealignment* (Cambridge: Cambridge University Press).

Schuman, H., Ludwig, J. and Krosnick, J.A. (1986), 'The Perceived Threat of Nuclear War, Salience, and Open Questions', *Public Opinion Quarterly* 50: 519–36.

Schuman, H. and Presser, S. (1981), *Questions and Answers in Attitude Surveys* (New York: Academic Press).

Silver, B.D., Anderson, B.A. and Abramson, P.R. (1986), 'Who Overreports Voting?' *American Political Science Review* 80, 2: 613–24.

Swaddle, K. and Heath, A. (1989), 'Official and Reported Turnout in the British General Election of 1987', *British Journal of Political Science* 19, 4: 537–51.

Tourangeau, R., Rips, L.J. and Rasinski, K.A. (2000), *The Psychology of Survey Response* (Cambridge: Cambridge University Press).

Traugott, M.W. and Katosh, J.P. (1979), 'Response Validity in Surveys of Voting Behavior', *Public Opinion Quarterly* 43: 359–77.

Whiteley, P., Stewart, M.C., Sanders, D. and Clarke, H.D. (2005), 'The Issue Agenda and Voting in 2005', in P. Norris and C. Wlezien (eds), *Britain Votes 2005* (Oxford: Oxford University Press).

Wlezien, C. (2005), 'On the Salience of Political Issues: The Problem with "Most Important Problem"', *Electoral Studies* 24: 555–79.

Wright, G.C. (1990), 'Misreports of Vote Choice in the 1988 ANES Senate Election Study', *Legislative Studies Quarterly* 15: 543–63.

Wright, G.C. (1993), 'Errors in Measuring Vote Choice in the National Election Studies, 1952–88', *American Journal of Political Science* 37: 291–316.

Zaller, J.R. (1992), *The Nature and Origins of Mass Opinion* (Cambridge: Cambridge University Press).

Chapter 5
Measuring Religious Behaviour

Peter Brierley

The doyen religious sociologist, Durkheim, usefully defined religion in terms of affiliation, practice and belief. This chapter follows these three aspects of religion and seeks to show how each has been, and can be, measured or assessed. Before that is done, however, it may be helpful to describe briefly the various broad religious groupings frequently used in research or other publications.

Religious Groups

The adherents of two religions formed a majority, 51 per cent, of the world's population in 2000: Christianity and Islam (Barrett, Kurian and Johnson, 2001). The most numerous groups in the United Kingdom are Christians, Muslims, Hindus, Sikhs and Jews, in that order, followed by a large number of smaller entities (Brierley, 2008: 10.8f). Because the first group is large, the remainder are sometimes simply grouped as 'non-Christian religions'.

The Christian group is often divided into two (theological) categories, Trinitarian and non-Trinitarian. Trinitarian churches are those which 'accept the historic formulary of the Godhead as the three eternal persons, God the Father, God the Son and God the Holy Spirit, in one unchanging essence' (Wraight, 2006: Criteria for inclusion). The Trinitarian group is broken down into ten broad denominational categories:

1. Anglican (very largely the Church of England, Church in Wales, Scottish Episcopal Church and the Church in Ireland)
2. Baptists
3. Roman Catholics (including overseas Catholic churches in the UK, like the Croatian, Hungarian or Polish)
4. Independent churches (including the Christian Brethren, Congregational Churches, Fellowship of Independent Evangelical Churches, Churches of Christ, Liberal Catholics and many others)
5. Methodists (of which about 90 per cent is the Methodist Church in Great Britain)
6. New Churches (previously called House Churches)
7. Orthodox (including Greek and Russian)

8. Pentecostal (including Assemblies of God, Elim and the many black charismatic groups of which the New Testament Church of God is the largest)
9. Presbyterian (including the Church of Scotland, the Presbyterian Church in Ireland, the United Reformed Church, and several others)
10. Smaller, or other, denominations (the largest of which are, in order, the Salvation Army, Seventh-Day Adventists, Lutherans (collectively) and the Religious Society of Friends)

In 2006 there were 275 different Christian denominations in the UK (Brierley, 2008: Table 2.21.3). The ten Christian denominations are sometimes further sub-divided into institutional churches (numbers 1, 3, 7 and 9) and non-institutional or Free churches.

The non-Trinitarian churches include the Christadelphians, Christian Scientists (officially called the Church of Christ, Scientist), Church of Scientology, Jehovah's Witnesses, Mormons (Church of Jesus Christ of Latter Day Saints), Spiritualists, Swedenborgian New Church, Unification Church (Moonies), Unitarian (and Free Christian) Churches, and so on.[1]

The non-Christian religions include not just the main religions mentioned above, but smaller ones like the Baháis, Buddhists, Jains and Zoroastrians. They also include the many new religious movements, statistics of some of which are available (Brierley, 2008: 10.6, 10.7).

Addresses for many of these denominations, non-Trinitarian churches and other religions are given in the *UK Christian Handbook* (Wraight, 2006), so that researchers can contact them directly if necessary. Membership statistics, the number of churches or meeting places, and the number of ministers or full-time leaders are also given for each individual denomination in *Religious Trends* (Brierley, 2008). These figures effectively describe the entire church population, and thus allow an accurate sampling frame to be drawn up for research, and for the results to be weighted as required.

Affiliation: Community

'Affiliation' essentially means 'belonging', but belonging means different things to different people. Currently there are two broad measures of looking at religious belonging – community or membership. Both can be researched.

The Christian community has been defined as 'all those who would positively identify with belonging to a church even if they may only attend irregularly, or were just baptised as a child' (Lawson, 1991: 15). If we substitute mosque or temple for church, and where necessary an alternative rite for baptism, a similar definition would be acceptable for most, if not all, religions other than Christianity. Another definition is 'those who belong to a particular denomination, however

---

1   A more detailed list is given in Brierley, 2008: 10.2–5.

loosely. If Anglican, Roman Catholic, Lutheran, Orthodox or Presbyterian, they will usually approximate to the number baptised in that country' (Brierley, 1997: 10). The Methodists keep a 'Community Roll' for each church.

In the Northern Ireland Population Census, a question on religion has to be asked according to the 1920 Union Act. In 2001 this was worded as 'Do you regard yourself as belonging to any particular religion? If yes, …', and the official report of the findings treated the religious community as the total number who ticked the box indicating their 'religious allegiance' or preference (Brierley, 1994: 21). Some equate community to 'adherents' (Johnstone and Mandryk, 2001). The broad thrust of these definitions is clear – all those in a particular country or other geographical area who would name themselves as Christian, Muslim, Hindu, Buddhist, and so on.

The 2001 Population Census for England, Wales and Scotland asked a question on religion for the first time since the 1851 Census (Mann, 1854). In England and Wales the wording was 'What is your religion?' followed by seven options: Christianity, Islam, Hindu, Sikh, Jew, Buddhist, Other Religions, with a No Religion box. In Scotland the question was 'What religion, religious denomination or body do you belong to?' with the same options as in England and Wales but with Christian broken down into three components: Church of Scotland, Roman Catholic, Other Christian. The question in Northern Ireland also broke down the Christian component into denominations: Church of Ireland, Roman Catholic, Presbyterian Church in Ireland, Methodist Church in Ireland and Other Christian. The purpose of these questions was primarily to determine the size of the religious communities by type and geographical area, as well as having information that could very usefully be broken down by the other census characteristics.

The overall answers from the census are given in community numbers in Table 5.1 and as percentages of the population in Table 5.2.

Table 5.1 Community numbers by religion, by country, 2001

Religion	England	Wales	Scotland	N Ireland	TOTAL UK
Christianity	35,251,244	2,087,242	3,294,545	1,446,386	42,079,417
Islam	1,524,887	21,739	42,557	1,943	1,591,126
Hindu	546,982	5,439	5,564	825	558,810
Sikh	327,343	2,015	6,572	219	336,149
Jew	257,671	2,256	6,448	365	266,740
Buddhist	139,046	5,407	6,830	533	151,816
Other Religions	143,811	6,909	26,974	1,143	178,837
No Religion	7,171,332	537,935	1,394,460	45,909	9,149,636
Not stated	3,776,515	234,143	278,061	187,944	4,476,663
TOTAL (=Population)	49,138,831	2,903,085	5,062,011	1,685,267	58,789,194

Table 5.2 Community percentages by religion, by country, 2001

Religion	England %	Wales %	Scotland %	N Ireland %	TOTAL UK %
Christianity	71.74	71.90	65.08	85.83	**71.58**
Islam	3.10	0.75	0.84	0.12	**2.71**
Hindu	1.11	0.19	0.11	0.05	**0.95**
Sikh	0.67	0.07	0.13	0.01	**0.57**
Jew	0.52	0.08	0.13	0.02	**0.45**
Buddhist	0.28	0.18	0.14	0.03	**0.26**
Other Religions	0.29	0.24	0.53	0.07	**0.30**
No Religion	14.60	18.53	27.55	2.72	**15.56**
Not stated	7.69	8.06	5.49	11.15	**7.62**
Base (= 100%)	49,138,831	2,903,085	5,062,011	1,685,267	**58,789,194**

Table 5.2 shows that the Christian percentage was 72per cent of the entire UK population in 2001, and the total religious percentage was 78 per cent, percentages which have dropped from 85 per cent and 86 per cent respectively in 1910 (Brierley, 1999: Table 2.15). The 2001 figure compares with 68 per cent and 73 per cent respectively in Australia in 2001 (Hughes, 2007). The Christian percentage is available for every country in the world in the *World Churches Handbook* (Brierley, 1997).

While the 2001 Census gave figures which had not been available for many decades, it is not the only source of such information. The British Social Attitudes Survey, for example, uses the wording: 'Do you regard yourself as belonging to any particular religion?', and if the answer is 'yes', a list follows, of which 'No Religion' and 'Christian – no denomination' are two categories. The question has been asked, sometimes augmented with other related questions, every year since the survey began in 1983, which means that a useful historical series exists. For the latest report, see Park et al. (2008).

In Britain, a person going into hospital or prison is usually asked their religion. Many people simply reply 'C of E' (Church of England), or 'Methodist' or 'RC' (Roman Catholic), even if they have no current connection with that particular Christian church. The religious community figure represents the totality of all such people.

An exploration of what 'belonging' means, and suggesting that there is a large group of 'believing without belonging', has been undertaken by Professor Grace Davie (1994). More recently this has developed into a discussion of the differences between 'religion' and 'spirituality', with some claiming to be in one category but not the other, and some asking whether if to be 'Christian' means being both (see Avis, 2003; Heelas and Woodhead, 2005; and Savage et al., 2006). Is there a place for religion or spirituality in the public arena (N. Spencer, 2006)?

Affiliation: Membership

The second measure of affiliation is membership. This naturally means those who belong, who are members. In the Christian church, unfortunately, most denominations define membership differently! Thus in a Baptist church, membership may be limited to those baptized as adults. In an Anglican church, members are often taken as those on the electoral roll (not to be confused with the local authority electoral roll). In some Pentecostal churches, membership is confined to those who are baptized, born again, speak in tongues and give evidence of living an active Christian life over at least six months. The Roman Catholics, however, define their members as the 'baptized', which is equated above to church community; for detailed Catholic statistics, see A. Spencer (2007).

This problem of multiple definition probably relates more to Christianity than other religions, but even so it is not unique to it. Ethnic variation is sometimes a variable, which helps to distinguish one group from another (black people are more likely to be Christian, for example), and one of the two-way tables (S104) in the Census Report helpfully gives ethnicity by religion (Population Census, 2003).

Membership therefore, although widely collected in Christian churches, is but a heterogeneous collection of disparate numbers given the same appellation but not the same meaning. The variety of meaning may also be seen in the ages of those counted as members: Anglicans are those 16 and over, Baptists 14 and over, and so on, so membership figures, therefore, at least in some denominations, omit children and some young people.

The value of membership figures is that they are frequently available over time, sometimes for many decades, and occasionally even centuries (Currie, Gilbert and Horsley, 1977). They have usually been collected using the same definition *within a particular denomination* and therefore the trends in the figures may be judged as accurate.

It has been suggested that denominations which have the strictest membership criteria are likely to be those which grow fastest. There was some truth in this among the black Pentecostal denominations in the UK, first seen in the 1980s when the New Testament Church of God and the Church of Cherubim and Seraphim, for example, recorded attendance five times as great as their membership (Longley and Brierley, 1986: Table 9a, Footnote 2), which has continued since. This has been confirmed by two studies in America, one in the 1970s amongst Conservative churches, and the other in the 1990s amongst Lutheran churches. 'Churches that reflect solid quality and quantity growth are those that are clear to declare specific tenets of belief' (Hunter, 1996).

It should be noted that membership and attendance are not the same and that they are not necessarily causally linked! The Baptist Union in Scotland had a special outreach programme in the mid 1980s. In their report they said: 'During 1985 there was a marked increase in church membership (7.8 persons per church against 4.8 in 1982) and a total of 1,149 first commitments. It was disturbing to note that of these only 50% were recorded as being baptised, and only 33% as joining the church' (Baptist Union, 1988: 7).

In the United Kingdom, religious membership has been decreasing. In 1900 church membership was 33 per cent of the adult population and religious membership 34 per cent, but by 2005 it had dropped to 12 per cent and 16 per cent respectively (Brierley, 2008: Tables 2.21.2 and 12.8.1). These figures were obtained by writing to the individual Christian denominations asking for the number of members. Most of the larger denominations publish their own yearbooks at regular intervals, usually annually, and these invariably give membership details.

Practice: Historical Church Attendance

One way of measuring Durkheim's 'practice' is to assess attendance at religious services or meetings. Researching religious attendance is conceptually much easier than community – either people are there on a Sunday (for Christians), a Saturday (for Jews and some Christian groups) or a Friday (for Muslims), or not!

Counting those present on a particular day therefore gives a uniformity to the numbers. In Christian terms, this gives a homogeneous way of measuring between the many denominations. Attendance figures, however, are not always or universally collected by the different denominations, and even when regularly counted, will often be counted on different Sundays.

Large-scale measurements of church attendance in Great Britain are few (none has been attempted as yet in Northern Ireland). The first count of attendance was in 1851 as part of the Census of the Population of England and Wales (Mann, 1854). It was a count of *religious* worship, and the only non-Christian worshippers identified were the Jews, although several non-Trinitarian groups are also listed. Depending on how the figures are taken, the percentage attending church on that Census Sunday was 39 per cent, but this *included* those who went two or three times. If the same percentage of 'twicers' who were counted in 1903 applied in 1851 (and it could have been more then), then this figure would reduce to 24 per cent. Some partial studies of attendance prior to 1851 have been undertaken (Field, 2008a, 2008b).

A major large-scale study of London was undertaken by the *Daily News* between November 1902 and November 1903 (Mudie-Smith, 1904). This sought to count everyone entering every place of worship in a specific borough of London for every service, counting a different borough each week. It was therefore only a Christian survey. *Excluding* twicers, the percentage of the population who attended church in London was 19 per cent each Sunday.

A Mass-Observation survey in 1948–49 found that 15 per cent of the population attended church (Mass-Observation, 1949).[2] The English Church Census of 1979

---

2   The original report is in the Mass-Observation Archive in the University of Sussex, Brighton.

found that 12 per cent of the population attended; the 1989 Census that 10 per cent did; the 1998 survey that 7.5 per cent did; and the 2005 Census that 6.3 per cent did. The gentle slope of decline over the last 150 years has thus started to accelerate. All four census counts excluded those who attended twice on a Sunday.

The 1989 figure compares with 25 per cent in Australia (Kaldor et al., 1994: 263) and 42 per cent in the United States (Barna, 1995: 3), and the 2005 figure with an estimated 20 per cent in Australia (Hughes, 2005), 34 per cent in Canada (Bethune, 2006) and 40 per cent in the United States (Barnes and Lowry, 2007, quoting Gallup but maintaining that a truer figure was 18 per cent).

Attendance: Church Censuses

There have been nine large-scale surveys of church attendance in Great Britain since 1975: four have focused on England (1979, 1989, 1998 and 2005), two on Wales (1982[3] and 1995), and three on Scotland (1984, 1994 and 2002). (See, respectively, for England: Nationwide Initiative in Evangelism, 1980 and 1983; Brierley, 1991a and 1991b; Brierley, 1999, 2000 and 2001; and Brierley, 2006a and 2006b; for Wales: Evans and Brierley, 1983; and Gallagher, 1997; for Scotland: MacDonald (1985), MacDonald and Brierley, 1995; and Brierley, 2003a and 2003b.)

As the results of this set of surveys allow very detailed sampling frames, it may be helpful to give the various parameters used in these studies:

- Geography: *County* or equivalent area – England 1979, 1989, 1998, 2005; Wales 1982; Scotland 1984, 1994, 2002; Local Authority *District*: England 1989 (Brierley, 1995), 1998, 2005; *Region*: England 1989, 1998
- Denomination: all surveys; by Geography – all except Wales 1995; and by coloured maps: England 2005
- Age of churchgoers: all surveys; by Geography – all except Wales 1995; by Denomination – all surveys
- Churchmanship (type of belief system such as anglo-catholic, broad, catholic, charismatic, evangelical, liberal, low church, orthodox, radical, reformed): England 1989, 1998, 2005; Scotland (slightly different categories) 1994, 2002; by Geography, Denomination and by Age of churchgoer – the same five
- Size of church: England 1989, 1989, 2005; Scotland 1994; by Geography – England 1989, 2005; Scotland 1994; by Denomination, Churchmanship and Environment: England 2005
- Church environment (city centre, inner city, council estate, suburban, town centre, rural commuter and other rural): England 1989, 2005; Scotland (slightly different categories) 1994, 2002; by Geography and by Churchmanship – the same four

---

3   Carried out on behalf of Wales for Christ.

- Year of foundation: England 1989, 1998; Scotland 1994; by Geography, Denomination and by Churchmanship – England 1989; Scotland 1994
- Third world support: as for Year of foundation, though not in England 1998
- Frequency of attendance: England 1998, 2005; by Geography – the same; by Churchmanship, Denomination, Environment, Age-group, Gender – 2005
- Ethnicity of attendance: England 1998, 2005; by Geography and Denomination – the same; by Churchmanship – 2005
- Growth of churches by Denomination: England 1998, 2005; by Churchmanship, Ethnicity and Frequency of attendance – 2005; Scotland by Geography – 2002
- Fringe attendance (those who came to church premises during the week but not to a Sunday service): England 1998, 2005
- Mid-week attendance: England 1998, 2005
- Youth worship service: England 1998
- Youth meeting: England 2005
- Healing services: England 1998
- Financial giving in past year: Scotland by Geography – 2002
- Attendance by age-group across 16 specimen towns: England 2005
- Percentage of population in church by Geography: England 1989, 1998, 2005; Scotland 1984, 1994, 2002; by Age-group – 2002
- Lay leadership: Scotland 2002
- Ministers, age and gender: England 2005
- Alpha and other training course attendance: Scotland 2002; England 2005
- Bible Reading, by Denominations, Churchmanship, Environment: England, 2005
- Church change 1998 to 2010: England 1998; Scotland 2002

Copies of the questionnaires used for all these studies are in the volumes mentioned. The last topic in the above list may be of interest. We were asked by one sponsor to ascertain whether a church was likely to survive till 2010. Such a direct question could hardly be asked! Instead it was put in the form: 'By 2010 do you expect your church to have ... Grown significantly/ Grown a little/ Remained static/ Declined/ Closed' which was answered without any apparent problems.

Another element is the importance of distinguishing between the number of attend*ers* and the number of attend*ances*. The numbers are not the same! The Church Censuses have used the question: 'Please estimate the average number on a typical Saturday/Sunday in *this* church. Count any adults or children who attend more than one service only once.'

Practice: Attendance Frequency

Asking if a person attends church directly can lead to bias in that the respondent tries to give answers which they think the interviewer wants. In such surveys the percentage saying they attend church can be twice as high as the number who actually attend! It is better to ask, as in the E-MORI form, what activities a respondent undertakes with a given frequency and provide a comprehensive list of 20 or 30 items, of which churchgoing is one. This rough 'twice as high' figure has been measured more exactly in America where the same phenomenon occurs and where the results are very similar (Hadaway, Marler and Chaves, 1993; Hadaway and Marler, 1998 and 2005).

Alternatively one can ask: 'Did you do any of the following last weekend ...?' and list a number of items, of which going to church is *not* included. Then ask: 'Did you do anything else not listed here?' and frequently if a person went to church they will then say so, but not if they did not.

While attendance is a variable readily understood, the English studies of 1998 and 2005 and especially the Scottish Census of 2002 have shown it is not as straightforward as might be expected. These surveys show that what it means to go to church has changed. Table 5.3 shows that Sunday church attendance may be less frequent than in 1989 or earlier –'church attendance' more or less meant weekly then, but not now.

Table 5.3 Percentage of the population attending church by frequency

Frequency	England 1998 %	England 2005 %	Scotland 2002 %
Weekly	7.5	6.3	11.2
Fortnightly	8.3	6.9	n/a
Monthly	10.2	7.3	14.3
Quarterly	11.3	8.0	15.5
Half-yearly	12.6	9.9	n/a
Annually	16.2	14.5	19.4

For frequency the question has been consistently worded: 'We appreciate that it is difficult, but it would be a great help if you could estimate the approximate numbers of your total adult congregation who attend Saturday/Sunday services on a weekly, fortnightly, monthly or less frequent basis.' The form for the 1989, 1998 and 2002 Censuses gave the following break points: twice weekly, weekly, fortnightly, monthly, quarterly, twice a year, visitors/first attendance. The 2005 form asked separately: 'Approximately how many additional people attend ... Quarterly, Twice yearly, Once a year?'

In order to facilitate getting such information accurately, a small slip of paper, reproduced below from the 2005 English Church Census, was printed five times on a sheet and sent to each minister. This could then be photocopied, cut and distributed to individual members of the congregation, asking for their return as they left church (or to put it in with the collection). Forty-one per cent of respondents used this form in 1998, and thus gave an accurate count. There was no significant difference however between these 41 per cent accurate counts and the 59 per cent estimates. In 2005 more than 500,000 churchgoers completed one of these slips, giving as accurate an overview of age, gender, and so on, as one could wish.

1)Age/gender	Under 11	11-14	15-19	20-29	30-44	45-64	65-74	75-84	85 or over
Male									
Female									
2) Frequency of attendance	Twice weekly	Weekly		Fortnightly	Monthly		Less often	Visitor/ First attendance	
3) Your ethnic group	White	Black Caribbean /African/ Other		Chinese/ Korean /Japanese	Indian / Pakistani / Bangladeshi		Other Asian	Other non-white	
4) Do you read the Bible personally (other than in church) at least once a week?			YES		NO		**Please tick one box in answer to each question. Thanks!**		

Figure 5.1 Slip distributed to churches for completion by individual churchgoer

The British Social Attitudes Survey always uses the wording: 'Apart from such special occasions as weddings, funerals and baptisms, how often nowadays do you attend services or meetings connected with your religion?' (Park et al., 2008: 347) to obtain frequency. Its break points are as above, though without quarterly but including annually, 'less often' and 'never or practically never'. These frequencies may be too many for the non-Christian religions. One survey of Mosque attendance used just three categories – Festival attendance, daily and Friday attendance (Holway, 1986).

Practice: Attendance Not Necessarily on a Sunday

Another radical change has also occurred during the last 20 years or so. While there have always been some churches holding services mid-week, many of those who attended also attended on a Sunday. However, measuring those who *only* come mid-week, as the more recent Church Censuses have done, shows that a cultural change has occurred in this respect also – church attendance may now be mid-week rather than on Sunday.

This has implications for counting Christian churchgoers, and for those of other faiths also. It suggests that what should be counted are the number of people (including children and young people) attending *worship* services either on Sunday or mid-week, averaged over, say, a month. If all denominations did this, we would then have national statistics, comparable to each other, useful to respondents (always important in getting a good response), which would be easy to collect (important for accuracy!). Since many funerals and weddings take place in a church or other religious building, we need to distinguish also between these types of service and normal worship services.

Attendance at mid-week services in England is increasing: 240,000 in 1998 and 310,000 in 2005, suggesting it is going up by about 10,000 people a year. These are people who do not attend on a Sunday – 310,000 people is 0.6 per cent of the population, so the number attending church weekly is 6.9 per cent, as opposed to the average Sunday of 6.3 per cent. Thus mid-weekers add about 10 per cent to the number of regular churchgoers, an extra proportion not to be missed when sampling.

Attendance: Immigration

The UK has experienced a huge increase in the number of immigrants, beginning in the latter quarter of the twentieth century, and especially in the twenty-first century. Many of these have found themselves welcomed by faith communities speaking their language and a proliferation of overseas national congregations has resulted. The most significant by far has been the growth of the so-called 'black' congregations, who have come from both the West Indies and Africa, as Table 5.4 indicates, taken from the 2005 English Church Census:

Table 5.4 Church attendance by ethnic background, England, 1998 and 2005

Denominational group	1998	Change	2005
1) Catholic Overseas National Churches	12,300	*+42%*	17,500
2) Black Charismatic Pentecostal Churches	104,300	*+46%*	151,900
3) Protestant Overseas National Churches	9,200	*+110%*	19,300
4) All Orthodox denominations	25,200	*+2%*	25,600
Total attendance at ethnic churches	**151,000**	**+42%**	**214,300**
5) Non-white churchgoers attending white churches	289,100	*+8%*	311,300
6) White churchgoers attending essentially white churches	3,274,600	*-19%*	2,640,600
Total church attendance	**3,714,700**	***-15%***	**3,166,200**

The largest congregations in the UK are in these (black) charismatic Pentecostal churches, with Kingsway International Christian Centre seeing over 12,000 people on an average Sunday, Ruach Ministries in Brixton with over 4,000, and so on. The phenomenal increase seen by some black congregations is matched by only a few white congregations, of which Hillsong (started by Australians) in the Dominion Theatre, with 5,000 plus on a Sunday, is one.

The huge increase in such congregations and the reasons for their growth have yet to be deeply researched, but one commentator is Sturge (2005). The immigration influx is not limited just to those joining Christian churches, for many Muslims have also come to Britain in recent years. They are also, to date, poorly researched, but one study is by Jayawera and Tufyal (2008).

Putting It All Together

The three categories described above (community, membership and attendance) may be illustrated as shown below, where the outside square represents the whole population. It is not drawn to scale. Regular attendance would mean at least monthly, mid-week or on Sunday.

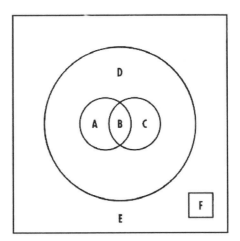

Figure 5.2 Community, membership, attendance and the population

The different spaces should be labelled as follows:

A = Those who are regular church attenders but who are not, or who are not
yet, members.

B = Those who are both regular attenders and members of their church.

C = Those who are not regular attenders but who remain members of their
church.

D = Those who call themselves Christian but who are not members or
attenders of any church on a regular basis (they may go at Christmas or
Easter).

E = Those who are those not in any faith community and who may therefore
be described as non-religious.

F = Those who are not Christian but who are members of another faith
community, like the Muslims or Hindus, or who belong to one
of the non-Trinitarian churches, like the Jehovah's Witnesses or
Mormons.

**Table 5.5 Religious structure of the population of Great Britain, 1980, 2000
and projected to 2020**

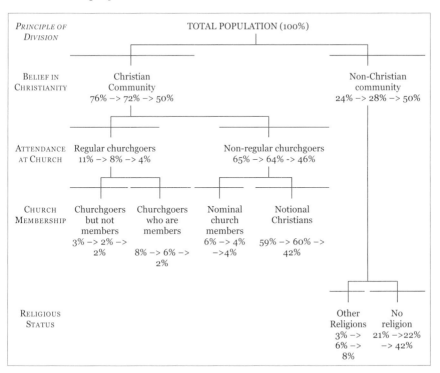

This information can also be arranged as shown in Table 5.5.

This table projects trends forward to 2020 assuming present trends continue. Sources for the data are given in Brierley, 2004 (Table 2.2) and 2008 (Table 12.8.2).

One area of interest is to consider how people might move from one category to another. Thus it might be expected that, over a period of time, people in Group A might become like those in Group B. Do those in Group B become like those in Group C as they get older? It has been noticed that some people move from Groups A or B to Group D. These people, sometimes described as 'de-churched' because they have largely left regular church attendance, have been extensively researched by Philip Richter and Leslie Francis (Richter and Francis, 1998; Francis, 2008).

Other factors which are worth exploring are the size of churches (and the increasing strategic importance of the largest churches) and the age and gender of churchgoers (why are the young people leaving and middle-aged women attending much less frequently? How can the energies of the many older people be used creatively?)

Practice in Other Ways

There are many other ways of measuring the behavioural manifestation of a person's religiosity other than attendance at services and the frequency of such. For example, how often do (religious) people read the Bible or Koran? How often do (religious) people pray? What do they pray for? For how long do they pray? Does a person's religious faith affect the ethics with which they conduct their personal life? Does it affect the principles by which they work? Does it impinge on how they treat their family? Or live with others? Or view their neighbour? Bible reading by churchgoers was measured in the 2005 Census (Brierley, 2006b: 5.9).

Many surveys have been undertaken which ask such questions. The very large majority use normal quota or other sampling methods and typically will get answers from 1,000 or fewer people. They are reported in the religious press, in the annual British Social Attitudes (BSA) volume, in the biannual *Religious Trends*, in specialist studies (a number of which are listed in each issue of *Religious Trends*), or in normal academic journals. Sometimes the actual questionnaire used is given (as in the BSA report); other times it is necessary to contact the original researcher.

The techniques of researching these kinds of social behaviour, attitudes and motives are little different if the subject is religion from those of any other dimension. Likewise the techniques of questionnaire design. For those interested in historical studies in such areas, this author knows three printed sources as well as their respective websites: British Social Attitudes, for the first 60 years of Gallup surveys (Wybrow, 1989) and generally for religious studies (Barley, 1987).

Belief

Belief has been regularly and frequently measured in numerous surveys, social and otherwise, and although it may be questioned what it actually means when someone says that they believe in God, the actual basic statistics resulting from such questions, as well as the wording used in such questions, are fairly commonplace and require little attention other than that which is generally available in questionnaire design.

The results of questions on belief are given in the volumes mentioned in the last two paragraphs of the previous section. An important analysis of belief (part of a major series on religious topics) and churchgoing gives data not only in positive response to the question: 'Do you believe in God?', but negative also, and this has been summarized across the last half of the twentieth century (Gill, 1999). European religious belief has been explored by Davie (2002) and Jenkins (2007).

Leadership

Leadership is crucial for successful religious growth and worship. There were some 35,000 ministers in the UK who were responsible for some 48,000 churches in 2006, with the number of ministers increasing and the number of churches decreasing. Some research on the beliefs, practices and strategies has been undertaken, largely along denominational lines – see, for example, Jackson (2002), Low and Gardom (2002), Francis (2005) and Barley (2006a and 2006b) for the Church of England; Louden and Francis (2003) and Horwood (2006) for the Roman Catholic Church; Brierley (2007) for the Baptist Union; Haley and Francis (2006) for the Methodist Church; Brown (2003) for the Christian Brethren; Kay (2000) and Martin (2002) for the Pentecostals; Love (2006) for the New Churches; Sturge (2005) for the black churches, and so on.

Researching Religion

Why, then, research this important subject? It is a key topic, essential for understanding current society, whether as something people have turned away from (though whether this thus creates a secular society is debatable) or something they are turning towards. Religion is not an optional extra; it is a vital component of life, and measuring it in all its diversity therefore an ever urgent challenge.

There are whole areas of religious activity which are not touched by the above comments, all deserving and warranting a far greater amount of research than has hitherto been bestowed upon them – subjects like:

- Church or faith schools (29 per cent of primary and 17 per cent of secondary schools can be so described)

- Religious publishing (one book bought in every 30 is religious)
- Christian mission workers serving overseas (almost 6,000 of them in 2006; What do they do? Why do they go? Are they effective?)
- Religious education (and the increasing numbers taking this subject for GCSE and A level)
- Marriages in church (nine out of every ten are probably by non-regular churchgoers)
- The explosion of the Alpha Course (more than ten million worldwide have now taken it) and other teaching courses (Brookes, 2007)
- Faith and the environment (do religious people care?) (Spencer and White, 2007)
- The geography of religion (Why are some of the most remote rural areas seeing church attendance increase?) (an early study is Gay, 1971)
- The psychological type of Christian or religious people (a list of surveys published with data is given in Brierley, 2008: 5.15)
- Church fires (why are proportionately more in the north?)
- Succession in senior church leadership positions
- Religion in the prisons and Armed Forces
- Christian camps (are they effective?)
- How people come to faith, and/or return to the church (is the proportion still the 40 per cent it was in the early 1990s?)
- Christian family life (is it really the second child who most likely does not follow in the faith?)

and so on.

'Facts are the fingers of God. To know the facts ... is the necessary condition of intelligent interest. Knowledge does not always kindle zeal, but zeal is "according to knowledge" and will not exist without it.' This was penned by the American Presbyterian minister, A.T. Pierson, who had wide religious interests, in 1886. It is still true well over a century later as people search to know the 'big picture'! Only by knowing the facts can the best strategic decisions be taken for the future.

References

Avis, P. (ed.) (2003), *Public Faith? The State of Religious Belief and Practice in Britain* (London: SPCK).

Baptist Union (1988), *Scotreach Programme Report* (Edinburgh: Baptist Union of Scotland).

Barley, L. (1987), *Reviews of UK Statistical Sources: Religion* (Oxford: Pergamon Press).

Barley, L. (2006a), *Churchgoing Today* (London: Church House Publishing).

Barley, L. (2006b), *Christian Roots, Contemporary Spirituality* (London: Church House Publishing).

Barna, G. (1995), *Casting the Net: The Unchurched Population* (Los Angeles: Barna Research Group).

Barnes, R. and Lowry, L. (2007), 'Special Report: The American Church in Crisis', *ChristianityToday.com*, 22 March 2007.

Barrett, D.B., Kurian, G.T. and Johnson, T.M. (2001), *World Christian Encyclopaedia* (2nd edition) (New York: Oxford University Press).

Bethune, B. (2006), 'Praise the Lord and Call the Psychic', *Macleans*, 119, 27/28.

Brierley, P.W. (1991a), *'Christian' England* (London: MARC Europe).

Brierley, P.W. (1991b), *Prospects for the Nineties* (London: MARC Europe).

Brierley, P.W. (1994), *Irish Christian Handbook* (1995/96 edition) (London: Christian Research).

Brierley, P.W. (1995), *English Church Attendance District by District* (London: Challenge 2000 and Christian Research).

Brierley, P.W. (1997), *World Churches Handbook* (London: Christian Research and Lausanne Committee for World Evangelization).

Brierley, P.W. (1999), *Religious Trends* No 2 (2000/2001 edition) (London: Christian Research and HarperCollinsReligious).

Brierley, P.W. (2000), *The Tide is Running Out* (London: Christian Research).

Brierley, P.W. (2001), *Religious Trends* No 3 (2002/2003 edition) (London: Christian Research).

Brierley, P.W. (2003a), *Turning the Tide* (Edinburgh: Church of Scotland; London: Christian Research).

Brierley, P.W. (2003b), *Religious Trends* No 4 (2003/2004 edition) (London: Christian Research).

Brierley, P.W. (2004), *Religious Trends* No 5 (2005/2006 edition) (London: Christian Research).

Brierley, P.W. (2006a), *Pulling Out of the Nosedive* (London: Christian Research).

Brierley, P.W. (2006b), *Religious Trends* No 6 (2006/2007 edition) (London: Christian Research).

Brierley, P.W. (2007), *The Baptist Union of Great Britain* (Didcot: Baptist Union and London: Christian Research).

Brierley, P.W. (2008), *Religious Trends* No 7 (2007/2008 edition) (Swindon: Christian Research).

Brierley, P. W. (2010), *God's Questions* (Milton Keynes: Authentic).

British Social Attitudes (1992), *Cumulative Sourcebook: The First Six Surveys* (Aldershot: Gower; London: Social and Community Planning Research).

Brookes, A. (2007), *The Alpha Phenomenon* (London: Churches Together in Britain and Ireland).

Brown, G. (2003), *Whatever Happened to the Brethren? A Survey of Local Churches in 1998/99* (Carlisle: Paternoster Press).

Currie, R., Gilbert, A. and Horsley, L. (1977), *Churches and Churchgoers* (Oxford: Oxford University Press).

Davie, G. (1994), *Religion in Britain since 1945* (Oxford: Blackwell).

Davie, G. (2002), *Europe: The Exceptional Case: Parameters of Faith in the Modern World* (London: Darton, Longman and Todd).

Evans, B. and Brierley, P.W. (1983), *Prospects for Wales* (London: Bible Society and MARC Europe).

Field, C.D. (2008a), 'Churchgoing in the Cradle of Christianity: Kentish Evidence from the 16th to the 20th centuries', *Archæologia Cantiana*, Vol. XXVIII; for further information contact the author on c.d.field@bham.ac.uk.

Field, C.D. (2008b), 'A Shilling for Queen Elizabeth: The Era of State Regulation of Church Attendance in England, 1552–1969', *Journal of Church and State* 50, Spring.

Francis, L. (2005), *Fragmented Faith? Exposing the Fault-Lines in the Church of England* (Milton Keynes: Paternoster).

Francis, L. (2008), *Gone for Good* (Peterborough: Epworth Press).

Gallagher, J. (1997), *Challenge to Change* (Swindon: Bible Society, Cytûn and Evangelical Alliance).

Gay, J.D. (1971), *The Geography of Religion in England* (London: Duckworth).

Gill, R. (1999), *Churchgoing and Christian Ethics* (Cambridge: Cambridge University Press).

Hadaway, C.K. and Marler, P.L. (1998), 'Did You Really Go to Church This Week?' *The Christian Century*, 6 May: 472–5.

Hadaway, C.K. and Marler, P.L. (2005), 'How Many Americans Attend Worship Each Week? An Alternative Approach to Measurement', *Journal for the Scientific Study of Religion* 44: 307–22.

Hadaway, C.K., Marler, P.L. and Chaves, M. (1993), 'What the Polls Don't Show: A Closer Look at US Church Attendance', *American Sociological Review* 58: 741–52.

Haley, J.M. and Francis, L.J. (2006), *British Methodism: What Circuit Ministers Really Think* (Peterborough: Epworth).

Heelas, P. and Woodhead, L. (2005), *The Spiritual Revolution: Why Religion is Giving Way to Spirituality* (Oxford: Blackwell).

Holway, J. (1986), 'Mosque Attendance', in *UK Christian Handbook* (1987/88 edition) (London: MARC Europe), 150–53.

Horwood, T. (2006), *The Future of the Catholic Church in Britain* (Laicos <www.futurecatholic.org.uk>).

Hughes, P. (2005), 'Evolving Understanding of Religious Faith in the Australian Culture', *Occasional Research Paper* No. 6 (Australia, Victoria: Christian Research Association).

Hughes, P. (2007), 'What Do the 2006 Census Figures about Religion Mean?' *Pointers* 17, 3: 1–6 (Australia, Victoria: Christian Research Association).

Hunter, K. (1996), 'Ask the Church Doctor', *Strategies for Today's Leader* XXXIII, 2, Fall.

Jackson, B. (2002), *Hope for the Church: Contemporary Strategies for Growth* (London: Church House Publishing).

Jayawera, H. and Tufyal, C. (2008), *Immigration, Faith and Cohesion: A Report on Muslims in Britain* (Oxford: Oxford University Press; York: Joseph Rowntree Trust).

Jenkins, P. (2007), *God's Continent: Christianity, Islam and Europe's Religious Crisis* (Oxford: Oxford University Press).

Johnstone, P. and Mandryk, J. (2001), *Operation World* (21st century edition) (Carlisle: Paternoster Publishing; Gerrards Cross: WEC International).

Kaldor, P., Bellamy, J., Powell, R., Correy, M. and Castle, K. (1994), *Winds of Change: The National Church Life Survey* (New South Wales: Lancer).

Kay, W. (2000), *Pentecostals in Britain* (Carlisle: Paternoster Press).

Lawson, M. (1991), *Austrian Christian Handbook* (London: MARC Europe).

Longley, D. and Brierley, P. (eds) (1986), *UK Christian Handbook* (1987/88 edition) (London: MARC Europe).

Louden, S.H. and Francis, L.J. (2003), *The Naked Parish Priest: What Parish Priests Really Think They're Doing* (London: Continuum).

Love, M. (2006), *The Body Book* (11th edition) (Leatherhead: Pioneer).

Low, R. and Gardom, F. (2002), *Believe It or Not! Part of the Mind of Anglicans Study* (London: Christian Research).

MacDonald, F. and Brierley, P.W. (1985), *Prospects for Scotland* (Edinburgh: National Bible Society of Scotland; London: MARC Europe).

MacDonald, F. and Brierley, P.W. (1995), *Prospects for Scotland 2000* (Edinburgh: National Bible Society of Scotland; London: MARC Europe).

Mann, H. (1854), *Religious Worship in England and Wales* (London: George Routledge).

Martin, D. (2002), *Pentecostalism: The World Their Parish* (Oxford: Blackwell).

Mass-Observation (1949), Report of survey was published originally in *British Weekly*, January/February 1949, and then in *Journal of the Free Church of England, Vision* III, 1, Winter 1952.

Mudie-Smith, R. (1904), *The Religious Life of London* (London: Hodder & Stoughton).

Nationwide Initiative in Evangelism (1980), *Prospects for the Eighties*, Vol. 1 (London: Bible Society).

Nationwide Initiative in Evangelism (1983), *Prospects for the Eighties*, Vol. 2 (London: MARC Europe and Bible Society).

Park, A., Curtice, J., Thomson, K., Phillips, M., Johnson, M. and Clery, E. (eds) (2008), *British Social Attitudes: The 24th Report* (London: SAGE Publications and the National Centre for Social Research).

Population Census (2003), *National Report for England and Wales*, Part 2 (London: National Statistics; Basingstoke: Palgrave Macmillan).

Richter, P. and Francis, L. (1998), *Gone But Not Forgotten: Church Leaving and Returning* (London: Darton, Longman and Todd).

Savage, S., Collins-Mayo, S., Mayo, B. and Cray, G. (2006), *Making Sense of Generation Y: The View of 15–25 Year-olds* (London: Church House Publishing).

Spencer, A.E.C.W. (ed.) (2007), *Digest of Statistics of the Catholic Community of England and Wales, 1958–2005*, Vol. 1: Population and Vital Statistics, Pastoral Services, Evangelisation and Education (Devon: Pastoral Research Centre and Russell-Spencer Ltd).

Spencer, N. (2006), *'Doing God': A Future for Faith in the Public Square* (London: Theos).

Spencer, N. and White, R. (2007), *Christianity, Climate Change and Sustainable Living* (London: SPCK).

Sturge, M. (2005), *Look What the Lord Has Done!* (Bletchley: Scripture Union).

Wraight, H. (2006), *UK Christian Handbook* (2007/2008 edition) (London: Christian Research).

Wybrow, R.J. (1989), *Britain Speaks Out 1937–87: A Social History As Seen Through the Gallup Data* (Basingstoke: Macmillan).

Chapter 6

Measuring Social Class

Eric Harrison*

Introduction

This chapter deals with the issues raised when social scientists wish to make use of survey instruments to measure social class and explore its effects. It is organized in the following way. It starts by explaining the continuing salience of class as a sociological variable, and its importance as a core component of large-scale social surveys. The following section explains the need for conceptually grounded models of class, and discusses one such model (EGP) based on the theory of employment relations. Part three discusses the data requirements for its full operationalization via a combination of information on occupation, employment status and supervisory responsibility. The next part goes on to explore the limitations of real-world survey data and some pragmatic steps that can be taken to deal with incomplete and imperfect information from questionnaires. Part five explores the concept of 'validation' in relation to measures of class, and the extent to which this is achieved in practice. The final section evaluates the current relationship between class analysis and survey research and makes suggestions for future improvements.

The Continuing Significance of Class

Class holds a unique position in the canon of sociological concepts. It is arguably the discipline's most hotly contested concept, and yet it also remains its most powerful. As has often, rather wistfully, been remarked, class is 'sociology's only independent variable'. If this really is a paradox, then it has always been so. Indeed, 'talk of class being in decline is not novel, it is one of the constants' (Roberts, 2001: 11). Most, if not all, of this kind of debate stems from a lack of clarity about what class actually *is*, or perhaps which elements of class are being discussed. As this is a book about measurement, it seems worthwhile dwelling on this point.

_____

* This chapter draws heavily on joint work carried out with David Rose since 2004 and I would like to thank him for his help and support during that time. I am responsible for any errors and omissions, however.

Roberts argues that while sociologists who study class have much in common:

> there has been a rough division of labour between, on the one hand, those who study the shape of the class structure, mobility flows and rates, and who typically conduct large-scale surveys with representative samples, then, on the other hand, those who study class consciousness and related behaviour, typically using case-study methods. Yes, there is a difference, but these are not competing groups of class researchers (2001: 9).

Indeed. To a great extent the study of class as a structural economic location, and the study of class as 'lived experience' are entirely complementary. And it is very difficult to break into the circle and disentangle the two.

Many opinion polls show that, despite a rising tide of affluence and a widespread perception that 'we are all middle-class now', a high proportion of respondents report themselves as belonging to the working class, even when they have jobs sociologists would consider to be middle class. Clearly many of the individuals we try to classify have their own experiences and their own ideas about class, the class structure and their place within it. Part of the problem here is a lack of clarity about what is being measured. There is a tendency in everyday language (and too often in social science) to confuse or conflate class with *status*. Individuals and groups adopt many strategies to signal that they are of greater worth or at least distinct from others. One of the most common is to purchase 'positional goods', the value of which stems not from their use but also from their scarcity or the associations they have and the messages they therefore transmit to others. Such patterns of consumerism, in combination with other cultural tastes, leisure pursuits, modes of dress and ways of speaking, become identifiable as discrete 'lifestyles'. These 'lifestyle packages' can cut across class differences, often being cultural markers for youth, ethnic groups or some other 'identity'. More often, though, they enforce class distinctions, hence the enduring notion of 'working-class culture' in popular parlance.

Thus two conceptions of class compete for our attention, but which is the correct one to measure? To use the language of quantitative social science, which is the independent variable? The answer is not immediately obvious. On the one hand, one's location in the occupational division of labour will have a substantial impact upon the monetary rewards accruing over a lifetime and consequently the resources a person can command. This fact, along with their social interactions with work colleagues elsewhere in the division of labour, is likely to limit and shape their lifestyle and their attitudes to the social world. Equally, however, something must explain the initial distribution of individuals throughout the occupational division of labour, and the fact that those growing up with parents in particular economic locations will, with overwhelming probability, 'choose' to reproduce that type of labour market trajectory. Does the experience of working-class employment produce working-class cultures, or do those working-class attitudes and values predict the labour market futures of those who hold them? The answer is probably that elements of both propositions are true. The point is that, in short, 'class matters' – in so far as it has an extraordinary relationship with almost every meaningful measure of what Max Weber called 'life-chances', the mix of resources, experiences and opportunities that individuals compete to acquire and control in modern societies. As Roberts graphically illustrates in relation to the UK:

> Compared with children of top professionals and managers, the children of unskilled workers are 50 per cent more likely to die in infancy. As adults, the unskilled group are roughly twice as likely to die before reaching retirement age, and ten times more likely to have no natural teeth ... Class is related to many other things – the ages at which people marry, how they vote, church attendance and risks of criminal conviction. These inequalities may not, in themselves, prove that society is divided into separate classes. The challenge is: can anyone explain these inequalities without a theory of class? (2001: 1).

So while debates persist over the weakening of class effects over time, it is clear that one of the reasons the concept of class remains so influential is its remarkable predictive power. Not only does class *matter*, but pragmatically from a survey researcher's perspective, class *works*. It therefore has come to sit alongside age, gender and education as an indispensable part of any social survey, be it general or highly specific in its purpose. In the world of survey methodology these are often referred to as 'demographic' or 'background' variables. Given their explanatory power and central position in sociology, it is preferable to use the term 'socio-structural variables', but the argument stands nonetheless. It is important to measure social class.

Theorizing Social Class

It is important that class measurement be built on a clear conceptual framework. Why is this? The primary reason is that if we wish to examine the variation in life chances across different groups within a population or across different national populations, and show what these patterns *mean*, it must be clear what it is measuring. There are two contrasting approaches to the derivation of social classifications – official and otherwise – which reflect deeper disputes in social science methodology. The first approach works by intuition, is rooted in experience and empirically informed, that is to say, the classification emerges from the shape of the data. This could be described as part of the 'inductive' approach to social science. The second proceeds from a set of theoretical premises which implies that individuals who are similar on some measure or set of measures should be placed together in the same category within the classification. This theory-driven procedure is commonly described as a 'deductive' approach. The sorts of public-use classifications that have traditionally been most common take the former approach. While these have the merit of being intuitive and rooted in common-sense knowledge about a society, they are inadequate for social scientific purposes, especially as we shall see later, when these involve cross-national comparisons.

A key shortcoming of 'inductive' classifications is that while they will have the capacity for displaying variation, they are altogether lacking in analytic transparency (Rose, 2005; Rose and Harrison, 2009). In other words, in the absence of a clear conceptual rationale it is not possible to identify the causal mechanisms which lead to the variation in outcomes shown in the data, what sociologists call 'empirical regularities'. To put it very simply, we see that clusters of people have similar experiences but we have no firm idea why. A further consequence of this is that if we cannot identify the cause of the observed phenomenon, then there is little scope for policy interventions to effect changes. One cannot imagine launching education initiatives or public health programmes in order to tackle persistent inequalities, without being able to identify the right 'policy levers' to pull. Herein lies the key distinction between descriptive and analytical classifications.

Clearly having a strong conceptual basis is not a cure-all for the limits of social explanation. The more specific and well-defined the measure, the smaller the range of phenomena it is likely to explain. However, this is also its strength. The more tightly bounded and clearly defined a concept, the more testable it becomes, and the greater confidence we can have in the results of those tests. And by treating it as an isolated concept, the greater the number of discrete variables we have at our disposal while seeking to explain the remaining variation. In short we are in a better position to specify our model.

Furthermore, working without a conceptual rationale renders the task of *validating* a classification impossible and of *maintaining* a classification over time much harder, if not impossible. As we shall explain in the final section of this chapter, validation involves both demonstrating that a measure does indeed measure what it is supposed to (criterion validity) and that it usefully discriminates other variables in theoretically predicted ways (construct validity). In addition, once (criterion-) validated, a measure may be re-validated to assist with maintenance over time.

There are many varieties of class schema from which to choose, some influenced by the Marxian tradition, others more by the work of Max Weber (see Wright, 2005 for a review), but they all start from firm theoretical foundations. The formulation that has most application to survey research is usually thought of as 'neo-Weberian', and draws on a body of literature concerning the buying and selling of labour, along with the variation in employment regulation for those who work as employees. In its initial form this approach goes back 50 years to David Lockwood's (1958) seminal distinction between work situation and market situation in relation to class, through a series of more formal re-statements of the issues, and their operationalization in numerous versions associated with the work of British sociologist, John Goldthorpe. In international circles such approaches are normally named after the authors of an early application of the schema to social mobility research (Erikson, Goldthorpe and Portocarero, 1979, or simply EGP).

More recently, the EGP schema has become more formally presented in terms of 'employment relations'. The primary distinction made by EGP is that between: (1) *employers*, who buy the labour of others and assume some degree of authority and control over them; (2) *self-employed* (or '*own account*') *workers* who neither buy labour nor sell their own to an employer; and (3) *employees*, who sell their labour and thus place themselves under the authority of their employer. These three basic positions are common to any society based on the institutions of private property and a labour market. Most recent schemas have responded to recent periods of mass unemployment in capitalist societies by allowing for a fourth basic class position, the '*excluded*', that is, those who are barred from an employment relationship because they have never worked (involuntarily) or are long-term unemployed (conventionally defined as a period of more than 12 months).

In addition, EGP makes a set of secondary distinctions in order to differentiate further the available analytical categories. For a start, in many EU Member States, employees account for anything up to 90 per cent of the economically active population. Clearly, however, they do not all hold identical class positions. As already argued, employees occupy different *labour market situations* and *work situations* as expressed through employment contracts. Labour market situation equates to issues such as source of income, economic security and prospects of economic advancement. Work situation refers primarily to location in systems of authority and control at work (see Lockwood, 1958/1989). Thus class categories comprise not of persons but positions or 'slots' defined by the pattern of contractual regulation in the workplace (see Goldthorpe, 2000).

Two basic forms of contract or employment regulation are distinguished: the *labour contract* and the *service relationship*. Each is seen as a response by employers to certain problems they face in ensuring employees perform as required, or to use a Marxian notion, in converting labour power to labour. These fall under two headings, 'asset specificity' and 'monitoring problems'. *Asset specificity* concerns the level of job or organization specific skills, expertise and knowledge ('human capital') required by employees and/or the required investment by the employer in employees' work competences (in other words, education and training). The higher this asset specificity, the more both employers and employees have a vested interest in maintaining a long-term employment relationship. In terms of Lockwood, this represents the employee's market situation. *Monitoring problems* are particularly difficult when the amount and quality of work cannot be overseen directly or easily, as in the case of higher professional and higher managerial occupations. This situation can easily be contrasted to, for example, assembly-line work which, with its standardized work tasks and fixed production pace, may be easily monitored. This is a recasting of Lockwood's concept of work situation, but it has also been set out in Marxian labour process sociology as the distinction between managerial strategies of 'direct control' and 'responsible autonomy' (Friedman, 1977).

Two ideal-types of employer response thus emerge. The presence of low levels of both monitoring problems and asset specificity leads to a 'labour contract', characterized by the short-term purchase of labour by the hour or the 'piece', the most typical example being the case of 'unskilled' ('manual') work. In contrast, where there exist both high monitoring problems and high asset specificity, as in higher professional and higher managerial work, the 'service relationship' is a more adequate and better suited response, that is, a contractual exchange of a relatively long-term and diffuse kind in which employees exchange service over a longer time-horizon in return for a salary and important prospective elements, such as structured pay progression, occupational pensions and expectations of continuity of employment.

These are 'pure' forms of contract which will also appear in modified forms with lower technical ('skilled') occupations and routine non-manual occupations (lower sales, services and clerical) in the case of the labour contract; and lower-level professional and managerial occupations and higher level technicians in terms of the service relationship. That is, the service relationship and labour contract may each be actualized to different degrees (Erikson and Goldthorpe, 1992: 43). In addition, there is the potential for 'mixed' forms of employment regulation where employers are faced with only one of the contractual problems. An example of this would be clerical work in large bureaucratic organizations, where tasks require relatively few skills but are more difficult to directly monitor.

EGP is best thought of, not as a classification in itself, but as a set of theoretical principles from which analysts may construct classifications on the basis of argument and evidence. Much of what follows makes reference to two recent classifications which could be described as part of the EGP family: the National Statistics Socio-economic Classification (NS-SEC) developed for the UK government (Rose and Pevalin, 2003; Rose and Pevalin with O'Reilly, 2005); and a collaboration between academics and national statistical institutes to produce a prototype for a harmonized European Socio-economic Classification (ESeC) which might be considered for adoption by Eurostat as an official classification (Rose and Harrison, 2007).

Operationalizing Social Class through 'Occupation +'

While it is true to say that a classification without a rationale will be impossible to validate, it is equally the case that a classification without a simple and flexible method of operationalization will be nigh on impossible to implement. When the worlds of class analysis and survey methodology meet, a classification is exposed to additional criteria for evaluation. It is not sufficient that it be conceptually coherent and sociologically satisfactory; it must also be widely applicable. Class schemas of the type discussed in this chapter are occupationally based classifications. This is for two reasons. Firstly, patterns of employment relations are embedded in occupations, in so far as these typically share the same sorts of levels of asset specificity and monitoring problems. Put in Lockwood's terms, it is the organization and content of an individual's occupation which puts him or her in a particular market and work situation. The second reason is more pragmatic. Given that class is rooted in employment relations, the purest form of class schema would attempt to measure the employment relations of each individual respondent through a series of questions about their employment contract, working conditions and organization of their tasks. They could then be grouped according to some predetermined criteria, such as ascending threshold scores, or by weighting certain variables over others. But adopting this approach would rule out the inclusion of class measures on all but the most specialist surveys of employment, so instead class is operationalized through a series of labour market variables of which occupation is the principal driver.

The basic information needed to derive social class is data on occupation, establishment size and employment status. This places a premium on the consistent measurement of these between surveys in individual countries, and between countries in comparative social surveys. This is achieved with more or less success by different survey instruments. Considering that occupation combined with employment status is regarded as a 'convenient proxy' for typical employment relations, it actually requires up to eight questionnaire items to obtain the necessary information (see Appendix).

On the basis of textual information supplied by the respondent, occupation is coded to a standardized classification. This might be a nationally specific framework, such as the UK's SOC2000, or a harmonized international standard, known in the EU as ISCO-88 (COM). Both these organize occupations into a hierarchical framework. The lowest level, the 'job', comprises a set of tasks or duties designed to be executed by one person. Jobs that are sufficiently similar are then combined into Occupational Unit Groups (OUGs) which form the most detailed level of statistical measurement. Occupations are situated within different levels of this hierarchy by making a judgment about the level of skill required to perform the duties of the job (as distinct from the skills or qualifications possessed by the jobholder). Both SOC2000 and ISCO-88 (COM) have four levels of precision. The highest level of aggregation is the major group of nine (SOC2000) or ten (ISCO-88) clusters covering the entire range of possible occupations. Levels below this then differentiate further into sub-major groups, minor groups, and finally the OUGs described above.

In addition to occupation, it is necessary to distinguish whether a respondent is an employer, working for themselves without employees, or is an employee of another individual or an organization. In order to distinguish 'large' from 'small' employers, respondents will be asked (if self-employed) whether they have employees and, if so, how many. Armed with this information, the data user must then decide what constitutes a large employer. In the UK Labour Force Survey the cut-off size for a small establishment is fewer than 24 employees. In harmonized European datasets it is more conventional to define this as fewer than ten employees. Of course, if in addition to being coded into 'large' or 'small' firms, establishment size is recorded as a continuous variable (that is, the exact number offered by the respondent) then data users can make datasets comparable.

Finally, in EGP-based classifications, those who have responsibility for supervising the work of others are placed in a class different from those colleagues, despite being in the same occupation. This makes it necessary to collect information about supervisory status, an aspect of measurement also prone to difficulty. From a theoretical point of view, we wish to identify individuals whose primary task is to supervise the work of others, in the manner of the traditional industrial 'foreman' or the head of a typing pool. However, the changing organization of many workplaces has encouraged the development of greater teamworking, and the increasing delegation of responsibility to 'line managers' has blurred these once clear delineations. Whether this heralds the 'death of the supervisor' or conversely means that 'we are all supervisors now' is a matter for conceptual debate. Empirically it is the case that on average those with supervisory responsibility enjoy better employment relations than their subordinates, and class analysts therefore wish to identify them separately. Recent work within a project to develop a European Socio-economic Classification (ESeC) has shown that the number of respondents recorded as supervisors is quite sensitive to the nature of the question asked; for instance, setting a threshold for the number of employees one is responsible for reduces the number of 'false positives' in the data (Pollak et al, 2009).

Using the data resulting from this series of questionnaire items, it is possible to create a 'derivation matrix' (or look-up table) which can allocate a class position to every combination of many hundred OUGs and five possible employment statuses (large employer, small employer, self-employed working alone, supervisor, employee). The matrix can be used to produce syntax that, by plugging in the variable names specific to that dataset, will easily generate a social class variable. The full version of the schema is presented in Table 6.1.

Table 6.1 The European Socio-economic Classification

	ESeC Class	Common Term	Employment Regulation
1	Large employers, higher grade professional, administrative and managerial occupations	Higher salariat	Service relationship
2	Lower grade professional, administrative and managerial occupations and higher grade technician and supervisory occupations	Lower salariat	Service relationship (modified)
3	Intermediate occupations	Higher grade white-collar workers	Mixed
4	Small employer and self-employed occupations (excl. agriculture, etc)	Petit bourgeoisie or independents	Not applicable
5	Self-employed occupations (agriculture, etc)	Petit bourgeoisie or independents	Not applicable
6	Lower supervisory and lower technician occupations	Higher grade blue-collar workers	Mixed
7	Lower services, sales and clerical occupations	Lower grade white-collar workers	Labour contract (modified)
8	Lower technical occupations	Skilled workers	Labour contract (modified)
9	Routine occupations	Semi- and non-skilled workers	Labour contract
10	Never worked and long-term unemployed	Unemployed	Not applicable

Source: Adapted from Rose and Harrison (2007): 464.

Deriving Class Schemas in Conditions of Incomplete Information

So far we have emphasized the conceptual rigour of measures of social class, and set out the information required to construct an optimal class variable on existing data. However, those familiar with secondary analysis know that survey data is frequently imperfect and always incomplete. This section describes the way that recent classifications dealt with these problems.

Both NS-SEC and ESeC are intended to be comprehensive socio-economic classifications and therefore it is very important to be able to code as high a proportion of cases as possible. In any representative survey sample of adults we would expect to find no more than 55 per cent of the respondents in paid work. The remainder will be students, retired, caring for relatives, looking after the home or currently unemployed. Those who are not class analysts sometimes assume that questions on occupation must only relate to the workforce and concern the experience of working life. Of course it is essential to know a person's occupation as a key to allocating them a class. So wherever a respondent is not working, they should be asked what they did in their last job. If it has been some time since they worked, interviewers should ask respondents what type of work they normally do. This also pertains in the case of retired respondents who are either not working or perhaps whose labour market trajectory is tapering off. In each case occupation is not standing solely as a measurement of a week's work tasks, it is also acting as a proxy for the sort of employment relations experienced in a person's life course and the levels of resources these have allowed them to command. It is therefore the 'career-typical' occupation that we are seeking to capture.

In some cases respondents (usually but not exclusively female) will be coded as 'not applicable' because they have been permanently inactive (outside the labour market) or unemployed since they left full-time education. The default approach to this problem is to remember that, while we collect information from individual respondents, the unit of class composition is the household. Class analysis takes as axiomatic the fact that the household is the unit of class 'fate' because of the inter-dependence of its members and the fact that key resource decisions are often taken at the household level (Rose and Pevalin with O'Reilly, 2005: 40). Because of this it would be an improvement if researchers saw classifications as relating not only to individual labour market positions but those of households. Where individuals are not working, they should be reallocated to the class of the Household Reference Person (HRP), but equally where more than one household member is working, they can both be seen as meriting the class position of the economically dominant partner (see Rose and Pevalin with O'Reilly, 2005, and Rose and Harrison, 2009 for a fuller explanation of these issues).

A key concern during the construction of both NS-SEC and ESeC was that it should be useful even when the base information varied in precision or was absent altogether. This may happen in a number of ways: Firstly, the occupational variable may not be coded with full precision; secondly, there may be no information about supervisory responsibility; thirdly, the establishment size variable may either be absent or in categories that do not dovetail with the classification's thresholds for large/small firms. One or all of these may be true of all or part of a data set. In a national survey users may be concerned if there is high item non-response ('missing data') on one or more of these variables, especially if the non-response is systematic in terms of key demographics. In a cross-national survey a country or group of countries may have deviated from the specification or have coding conventions different to the others participating in the survey. As Davies and Elias (2009) found in applying ESeC to cross-national data, practice varies. In seven of the twelve European countries that took part in the first wave, the ECHP records information on current occupation at the two-digit level of ISCO. For the other countries who participated in the first wave, occupational information was recorded for groups of two-digit ISCO categories. This is largely in order to comply with requirements concerning respondent anonymity. In the European Labour Force Survey (EU-LFS) occupational data is collected at three or four digits, but this is offset by the absence, until relatively recently, of an item measuring supervisory responsibility.

A flexible classification needs to have ways of coping with sub-optimal data. In a national classification such as NS-SEC the main problem is the absence of establishment size or employment status information, and so there is both a 'reduced' (no size variable) and a 'simplified' (occupation only) method of derivation. In the development of the ESeC, these problems were compounded by inconsistencies in the way countries used ISCO-88, both in terms of their ability to code to four-digit precision, and their ability to agree on a single 'European' class position for the lowest level of measurement, the OUG. As a response to these problems, the final derivation matrix for ESeC only operates at '3 digit ISCO', the minor group level. Inevitably this leads to occupations within a single minor group ending in the same class, even though in a 'pure' matrix they would be in different classes. The decisions about the 'correct' allocation are made according to the 'modal class' for a minor group, that is, given that it may comprise two or more occupations, which are typically more numerous in a society? The modal allocation process is also used to derive class allocations for two-digit occupational codes. It should be noted that a data set with fuller occupational information may not necessarily be as accurate, or consistent, as one with coarser-grained distinctions. Particularly in comparative research, it may be well worth trading some precision for reliability.

Collapsing Class Schemas

A good class measure has not only flexibility with regard to the precision with which it is derived, but flexibility with regard to the detail in which it is specified. The less consistent/comparable the derivation method used to derive the measure, the more movement there will be across class categories. In such circumstances it may be advisable to tailor the precision of the class schema to the precision of its base information. For this reason, and because analysts do not always need to make such fine distinctions, most class schemas come in long and short forms. That is to say the full number of categories can be aggregated or, to use the usual term, 'collapsed' into a smaller number of classes, as shown in Table 6.2.

Table 6.2 Collapsing ESeC from 9 to 6 to 5 to 3 class models

ESeC Class	9 class version	6 class version	5 class version	3 class version
Higher salariat	1	1 + 2	1 + 2	1 + 2
Lower salariat	2			
Higher white collar	3	3 + 6	3 + 6	
Petit bourgeoisie	4	4 + 5	4 + 5	3 + 4 + 5 + 6
Small farmers	5			
Higher blue collar	6	3 + 6	3 + 6	
Lower white collar	7	7	7	
Skilled manual	8	8	8 + 9	7 + 8 + 9
Unskilled manual	9	9		
Unemployed	(10)	(10)	(10)	(10)

Source: Rose and Harrison (2007): 470.

Research with both the UK NS-SEC and the ESeC has shown that most of the 'churning' between classes caused by incomplete or imprecise information is within rather than across types of contract as described earlier in the chapter. Therefore by collapsing a schema into its more basic class positions, it becomes more insensitive to the reliability of the building block information over time, across countries and between different data sets. This is formed by merging classes 1 and 2 into a single service class and merging classes 3 and 6 into an intermediate, supervisory and technical class. The self-employed classes 4 and 5 combine into the new collapsed class 3; lower sales and service occupations become class 4 and the skilled and unskilled 'manual' occupations constitute class 5. Collapsing this hierarchy once more would yield three classes comprising more or less equal shares of the workforce: the service, intermediate and working classes. The ultimate aim of a classification should still be a robust and accurate long form, but the greater stability of the collapsed forms offers a useful fallback position when data quality or research focus dictate.

A Measure for Measures: Validating Classes Using Survey Data

As mentioned earlier in this chapter, the attraction of a schema with a theoretical grounding is that it is testable. Both NS-SEC and ESeC were initially derived through expert judgment, informed by data about employment relations in the UK. Once so derived it is essential for the measure to be validated as a measure with recourse to new data independent of that used to inform the choice of class positions for occupations and employment statuses. Validation of a class measure involves it passing two tests: first, it has to be shown that it is an adequate measure of employment relations (as defined and discussed earlier) and that it has internally homogeneous categories, each as different as possible from one another. Second, it has to be established that the class schema adds value by offering an improved understanding of other variables (such as health, income, employment, poverty and education variables). The first issue is that of *criterion validation* and the second of *construct validation*. Construct validation would also involve other issues, such as an assessment of ESeC as a comparative measure. There is in addition a third issue. What makes recent attempts to construct socio-economic classifications distinct from previous work on class is their avowed intention to be *public classifications*. NS-SEC and ESeC are conspicuous in the transparency of their construction, the clarity of their supporting documentation, and their user-friendly design for users of survey data. In order to be judged against this aspiration, they require *operational validation*, and the previous section dealt with this in some detail. Further discussion of the various types of validity may be found in Rose and Pervalin with O'Reilly (2005: Appendix 8).

Let us start with criterion validity. A measuring instrument 'is valid if it does what it is intended to do. An indicator of some abstract concept is valid to the extent that it measures what it purports to measure ... Validity concerns the crucial relationship between concept and indicator' (Carmines and Zeller, 1979: 12). In the case of ESeC, therefore, we need to know that it is a reasonably adequate index of the class concept as formulated in EGP. However, subjecting ESeC to the test of independent data in order to see if it measures the concepts that underlie it in terms of employment relations was not an easy task. The exercise revealed the limitations of existing cross-national data.

Ideally, the most direct indicators of the type of employment regulation contained or implied in contracts are form of payment (incremental salary against weekly wage calculated by time worked or payment by the piece), perquisites (final salary pension, private health care, company car, profit-related bonuses, and so on, or none of these), control over working time/pace of work (whether this is determined mainly by the employer or the employee), job security (for example, length of notice required to terminate contracts, protection against redundancy), and promotion/career opportunities (an internal organizational career ladder), that is to say, the types of measure that were used to construct the UK NS-SEC (Rose and Pevalin, 2003: 48–9). However, such indicators are not easily available in either European or national datasets.

In these circumstances we are reduced to relying on two more indirect measures: those that indicate the presence of the basic problems of monitoring and asset specificity (worker autonomy and qualifications required to do the job); and those that are indicative of an employer response to such problems (elements of a service relationship or a labour contract). The European Social Survey, primarily a cross-sectional survey of social attitudes (Jowell et al., 2007), has carried work-related items in its core questionnaire over four rounds and also in a dedicated 'rotating' module on work, family and well-being in round two (2004–2005). These have been used extensively by national teams within the ESeC project to measure the performance of the schema (see Rose and Harrison, 2009: chapters 4–7).

The second issue is construct validity. As outlined at the start of the chapter, a source of enduring reassurance to those engaged in class analysis (and no doubt a source of irritation to their critics) is that for all the debate about the concept, it repeatedly 'works' in so far as it is able 'to structure and discriminate in respect of a range of outcome variables' (Rose and Harrison, 2007: 479). Here the emphasis is not on whether a classification 'measures what it purports to measure', but whether it can, through its ability to predict and explain patterns of life-chances. Construct validity involves a judgment of a concept and its measurement in terms of empirical consequences.

> If the variable is intended to reflect a particular *construct*, to which attach certain *meanings*, then hypotheses can be constructed and tested based on what we understand about the construct. In other words, 'construct validity focuses on the assessment of whether a particular measure relates to other measures consistent with theoretically derived hypotheses concerning the concepts (or constructs) that are being measured' (Rose and Pevalin with O'Reilly, 2005: Appendix 8).

This type of validation is easier to undertake because, and only because, in addition to the major general-purpose social surveys, even surveys designed to collect quite specific information include the sorts of items required to create a social class variable. To recap, the argument is that employment relations and conditions are central to delineating the structure of socio-economic positions in modern societies. That is, the life chances of individuals and families depend mainly on their position in the division of labour and on the material and symbolic advantages that derive from it. Thus, for example, health inequalities are differences between class categories in respect of morbidity and mortality. The study of these inequalities makes visible the social forces acting to produce health outcomes. Moreover, it informs public policy by illuminating not merely the problem, but the appropriate levers for effecting change. Research using both NS-SEC and ESeC has clearly shown that class has plausible, instructive and informative relationships with key outcomes of interest in areas as diverse as income, poverty and deprivation, unemployment risks, and health and educational inequalities (Rose and Pevalin, 2003; Rose and Harrison, 2009).

Class Analysis and Large-scale Data Sets: Towards a Sociological Alliance?

This chapter has offered a number of arguments designed to show the importance of social class as a variable central to empirical research in the social sciences. It has shown that from an academic perspective, class should be theorized and measured in ways that allow it not just to describe systematic differences across and between populations, but to assist in the explanation of those differences. In order to do this kind of macro-sociology, it is crucial that there are frequent large-scale surveys that collect relevant data, and that this is recorded and coded with sufficient precision and reliability to allow analysts to produce descriptive and inferential statistics that are scientifically credible. It is also important that they are able to repeat this work with comparable data in order to validate and maintain their measures both over time and across space. It is no surprise that one of the central protagonists in class analysis is also one of the most influential lobbyists for the quantitative analysis of large-scale data sets in sociology (Goldthorpe, 2000).

The chapter has also argued that such is the explanatory power of social class – in relation to a host of outcomes related to health, educational achievement, social mobility, earnings, political behaviour and a range of social attitudes – that it is important for all social surveys, even if they are not explicitly designed for that purpose, to field items that permit analysts to construct a variety of social class schemas. Survey research, done well, is an expensive activity by social science standards, and it justifies itself partly through its influence on, and reputation with, end users.

Thus, survey methodology and social stratification communities are locked into an uneasy but potentially fruitful alliance. The research drawn upon in this chapter has illustrated some of the conflicts. Academics want comprehensive and comparable measures of class that allow them to distinguish up to ten or more classes. Some studies of the workforce may want to go further and look at the fortunes of different sub-groups within classes, such as individual occupational groups, or those in larger firms. This alone requires up to eight items on a questionnaire. In order to create a household class, they may require the same information relating to the respondent's partner. And to trace patterns of class inheritance, the same again for the respondents' father and mother! Survey managers have their own concerns. Fieldwork, especially face-to-face, is time-consuming and expensive. The public seem less and less inclined to participate in surveys and anything that increases the length and complexity of a questionnaire is not helping them in this regard. The content of many commercially funded surveys is very client-driven, and while such organizations pay much attention to 'demographics', these are not the sort of robust, conceptually driven and well-validated measures of the type discussed here.

The classifications alluded to in this chapter aim to build bridges between these two worlds by being not just conceptually sound but of broad empirical applicability. That is to say they require few enough variables, defined with reasonable enough precision, to be able to derive it simply and reliably on as many datasets as possible. Experience shows that this has largely been achieved, but there remain challenges to more accurate and reliable measurement in many respects. Firstly, too little is known authoritatively about international coding practices in relation to occupation, a worrying omission given its centrality in deriving class allocations. Secondly, there is a shortage of sound measures of employment relations to allow ongoing criterion validation of class schemas. Much recent work has relied on a limited number of not entirely ideal items from a small number of surveys. Many of the surveys with large samples, such as the EU-LFS, do not regard the collection of employment relations questions as a priority. Most others have samples too small for meaningful analysis of occupational groups (even at minor group level). There needs to be better provision of such variables across the European research area. Finally, there needs to be more integration between the different stakeholders in terms of conducting methodological research of this type. Survey agencies and polling companies are primarily production-centred; they concentrate on getting out into the field and back again. Social researchers are largely consumption-oriented; their attention is focused on what the data might reveal and they pay scant attention to how it gets to them. A better awareness of each other's activities and concerns could be the start of a more fruitful relationship.

References

Carmines, E. and Zeller, R. (1979), *Reliability and Validity Assessment* (London: Sage).

Davies, R. and Elias, P. (2009), 'The Application of ESEC to Three Sources of Comparative European Data', in D. Rose and E. Harrison (eds), *Social Class in Europe: An Introduction to the European Socio-economic Classification* (London: Routledge).

Erikson, R. and Goldthorpe, J. (1992), *The Constant Flux: A Study of Class Mobility in Industrial Societies* (Oxford: Oxford University Press).

Erikson, R., Goldthorpe, J. and Portocarero, L. (1979), 'Intergenerational Class Mobility in Three Western European Societies', *British Journal of Sociology* 30, 4: 415–41.

Friedman, A. (1977), *Industry and Labour* (London: Macmillan).

Goldthorpe, J. (2000), *On Sociology* (Oxford: Oxford University Press).

Harrison, E. and Rose, D. (2006), *The European Socio-economic Classification (ESeC) User Guide*, Institute for Social and Economic Research, Colchester. Available online at <http://www.iser.essex.ac.uk/research/esec/user-guide>.

Jowell, R., Roberts, C., Fitzgerald, R. and Eva, G. (2007), *Measuring Attitudes Cross-Nationally: Lessons from the European Social Survey* (London: Sage).

Lockwood, D. (1958), *The Blackcoated Worker: A Study in Class Consciousness* (London: Allen and Unwin).

Pollak, R., Bauer, G., Müller, W., Weiss, F. and Wirth, H. (2009), 'The Comparative Measurement of Supervisory Status', in D. Rose and E. Harrison (eds), *Social Class in Europe: An Introduction to the European Socio-economic Classification* (London: Routledge).

Roberts, K. (2001), *Class in Modern Britain* (Basingstoke: Palgrave).

Rose, D. (2005), 'Socio-economic Classifications: Classes and Scales, Measurement and Theories'. Paper presented at the First Conference of the European Survey Research Association, Pompeu Fabra University, Barcelona, 18–22 July 2005. Available online at <www.iser.essex.ac.uk/research/esec/presentations-and-publications>.

Rose, D. and Harrison, E. (2007), 'The European Socio-economic Classification: A New Social Class Schema for Comparative European Research', *European Societies* 9, 3: 459–90.

Rose, D. and Harrison, E. (eds) (2009), *Social Class in Europe: An Introduction to the European Socio-economic Classification* (London: Routledge).

Rose, D. and Pevalin, D. (eds) (2003), *A Researcher's Guide to the National Statistics Socio-economic Classification* (London: Sage).

Rose, D. and Pevalin, D. with O'Reilly, K. (2005), *The National Statistics Socio-economic Classification: Origins, Development and Use* (London: ONS).

Wright, E.O. (ed.) (2005), *Approaches to Class Analysis* (Cambridge: Cambridge University Press).

Appendix

Eight questions required to construct NS-SEC and ESeC

Questions to ask

4.13 The following are the questions ideally required to create ESeC. They should correspond to what is required for the purposes of the EU LFS and other harmonized European surveys. However, not all these questions may appear on other surveys. It is partly for this reason that we have designed ESeC so that it may be created using either the full or simplified methods.

4.14 The instructions for interviewers are shown in italics. Two series of questions are needed in order to derive ESeC using the full method: three questions on occupation, and five questions on employment status/size of organization.

Occupation

4.15 Questions 1 to 3 collect information for coding to national classifications or to ISCO. They are asked about current job for those in paid work or about last main job for those who have ever had paid work, with the exception of full time students.
(*The ESeC User Guide*, 2006, pp. 12–14)

Question 1 – Industry description

'What did the firm/organization you worked for mainly make or do (at the place where you worked)?'
(Open)

DESCRIBE FULLY – PROBE MANUFACTURING or PROCESSING or DISTRIBUTING ETC. AND MAIN GOODS PRODUCED, MATERIALS USED, WHOLESALE or RETAIL ETC.

Question 2 – Occupation title current or last main job

'What was your (main) job?'
(Open)

Question 3 – Occupation description current or last main job

'What did you mainly do in your job?'
(Open)
CHECK SPECIAL QUALIFICATIONS/TRAINING NEEDED TO DO THE JOB

Employment status/size of organization

Questions 4 to 8 collect information for deriving the employment status/size of organization variable. The interviewer asks questions 5 and 6 when the respondent answers 'Employee' to question 4. The interviewer asks question 7 when the respondent answers 'Self-employed' to question 4; and question 8 when the respondent answers 'With employees' to question 7.

Question 4 – Employee or self-employed

'Were you working as an employee or were you self-employed?'
1 Employee Go to question 5
2 Self-employed Go to question 7
The division between employees and self-employed is based on RESPONDENTS' OWN ASSESSMENT of their employment status in their main job.

Question 5 – Supervisory status

'In your job, did you have any formal responsibility for supervising the work of other employees?'
1 Yes Go to question 6
2 No Go to question 6
Include people who say they are managers
DO NOT INCLUDE:
– supervisors of children, e.g. teachers, nannies, childminders
– supervisors of animals
– people who supervise security or buildings only, e.g. caretakers, security guards

Question 6 – Number of employees (Employees)

'How many people worked for your employer at the place where you worked?'
This should be coded to 1–9; 10+. If categories are 1–10; 11+, then code to this. If
1–4; 5–19, code to 1–19, 20+.
*We are interested in the size of the 'local unit of the establishment' at which
the respondent works in terms of total number of employees. The 'local unit' is
considered to be the geographical location where the job is mainly carried out.
Normally this will consist of a single building, part of a building, or at the largest
a self-contained group of buildings.*

*It is the total number of employees at the respondent's workplace that we
are interested in, not just the number employed within the particular section or
department in which he/she works.*

Question 7 – Self-employed working on own or with employees

'Were you working on your own or did you have employees?'
1 On own/with partner(s) but no employees
2 With employees Go to question 8

Question 8 – Self-employed working on own or with employees

'How many people did you employ at the place where you worked?'
Were there ... (RUNNING PROMPT) ...
0, 1–9, 10+. For other size bands, see question 6 above

Chapter 7
Measuring Race and Ethnicity

Martin Bulmer

Introduction

Social variables differ in their characteristics and in the extent to which they can be measured with precision. The measurement of ethnicity and 'race' is particularly fuzzy and problematical, because it is closely tied up with the conceptual definition of those terms, and the meaning which is accorded to the categories which are used to distinguish different groups within the population. The question is also fraught with political difficulties. Why is it deemed necessary to draw attention to such differences at all? The Nazi rule of occupied Europe, in which population registration data was used to identify and deport members of the Jewish population in the implementation of the Final Solution, remains as a warning of the misuses to which data on race and ethnicity may be put. This area probably has more political overtones than almost any other considered in this book.

Indeed, the justification for asking such questions is often put in the policy context in terms of the existing social inequalities in a society such as the UK formally committed in various legislation to the absence of overt discrimination, the banning of treatment of people on the basis of their physical attributes such as skin colour alone, and the need to reduce social inequalities. It is commonly argued that because there are significant differences in social condition between members of different ethnic groups, this provides the justification for the continued collection of data on the subject. It was this line of argument in the 1980s which led to the introduction of the ethnic group question into the 1991 Census, as previous indicators such as country of birth became inadequate to distinguish the ethnic minority population.

This chapter does not provide a long historical perspective upon the measurement of race and ethnicity, and does not enter at all into the history of physical anthropology, a discipline which has attempted to identify the 'races' of mankind, but which to a large extent is no longer taken seriously by twenty-first-century social scientists. There is a review of the early history of such classifications in Bulmer (1986a), focusing upon definitions used by UK social scientists, and a detailed account of the introduction of the measurement of ethnicity into the 1991 Census of Population, the first time this was done on a large scale, in Bulmer (1996). Current UK government practice is usefully reviewed in *Ethnic Group Statistics* (Office for National Statistics, 2003), which provides a guide to the collection and classification of ethnicity data. It will be evident that this discussion is focused upon the UK, and does not encompass an international overview of problems of measurement in this area. Such an international focus would be a worthwhile and desirable aim but one which is extremely challenging, because different societies differ markedly in their approach (cf Aspinall, 2007). To take but three examples, if one puts the UK alongside the USA and France in relation to this subject, the variation is very marked. Each country embodies a different history and a different approach entailing different assumptions (cf Petersen, 1997; Kertzer and Arel, 2002). Hence the focus here confines itself to the UK.

This chapter focuses on the UK experience in the last 20 years or so. It discusses both the form taken by the ethnic group question in the population censuses of 1991 and 2001, and the introduction of such a question into virtually all the continuous government surveys conducted by the Office for National Statistics (ONS), the National Centre for Social Research, and other agencies conducting government surveys, such as the British Market Research Bureau. This dual focus upon censuses and surveys is necessary because in some respects the census has been the standard bearer, but once the route was pioneered, it was the continuous surveys which then carried forward the measurement of ethnicity and its detailed implementation. (For different perspectives on this, see Sillitoe and White, 1992; Bulmer, 1986b; Booth, 1985; Ballard, 1996).

Conceptual Clarification

> Collecting data on ethnicity is difficult because of the subjective, multi-faceted and changing nature of ethnic identification and there is no consensus on what constitutes an 'ethnic group'. Membership of any ethnic group is something that is subjectively meaningful to the person concerned and the terminology used to describe ethnic groups has changed markedly over time. As a result, ethnic groups, however defined or measured, will tend to evolve depending upon social and political attitudes or developments. Therefore, we do not believe that basing ethnic identification upon an objective and rigid classification of ethnic groups is practicable (ONS, 2003: 7).

An ethnic group is a collectivity within a larger population having real or putative common ancestry, memories of a shared past, and a cultural focus upon one or more symbolic elements which define the group's identity, such as kinship, religion, language, shared territory, nationality or physical appearance. Members of an ethnic group are conscious of belonging to the group. There is no doubt that the inclusion of the question on ethnic minority group membership in the 1991 Census was aimed at identifying the size and distribution of the main visible ethnic minority groups in Britain, distinguishable in terms of skin colour from the majority population.

A similar definition was proposed by the authors of the Fourth Survey of Race Relations in Britain:

In principle, an ethnic group would be defined as a community whose heritage offers important characteristics in common between its members and which makes them distinct from other communities. There is a boundary, which separates 'us' from 'them', and the distinction would probably be recognised on both sides of that boundary.

Ethnicity is a multi-faceted phenomenon based on physical appearance, subjective identification, cultural and religious affiliation, stereotyping, and social exclusion. But it is not possible in advance to prescribe what the key distinguishing characteristics might be; the components of ethnicity will be different in Britain compared with, say Northern Ireland, Belgium, Bosnia, the United States, Rwanda, India or Singapore. So it is necessary to adopt a flexible and practical approach to choosing the specific criteria to identify the important ethnic boundaries in any particular society (Berthoud, Modood and Smith, 1997).

To that extent the census question is concerned with 'race' rather than 'ethnicity'. 'Race', however, is a controversial term, not least because of the political misuses that have been made of the concept, particularly in Nazi Germany. The idea that an objective classification of mankind's major biological categories into 'races' is either possible or useful, and that in turn individuals can be assigned to such categories, has been progressively discredited. Though there are discernible differences in skin colour, head form or type of hair among members of the human species, no satisfactory general classification of 'races' exists to which individuals may be assigned on the basis of these characteristics. This is evident, for example, in the wide variations in skin colour which exist within the population as a whole, or the variations within sub-groups originating from particular geographical areas. At the same time, it is the case that the visible difference in skin colour between most members of an ethnic minority group and the majority white population is an attribute to which social significance is attached.

Membership of an ethnic group is something which is subjectively meaningful to the person concerned, and this is the principal basis for ethnic categorization. The 1991 Census question – which was essentially a self-assessed classificatory one – reflects the fact that both members of ethnic minority groups and of the majority population perceive differences between groups in that society and define the boundaries of such groups, taking into account physical characteristics such as skin colour. What the census question reflected is the inability to base ethnic identification upon objective, quantifiable, information as in the case of age or income, and the necessity to ask people which group they see themselves as belonging to.

Terminology

In order to ask a successful self-identification question about ethnicity or 'race', one must use a clear terminology. One of the difficulties in this area is that the terminology in general use has changed markedly over time. If one traces the post-war shifts in terminology, the earliest studies of British race relations used the term 'Negroes' or 'coloured migrants' for persons of West Indian descent (Bulmer, 1986a). One study was entitled *Dark Strangers* (Patterson, 1963). As Asian migration from the Indian sub-continent increased in the 1960s, the term 'migrant' or 'coloured immigrants' or 'Commonwealth immigrants' became much more commonly used. The first national study of racial discrimination, published in 1968, referred to the 'Commonwealth coloured immigrant population' (Daniel, 1968). In the early 1970s, in official publications of statistics about ethnic minority groups, the term 'New Commonwealth and Pakistan ethnic origin' was intensively used for a period (compare with Moser, 1972).

In the mid-1970s, in the years preceding the 1981 Census of Population, there was a shift in empirical social research toward using terminology placing an emphasis upon area of origin. In the second Political and Economic Planning (PEP) National Survey of Race Relations (Smith, 1976) the terms 'West Indian', 'African Asian' and 'Indians and Pakistanis' were used. West Indians were defined as people born in the West Indies or Guyana, or (if born in Britain) people whose families originally came from there. African Asians were defined as people who were racially Asian and who either were born in Africa or were living there immediately prior to coming to Britain, or belonged to families that were originally African Asian. Indians and Pakistanis were defined as people who were not African Asians and were born in India or Pakistan or who belonged to families that originally came from India or Pakistan. 'Asian' was used to refer only to people coming from the Indian sub-continent. Other Asian groups such as Chinese or Japanese were not included in the classification. This classification had similarities with the Office of Population, Censuses and Surveys (OPCS) estimates of the population of New Commonwealth and Pakistan ethnic origin, which was broken down by geographical area of origin.

Other studies at the time used this terminology in one form or another. In Ken Pryce's study of West Indian lifestyles in Bristol (1979), those researched are referred to throughout as 'Jamaicans' or 'West Indians', whether born in the West Indies or Britain. John Rex and Sally Tomlinson (1979), and Peter Ratcliffe (1981), in their studies of Handsworth in Birmingham, used the terms 'West Indian' and 'Asian', with the term 'ethnic group' introduced as a more general term. The third National Survey of Race Relations, carried out by PSI in 1981 (Brown, 1984), used a broadly similar definition of 'West Indian', 'African Asian', 'Indian' and 'Pakistani' to that of the second PSI survey in 1974.

A question on ethnic minority group membership, in addition to being tested in the OPCS methodological research for the census, was introduced into a number of national surveys carried out by OPCS for government departments. The first occasion was the National Dwelling and Housing Survey, a very large-scale survey into the nation's housing carried out for the Department of the Environment in 1976 in the wake of the cancellation of the 1976 mid-term census (DoE, 1980: 316). This survey asked for the first time a question on ethnic origin. Respondents were handed a card and asked:

'To which of the groups listed on this card do you consider .... (person) belongs'

- 01 White
- 02 West Indian
- 03 Indian
- 04 Pakistani
- 05 Bangladeshi
- 06 Chinese
- 07 Turkish
- 08 Other Asian
- 09 African
- 10 Arab
- 11 Other (give details)
- 12 Mixed origin
- 13 Refused

Measurement and Operationalization

From the point of view of the census, the key issue was whether a workable question could be devised which would enable members of different ethnic groups to be identified. Various possible ways of operationalizing the concept were available, and have been used over the years. These will now be reviewed. The discussion relates to Great Britain, and this volume does not cover Northern Ireland. It is worth noting that Northern Ireland censuses have, exceptionally for the UK, included a question on religion. Before focusing on the evolution of the ethnic group question, which is now the standard approach in UK surveys, something should be said about earlier attempts to operationalize the measurement of ethnicity in the UK.

Alternative Approaches: Country of Birth and Parents' Country of Birth

The first question used to identify persons coming from outside the UK has traditionally been via a question on country of birth. This works for immigrants born overseas who move to the UK as adults or children, but many of the members of ethnic groups whose parents or grandparents had been such immigrants were themselves born in the UK, and could not, as the later decades of the twentieth century progressed, be accurately identified by this question. This had led in the

1971 Census to the introduction of a question on parents' country of birth from which, cross-tabulating country of birth and parents' country of birth, attempts were made to infer the size of the ethnic minority population. This proved extremely unwieldy, and only useful for basic population counts because other cross-tabulations become impossibly complex. The use of a proxy variable such as birthplace, it was apparent, was increasingly unsatisfactory, and other solutions needed to be sought.

An interesting instance of the inadequacy of birthplace data is to estimate the size of the Irish population in the UK, if this is taken to refer to people descended from those born in the island of Ireland. The size of the UK Irish population has not been clearly established, because such immigration has been going on for over 150 years. In recent years, there have been attempts, for example, in collecting local authority data, at a question based on self-identification, but birthplace alone cannot be used to measure the size of the Irish population in the UK.

Alternative Approaches: Skin Colour

Popular perceptions of ethnic difference in relation to non-white groups – and to an extent, for a period, social science researchers – used terminology referring directly to skin colour. For policy purposes, the interest has always been in differences between the white and non-white sections of the UK population. The term 'coloured' was widely used in the 1950s, but then fell out of use, being regarded as pejorative and inaccurate. The metaphor of colour retained a powerful idea, however, and early discussions of a possible census question in the mid-1970s included references to measures of the appearance of different types of beer as an analogue to the measurement problems faced in the census in relation to ethnic minority groups.

In fact, one attempt was made to gather data on skin colour by observation, in the General Household Survey (GHS). From its inception in 1971 until well into the 1980s, the interviewer in the General Household Survey was asked to record whether the respondent was white, coloured or not known. No assessment was made of persons not seen by the interviewer, and most of these were children. If both parents were seen, the interviewer imputed their children's colour from 1980 to 1983. This observational variable was then used to tabulate data. Its use was not particularly extensive, although some tables appeared in *Social Trends*. The question suffered both from the limitations of interviewer error in observation, and from the limited amount of information which it yielded. 'Coloured' was an ambiguous term, and it was not clear which ethnic groups it included. Did it, for example, include people of Maltese, Cypriot or Arab origin; how were people of mixed racial origin classified, and so on? When both interviewer data on colour and the ethnic origin question (see below) were included in the GHS in 1983, and one was tabulated against the other, 99 per cent of those describing themselves as West Indian, 98 per cent of Indians, and 97 per cent of Pakistanis and Bangladeshis were classified by the interviewer as coloured, but of the remaining ethnic groups (including 'mixed ethnic origin'), one quarter were recorded by the interviewer as white. The data did not provide a breakdown of the members of different ethnic minority groups, and this, together with its imprecision, accounted for its relative unpopularity.

A further development in the late 1970s and early 1980s was the use of the term 'black' to refer to members of non-white ethnic minority groups. Although this might be used in a loose way to indicate members of non-white ethnic minority groups, its use by members of ethnic minority groups themselves had more specific connotation in terms of promoting a positive self-identity among ethnic minority group members, and a sense of common political purpose. (Not all people of South Asian descent, however, welcomed the term, and this led to the use by some of the phrase 'black and Asian' to refer to the main ethnic minority groups.)

The report of the House of Commons Home Affairs Committee Ethnic and Racial Questions in the Census (1983a, b, c) recommended that four questions be asked to identify a person's ethnic group in the census. These were:

a. Are you white? Yes/no
b. Are you black? Yes/no
   If you are black, are you: British/West Indian/African/Other
   (tick as many boxes as apply)
c. Are you of Asian origin? Yes/no
   If yes, are you British/Indian/Pakistani/Bangladeshi/West Indian/Chinese/ Vietnamese/Other (please tick as many boxes as apply)
d. Other groups
   Are you Mixed race/Arab/Greek Cypriot/Turkish Cypriot/None of these
   (tick one box)

What remained ambiguous was whether 'black' referred primarily to persons of West Indian and African origin, or also included people of South Asian origin. Sometimes in political discourse it was more inclusive, but the tendency in research terms was to limit 'black' to the two former groups, and to talk about 'black and Asian' when referring to the main non-white ethnic minority groups in the UK. This indeed is the implication of the Select Committee question given above.

Alternative Approaches: National/Geographic

The Select Committee questions quoted above take the form of a direct question, relying on self-classification. This is the solution to the problem of trying to find a satisfactory ethnic origin question which has most commonly been adopted. It has been the practice, for example, in censuses in other multi-ethnic societies such as the United States and Canada. Instead of a proxy variable such as country of birth or nationality, a direct question is asked seeking the person's own categorization of their ethnic group, or in the case of the census, that of the member of the household completing the enumeration form.

When a question is framed in this way, the increasing tendency in the UK context in the last 15 years has been to rely on elements in the question which referred to national or geographical origin, with the accompanying assumption that these mapped onto ethnic groups. Thus 'West Indian' or 'Indian' are taken as short-hand terms for members of ethnic groups originating in those parts of the world. White persons born in, for example, India are taken not to belong to these groups, and would be expected to exclude themselves, choosing some other alternative such as 'white' or 'English'. In the case of migrant ethnic groups, combinations of more than one identifier, as in 'East African Asian', can be used to differentiate between groups in a multi-ethnic society. In a sense one might argue that this is, if not a proxy variable, proxy terminology, since one is using national or geographic origin to identify people of a particular ethnic group.

A further development has been to combine national or geographical origin with a colour term such as 'black', as in 'Black African', to identify more precisely what group one is referring to for people originating from a part of the world which is itself multi-ethnic, such as the West Indies. The term 'Black British' has given rise to particular difficulties of meaning and use, and will be discussed more fully in the next section.

Alternative Approaches: Racial Group

Finally, there are a small number of cases where a classification is used which is more than an identification in terms of national origin or geography. Some of the OPCS tests of questions used categories such as 'Chinese' or 'Arab' which arguably are in effect a racial classification of a kind, even if they also have to an extent certain geographical connotations. So the question as it evolved in the 1991 Census was really a composite question combining elements of skin colour, national origin, area of origin and a small number of racial categories. This gave rise to criticisms of inconsistency in the framing of the question, which is inherent in the attempt to construct a satisfactory question on ethnicity or ethnic origin.

The Direct Question: Self-identification by Ethnic Group

In recent years, the approach taken in large national surveys has been to frame a self-identification question in terms of which the respondent can identify their own ethnicity. (For more material on this topic, see the ESDS Guide to Ethnic Data [Afkhani, 2009]).But as the ONS Guide of 2003 makes clear, this cannot be on the basis of the respondent writing in their own ethnic identification in relation to an open-ended question:

> In the census and many surveys, respondents are invited to select, from a list of categories, the ethnic group to which they consider they belong. There

appear to be two factors determining the ethnic group that is recorded for each respondent:

- their own choice of how they view their own ethnicity and
- the list of options presented to them.

The first consideration is the most straightforward: the ethnic group that each person chooses as his or her own is intrinsically the ethnic group of self-identity, rather than being ascribed by anyone else.

The second consideration is apparently not so clear-cut. The ethnic group options presented to the respondent are not completely ones of self-identity, since the respondent is likely to have had no say in the names or the number of the different alternative ethnic groups in the 'menu'. Therefore, the freedom the respondent has to select their own group is constrained and influenced by the options on offer.

So it is important that the ethnic groups presented in a self-identification question are piloted and pre-tested. And a large part of the piloting should centre on testing alternative wording of the questions as well as the named categories in order to match respondents' own preferred ethnic descriptions of themselves. This way, the list of ethnic group options will be consistent with their own understanding of their ethnic group. There is a very good reason for compiling your questions in this way: some who would respond with their ethnicity when it means ticking a box may not be prepared to write in their ethnicity by hand were it not listed (ONS, 2003: 11).

Refinements in the categorization used were introduced into the 2001 Census, the principal change being the introduction of a category for those of mixed ethnic origin. This was a considerable departure from previous categorizations, which allowed 'mixed' as a write-in option but did not recongize it as a separate category. The change has wider implications, for the definition of what is a 'race', and for the homogeneity of the categories which are recognized in a society. There is not space to consider this further here, but the widening of the ethnic group category in this way is of considerable note.

The 2001 Census question on ethnic group in England and Wales was the following:

What is your ethnic group?

Choose ONE section from A to E, then tick the appropriate box to indicate your ethnic group.

A White

☐ British
☐ Irish
☐ Any Other White background, *please write in*

_____

B Mixed

☐ White and Black Caribbean
☐ White and Black African
☐ White and Asian
☐ Any Other Mixed background, *please write in*

_____

C Asian or Asian British

☐ Indian
☐ Pakistani
☐ Bangladeshi
☐ Any Other Asian background, *please write in*

_____

D Black or Black British

☐ Caribbean
☐ African
☐ Any Other Black background, *please write in*

_____

E Chinese or other ethnic group

☐ Chinese
☐ Any Other, please write in

Figure 7.1 Ethnic group question in the 2001 Census of Population
Source: ONS (2003): 39.

Another more recent development in official statistical circles is the recommendation for a question on national identity as well as on ethnic origin. The question recommended for England and Wales by ONS has the following form:

What do you consider your national identity to be? Please choose your answer from this card. Choose as many or as few as apply.

    ☐English
    ☐Scottish
    ☐Welsh
    ☐Irish
    ☐British
    ☐Other

If someone answers 'Other' there should then be a follow-up question:

How would you describe your national identity?

This question allows respondents to choose more than one identity (if they think of themselves as having more than one). This is because, like ethnicity, national identity is self-defined, i.e. it is something that is subjectively meaningful to the person concerned. The second part of the question 'How would you describe your national identity?' should be asked of those for whom it is relevant, even if these answers are not going to be coded.

Figure 7.2 National identity question recommended by the Office for National Statistics in 2003
Source: ONS (2003): 32.

The currently recommended question to determine a respondent's self-categorization in terms of ethnic group is the following. This gives prominence to the 'mixed' category, which is the second set of choices:

Standard ethnic group question for England and/or Wales – to be used in conjunction with national group questions.

What is your ethnic group?

Choose ONE section from A to E, then tick the appropriate box to indicate your ethnic group.

A White

☐ British
☐ Any Other White background, *please write in*

_____

B Mixed

☐ White and Black Caribbean
☐ White and Black African
☐ White and Asian
☐ Any Other Mixed background, *please write in*

_____

C Asian or Asian British

☐ Indian
☐ Pakistani
☐ Bangladeshi
☐ Any Other Asian background, *please write in*

_____

D Black or Black British

☐ Caribbean
☐ African
☐ Any Other Black background, *please write in*

_____

E Chinese or other ethnic group

☐ Chinese
☐ Any Other, please write in

Figure 7.3 Suggested question on ethnic group

Another format is recommended in situations where telephone interviewing is being used and it is not practicable to read out a long list of categories. In this case, a two-stage procedure is suggested as follows:

Q1. What do you consider to be your national identity?
Choose as many or as few answers as apply.
- English
- Scottish
- Welsh
- Irish
- British
- Other

Q2. To which of these ethnic groups do you consider you belong?
- White
- Mixed
- Asian or Asian British
- Black or Black British
- Chinese
- Other ethnic group

Q3. And to which of these ethnic groups do you consider you belong?
If White chosen:
- British
- Another White background

If Mixed chosen:
- White and Black Caribbean
- White and Black African
- White and Asian
- Another Mixed background

If Asian or Asian British chosen:
- Indian
- Pakistani
- Bangladeshi
- Another Asian background

If Black or Black British chosen:
- Caribbean
- African
- Another Black background

If Chinese chosen:
Note – no further question
If Other ethnic group chosen, ask Q4

Q4. Please can you describe your ethnic group?

Question 4 should be asked of those for whom it is relevant, even if these answers are not going to be coded.

**Figure 7.4 Suggested ethnic group question when conducting telephone
interviewing**
Source: ONS (2003): 46–7.

Conclusion

Research on ethnicity and race carries with it its own dynamic. In one sense, the justification for using ethnic classifications and deploying them in data analysis lies in the differences which they reveal and the patterns which they display. Like gender difference, if no ethnic differences were displayed by data analysis, little use would be made of the variable and it would fall into lack of use. Such differences do, however, continue to be displayed. Consider, for example, the evidence about ethnicity and health demonstrated in studies such as Nazroo, 1998 and 2001; Aspinall, 2001; Karlsen and Nazroo, 2002; Bradby, 2003. So long as such research continues to show that there are significant ethnic differences in health, ethnicity is likely to remain a key variable in sociological research.

The measurement of ethnicity will continue to develop and change. In recent years, ONS has added the measurement of national identity as part of its methodological toolkit, no doubt reflecting the growth of Scotland, Wales and Northern Ireland as more autonomous units within the United Kingdom of Great Britain and Northern Ireland. There continues to be demand for more refined ethnicity data for smaller sub-groups, for example, to distinguish between people of Indian, Pakistani, Bangladeshi and Sri Lankan origin within the UK South Asian ethnic group, or to have finer data available for people of Latin American origin. More work needs to be done on international dimensions of the measurement of ethnicity, to see whether a greater degree of standardization, permitting cross-national studies, is possible. The European Social Survey has made an encouraging start, but the challenges are formidable, and to present measurement difference is more characteristic than any convergence. Even within the EU, practice varies considerably, and the conceptual basis of ethnic measurement is founded on different principles. Many challenges remain.

Guides

The ESDS Introductory Guide to Ethnicity (updated December 2008) is well worth consulting. It can be reached via the following web page, from which PDF and Word versions may be downloaded.

URL: <http://www.esds.ac.uk/government/resources/themeguides.asp>

This focuses upon data sources and data sets, but includes some useful tabulated information about classifications used in data.

Questions in Major UK Surveys

These may be found in the Question Bank (Qb) and in the UK Data Archive, which are now on the same site. The main large-scale surveys about ethnicity held in the Qb are listed below, as well as other smaller surveys that may be of relevance. This is just a selection of surveys that cover this topic in some depth. Questions on ethnicity may also be found in other surveys held in the Qb that are not listed here. To vist the Question Bank, go to the following URL: <http://surveynet.ac.uk/sqb/introduction.asp>

Major Surveys with Questions on Ethnicity:

- British Social Attitudes Survey
- European Social Survey
- Fourth National Survey of Ethnic Minorities
- Millennium Cohort Study
- People, Families and Communities Survey

References

Afkhani, R. (2009), *Ethnicity: Introductory User Guide*, Version 1.3, November (Manchester: Economic and Social Data Service [ESDS] Government), consulted on 10 December 2009 at <www.esds.ac.uk/government/resources/themeguides.asp>.

Aspinall, P.J. (2001), 'Operationalising the Collection of Ethnicity Data in Studies of the Sociology of Health and Illness', *Sociology of Health and Illness* 23, 6: 829–62.

Aspinall, P.J. (2007), 'Approaches to Developing an Improved Cross-national Understanding of Concepts and Terms Relating to Ethnicity and Race', *International Sociology* 22, 1: 41–70.

Ballard, R. (1996), 'Negotiating Race and Ethnicity: Exploring the Implications of the 1991 Census', *Patterns of Prejudice* 30, 3: 3–33.

Berthoud, R., Modood, T. and Smith, D.J. (1997), *Ethnic Minorities in Britain* (London: Policy Studies Institute).

Booth, H. (1985), 'Which "Ethnic Question"? The Development of Questions Identifying Ethnic Origin in Official Statistics', *The Sociological Review* 33, 2: 254–74.

Bradby, H. (2003), 'Describing Ethnicity in Health Research', *Ethnicity and Health* 8, 1: 5–13.

Brown, C. (1984), *Black and White Britain* (London: Heinemann).

Bulmer, M. (1986a), 'Race and Ethnicity', in R.G. Burgess (ed.), *Key Variables in Social Investigation* (London: Routledge), 54–75.

Bulmer, M. (1986b), 'A Controversial Census Topic: Race and Ethnicity in the British Census', *Journal of Official Statistics* 2, 4: 471–80.

Bulmer, M. (1996), 'The Ethnic Group Question in the 1991 Census of Population', in D. Coleman and J. Salt (eds), *Ethnicity in the 1991 Census of Population* (London: HMSO).

Daniel, W.W. (1968), *Racial Discrimination in England* (Harmondsworth: Penguin).

Department of the Environment (DoE) (1980), *The National Dwelling and Housing Survey 1979* (London: HMSO).

House of Commons Home Affairs Committee (1983a, b, c), *Ethnic and Racial Questions in the Census* (London: HMSO), House of Commons Paper HC 33-I, II and III, Session 1982–83, Vol. 1, Report; Vol. 2, Minutes of Evidence; Vol. 3, Appendices.

Karlsen, S. and Nazroo, J.Y. (2002), 'Relation Between Racial Discrimination, Social Class, and Health Among Ethnic Minority Groups', *American Journal of Public Health* 92, 4: 624–31.

Kertzer, D.I. and Arel, D. (2002), Census and Identity: The Politics of Race, Ethnicity and Language in National Censuses (Cambridge: Cambridge University Press).

Moser, C. (1972), 'Statistics about Immigrants: Objectives, Sources, Methods and Problems', *Social Trends* 3: 20–30.

Nazroo, J.Y. (1998), 'Rethinking the Relationship Between Ethnicity and Mental Health: The British Fourth National Survey of Ethnic Minorities', *Social Psychiatry and Psychiatric Epidemiology* 33, 4: 145–8.

Nazroo, J.Y. (2001), *Ethnicity, Class and Health* (London: Policy Studies Institute).

Office for National Statistics (ONS) (2003), *Ethnic Group Statistics: A Guide to the Collection and Classification of Ethnicity Data* (London: Office for National Statistics), available at: <http://www.statistics.gov.uk/about/ethnic_group_statistics/default.asp>.

OPCS/GRO (S) (1993), *Ethnic Group and Country of Birth, Great Britain*. 2 volumes. Ref. CEN91 ECGB (London, HMSO).

OPCS/GRO (S) (1994), Supplement to Report on Ethnic Group and Country of Birth: 1991 Census (London, OPCS).

Patterson, S. (1963), Dark Strangers: A Study of West Indians in London (Harmondsworth: Penguin).

Petersen, W. (1997), *Ethnicity Counts* (New Brunswick, NJ: Transaction).

Pryce, K. (1979), Endless Pressure: A Study of West Indian Life-styles in Bristol (Harmondsworth: Penguin).

Ratcliffe, P. (1981), *Racism and Reaction: A Profile of Handsworth* (London: Routledge and Kegan Paul).

Rex, J. and Tomlinson, S. (1979), *Colonial Immigrants in a British City: A Class Analysis* (London: Routledge and Kegan Paul).

Sillitoe, K. and White, P.H. (1992), 'Ethnic Group and the British Census: The Search for a Question', *Journal of the Royal Statistical Society*, series A, vol. 155, part 1: 141–63.

Smith, D.J. (1976), *The Facts of Racial Disadvantage: A National Survey* (London: Political and Economic Planning), PEP Broadsheet no. 560.

Chapter 8
Measuring Sexual Behaviour

Catherine H. Mercer, Sally McManus and Bob Erens

There is a need for accurate and reliable estimates of the nature, extent and distribution of sexual behaviour in different populations. Kinsey's groundbreaking studies conducted from 1938 to 1963 were surrounded by controversy, yet they provided a first insight into the range of behaviour that was 'normal' and not 'deviant' as many had thought (Kinsey, Pomeroy and Martin, 1948; Kinsey et al., 1953). Subsequent surveys in the 1970s provided new insights into patterns of fertility and reproduction, which informed demographic projections and contraceptive service planning. The advent of HIV/AIDS in the 1980s then prioritized the need to understand the distribution of risky sexual behaviours for epidemiological and public health projections and was accompanied by a huge growth in research in this field. This 'legitimization' of the study of sexual behaviour facilitated data collection on a range of behaviours and attitudes to answer epidemiological, reproductive health, as well as psychosexual, questions, furthering understanding of all aspects of sexual behaviour.

There are a number of ways to research sexual behaviour including using qualitative, in-depth interviews, analysis of treatment, diagnosis and prescribing statistics, and even observation. However, in order to obtain accurate and reliable estimates of the nature, extent and distribution of sexual behaviour in different populations or groups, high quality surveys are often the most desirable data collection tool. As with surveys generally, data collection is a resource-intensive activity and, due to the sensitive subject matter for a survey on sex, additional resources may be required to obtain a representative sample and to boost numbers of population groups who practice relatively rare sexual behaviours, such as men who have sex with men.

This chapter discusses the key issues that need to be considered when designing a survey to obtain unbiased and accurate estimates of sexual behaviour. It begins by addressing practical issues such as: designing a sample; modes of data collection; making contact; administering the interview; and questionnaire structure, content and wording. Five important topics in this field are then addressed:

1. first sexual experiences
2. sexuality, attraction and identity
3. sexual partner numbers
4. sexual partnership characteristics
5. condom use

The chapter cites examples and data from the British national sexual behaviour surveys, the National Surveys of Sexual Attitudes and Lifestyles ('Natsal'), conducted in 1990–91 (Johnson et al., 1994; Wellings et al., 1994) and again in 1999–2001 (Johnson et al. 2001a; Wellings et al. 2001; Fenton et al. 2001; Erens et al. 2001).

Designing a Sample

To avoid the biases that are likely to result from a volunteer, convenience or quota sample, high quality surveys invariably use probability sampling methods. For a general population survey, this requires a suitable sampling frame such as a population or electoral register, or for the UK, the Postcode Address File. For a survey of particular subgroups of the population for which there is no suitable sampling frame, such as men who have sex with men or commercial sex workers, then door-to-door screening may be unfeasible, and a convenience or volunteer sample the only available option.

Consideration needs to be given to the age range to be included in the survey, based on the key research questions. For example, if the purpose of the survey is to improve understanding of the epidemiology of sexually transmitted infections (STIs), then it may be reasonable to limit the age range to individuals aged 16–34 years, since this is the group most at risk of STIs, at least in the UK (Health Protection Agency, 2007). However, if the research is concerned with understanding sexual dysfunction, then it may be more appropriate to focus on an older age range, as prevalence is known to increase with age (Laumann, Paik and Rosen, 1999; Mercer et al., 2005).

The target population's lower age limit may be determined by ethical considerations. For example, ethical approval may require the exclusion of young people aged under 16 years, or there may be a requirement for parental permission for young people aged 16–18 years to participate in the survey. This is unfortunate given that first sexual intercourse tends to occur in the mid- to late-teens in many countries (Wellings et al., 2006). This means that where the eligible population is restricted to a minimum age of 18 years, then data on first sexual experiences are likely to refer to a number of years, if not decades, ago for a sizeable proportion of the sample, impacting on recall and increasing the potential for error. Issues surrounding measuring first sexual experiences are discussed later in this chapter.

As with all surveys, it is necessary to undertake sample size calculations to ensure that the interviewed sample will be large enough to have adequate statistical power to look at important sub-groups in the population (for example, age and sex or regional breakdowns), to estimate the prevalence of relatively rare sexual behaviours with sufficient precision, and to identify significant associations between key predictors and major parameters. In this respect, over-sampling particular population sub-groups, such as young people or ethnic minorities, may be an appealing option for obtaining more robust estimates for these groups. However, over-sampling can be statistically inefficient in terms of obtaining estimates for the full population, and if data collection involves face-to-face interviews the need for extra door-to-door screening will increase fieldwork costs.

Mode of Data Collection

The importance of reassuring survey participants of confidentiality cannot be over-emphasized when undertaking surveys of sexual behaviour, and this has implications for how and where such data are collected. While it is widely established that the reporting of sensitive behaviours increases using self-completion component(s), there are risks associated with the survey being administered without any personal element. For sexual behaviour surveys in particular, the rationale for why the study is needed is best explained by a fieldworker who can tailor this appropriately, and so improve response. In this respect, some have argued for matching interviewers to participants on attributes such as sexual identity and ethnic origin for surveys of particular populations (Spencer, Faulkner and Keegan, 1988; Mitchell et al., 2007). However, there are risks associated with this approach, especially when surveying a small community. In particular, there may be pressure to conform to expectations of the group if interviewed by someone from the same community, and thus reluctance to report behaviours that are not culturally acceptable to that community, or fear of 'word getting out' if such behaviours are reported.

Postal surveys are problematic, not only because they do not have a face-to-face component, but they also tend to achieve low response rates, especially when covering sensitive topics (Bates and Rogstad, 2000; Dillman, 2000; Edwards et al., 2002). It is also necessary to consider the risk of disclosure if a completed postal questionnaire is found by another member of the respondent's household. In contrast, if an interviewer is present, then they can take any completed paper questionnaires away with them, thus reducing this risk. Using a postal questionnaire means that there is also little control over who completes the questionnaire and whether or not this is done in private – issues that also apply to internet-based surveys.

While internet-based surveys are increasing in number, they have coverage problems as the proportion of the population with private internet access is still far from universal. Furthermore, there are indications that those with access, that is, the young, those with higher incomes, and living in more metropolitan areas, are likely to differ from the rest of the population in their sexual behaviour profile. A similar issue exists for telephone surveys as households with residents who are younger, move more frequently, or on lower income levels, are more likely to just have mobile phones rather than landlines, and therefore will be excluded from most ways of generating a random telephone sample. This is not to say that telephone interviewing is not appropriate for a survey of sexual behaviour. If the participant cannot see the interviewer, then this may make reporting socially undesirable behaviours easier for some people, especially if questions are phrased in a manner so that the participant just needs to answer 'yes' or 'no', or if automated interviewing tools are used (Villarroel et al., 2008). Conversely, a major problem with telephone surveys is that they are poor for collecting complex retrospective data, such as sexual partnership histories. (Further information on telephone survey methodology is given in Groves et al., 1988.) For these reasons, the rest of this chapter focuses on using face-to-face, interviewer-administered surveys for measuring sexual behaviour.

Interviewer-administered surveys that use computer-assisted personal interviewing (CAPI) have been found to improve data quality in terms of internal consistency and the number of missed questions, relative to using pen-and-paper questionnaires (Johnson et al., 2001b). It is easy to incorporate filtering into the CAPI programme, so irrelevant questions are skipped, reducing error and making it quicker and easier to complete the survey. Of course, CAPI may not be feasible or practical in some survey settings.

Regardless of whether or not CAPI is used, a self-completion component for the more sensitive questions is essential. This may be a pen-and-paper questionnaire, a computer-assisted self-interview (CASI), or specifically audio-CASI (A-CASI) whereby the participant hears, as well as reads, the question, benefiting in particular those with literacy or sight problems. Some have found that using CASI results in higher rates of reporting sensitive behaviours than using pen-and-paper questionnaires (Turner et al., 1998), although others have found no difference between these two modes of administration (Johnson et al., 2001b). (See Couper et al., 1998, for a general discussion of using CASI for data collection).

Making Contact

Some people may be reluctant to take part in a survey on sexual behaviour, for example, if they consider it voyeuristic, so it is important to take steps to try to overcome these assumptions and concerns. One such step is to send a letter to sampled addresses in advance of a fieldworker calling to briefly introduce the survey and notify the household that a fieldworker will call to seek permission to participate in the survey. This letter should be sent on headed paper from the organization(s) conducting the survey, and should state who the study is being funded by, for example, a research council or government health department, as this demonstrates that the survey is legitimate and respectable. The letter should also include the organization's contact details, so that potential participants can verify the survey or find out more information about the survey or the organizations (see, for example, Erens et al., 2001, 42).

When the fieldworker makes contact on the doorstep, it is essential for them to have an information sheet or leaflet at hand. This should cover: how the potential participant's address was selected; why the topic is being studied, giving illustrations of the utility of the research; who is conducting the research; the potential participant's rights; assurances of confidentiality; and where they can obtain further information should they wish to do so (for example, see Erens et al.,

2001, 44–5). This leaflet should ideally be used *after* the potential participant has been selected, but it is possible that the person who answers the door may act as a 'gatekeeper' and so it may be necessary for the fieldworker to first 'sell' the survey to them. This is vital for obtaining a good response rate and so fieldworkers need to be trained in appropriate ways to tailor the selling of the survey. For example, if the gatekeeper is the parent of a young person who is selected to participate, then they may be reluctant for their son or daughter to do so – especially if they believe that their child is sexually inexperienced. Consequently, the fieldworker may in this instance choose to emphasize the importance of young people's participation in the survey for informing personal and social education in schools.

Administering the Interview

Given the sensitive nature of the interview, it is desirable that it is conducted in a private location where the participant feels comfortable. Usually this will be the participant's home, but sometimes they may prefer an alternative location such as their place of work, or perhaps a public place, like a local park. The interviewer needs to be able to assess whether an environment is sufficiently private and if not, be assertive in asking where the interview can be conducted in privacy. If other people are within sight or earshot of the interview, then this may inhibit participants from answering particular questions. During face-to-face interviewing, showcards with concealed response codes can be used so that neither the participant nor the interviewer has to articulate any sexually explicit terms or the participant disclose aloud any sensitive information. Young people need to be explicitly reassured by interviewers that their responses will be safeguarded. For example, if a parent is in the same room as a teenage participant, then it may be preferable to ask the participant to complete a pen and paper version of a face-to-face interview. Other steps to further reassure the participant of confidentiality during the interview include asking participants to put paper questionnaires in sealed envelopes before returning them to the interviewer, or if CASI is used, then designing the computer program to 'lock' once the participant has entered their responses, so that the interviewer cannot go back to access their data.

The end of the interview is an appropriate time to invite participants to provide biological samples, if this is of interest. For example, participants in Natsal 2000 were asked to provide a urine sample for testing for the STI *Chlamydia trachomatis* (Fenton et al., 2001), while the London Gay Men's Sexual Health Surveys invited men to provide a saliva sample for testing for HIV (Dodds et al., 2004). In Natsal 2000, all eligible participants received a verbal explanation from the interviewer and a leaflet describing the purposes of the urine test and what would be involved, along with an information leaflet about *Chlamydia trachomatis*. For ethical reasons, written consent was obtained from participants prior to their providing the urine sample. Further details on testing of the urine specimens and quality control measures are given in the Natsal 2000 Technical Report (Erens et al., 2001).

Participants are generally willing to provide biological samples such as urine and saliva that do not involve invasive collection, whereas requests for blood samples are less well received and may have the added complication of requiring a research nurse or phlebotomist to collect the sample, adding to the cost of administering the survey (Craig and Mindell, 2008). Technological advances are, however, facilitating the use of biological samples that can be obtained via unobtrusive methods of collection, expanding the range of biomarkers that can be studied as part of a survey.

Questionnaire Structure and Content

Starting the interview with relatively neutral questions, for example, about the participant's general health, their family and children enables the interviewer to establish a rapport with the participant and gets the participant comfortable with talking to the interviewer, before needing to ask more sensitive questions. Questions about learning about sex when they were growing up are a natural follow on, should this be of interest, which in turn can lead to questions about their first sexual experience.

In order to get estimates for the population, everyone should be invited to participate in the survey, not just those who are sexually experienced or sexually active at the time of the interview. However, it may not be necessary or desirable for everyone in the sample to answer the most sensitive questions. For example, to avoid probing about childhood non-consensual sexual experience, the Natsal surveys did not ask such questions to participants whose only sexual experience was before the age of 13 years. This is discussed in more detail later in the chapter.

Starting the sexual behaviour module of the questionnaire with questions about recent experiences focuses the participant. For example, the Natsal surveys asked participants about the number of occasions of sex that they had had in the four weeks prior to their interview. Participants were then asked about the number of sexual partners they had had, the number of these partners that were new, and whether or not condoms had been used in this time-frame. Questions on specific sexual practices that may have last occurred some time ago can then be asked. For example: 'When, if ever, was the last occasion you had vaginal sexual intercourse?' (Erens et al., 2001: 80). While the participant is recalling past events is a good time to ask about the number of sexual partners that they have had in different time-periods, such as lifetime, the last five years, the last year, and the last three months. This topic is discussed in more detail later on.

It is usually preferable that questions differentiate between heterosexual and homosexual partnerships and practices, beginning with the former because of its higher prevalence, at least in a general population survey. Questions on more specific sexual behaviours can then be asked, such as experience of having sex with people from other countries, or about paying for sex, or the characteristics of their most recent partnership(s). Asking about sexual health issues, such as whether participants have ever been to a sexual health clinic, been diagnosed with a sexually transmitted infection, been tested for HIV, or their experience of sexual function problems and induced abortion, are also highly sensitive questions and so these also need to be asked in the context of a self-completion component.

Attitudinal questions should be placed *after* questions on behaviours, so that participants can report their own behaviour before being asked to make moral judgments, for example, on different types of sexual relationships (such as, one-night stands, sexual relationships with someone other than one's own spouse or partner) or socially-sensitive issues such as abortion.

As with most surveys, it is usual to end by asking questions to collect standard demographic information such as economic activity, occupation, household income, educational background, and religious and ethnic identity. In addition, it is worth recording details of the interview setting, for example, whether or not others were present during the interview and if so, whether they could see the questionnaire or computer screen or hear the participant's answers. This information can then be used to inform the analysis in terms of possible biases in the data.

In concluding the interview, it is advisable to provide contact details of advice and support groups, such as helplines able to deal with rape/child-abuse issues, as well as details of local health centres if participants feel that they may have been at risk, so that they can obtain appropriate health care, advice and screening.

Developing and Testing Questions

The sensitive nature of the topic means that sexual behaviour surveys require considerable development work. Where possible, it is sensible to use questions that have been piloted and validated for other studies (see, for example, the resources available from the ESRC Survey Question Bank), which also enables comparative analyses (for example, Dodds et al., 2006; Gilbart et al., 2006; Evans et al., 2007) and helps to contextualize results. If questions need to be developed from scratch, then several stages of testing are essential, including a qualitative phase to look at the acceptability of asking about specific topics, as well as cognitive testing for meaning, before piloting the instrument in its entirety. Indeed, even if questions have been used before, it is advisable to pilot the questionnaire for acceptability and appropriateness if the target population differs to that of the original study (Bhopal et al., 2004), or if the original study was conducted some time ago, as language evolves and examples may become dated.

In terms of the *type* of language used, pilot work for the Natsal surveys revealed that people preferred the use of scientific language (for example, 'sexual intercourse') to the colloquial ('having sex') or romantic language ('making love') in the interview setting. Ultimately the language used should be non-judgmental, meaningful and widely acceptable, and thus may require piloting.

Because of the imprecision surrounding sexual language, often because of the use of euphemistic language, it is advisable to ask participants to read a list of definitions just before they answer questions on sexual behaviour, to clarify meanings and to ensure that everyone ascribes the same meanings to the terms used. For example, some people do not consider oral sex as sexual intercourse, as famously illustrated in 1998 when the then US President, Bill Clinton, stated: 'I did not have sexual relations with that woman', despite it later being revealed that he had in fact had oral sex with his intern, Monica Lewinsky (Baker and Harris, 1998). Similarly, cognitive interviewing for the Natsal surveys highlighted that many heterosexual participants interpreted the term 'having sex' or 'sexual intercourse' to refer just to vaginal intercourse (Mitchell et al., 2007), while the Natsal surveys define 'sexual intercourse' more broadly to include vaginal, oral and anal sexual intercourse (see Table 8.1).

Table 8.1 Key sexual behaviour terms as defined in the Natsal surveys

Term	Definition
Partners or sexual partners	People who have had sex together – whether just once, or a few times, or as regular partners, or as married partners.
Genital area	A man's penis or a woman's vagina – that is, the sex organs.
Vaginal sexual intercourse	A man's penis in a woman's vagina. This is what people most usually think of as "having sex" or "sexual intercourse".
Oral sex or oral sexual intercourse	A woman/man's mouth on a partner's genital area.
Anal sex or anal sexual intercourse	A man's penis in a partner's anus (rectum or back passage).
Sexual intercourse, or 'having sex'	This includes vaginal, oral and anal sexual intercourse.
Genital contact *not* involving intercourse	Forms of contact with the genital area NOT leading to intercourse (vaginal, oral or anal), but intended to achieve orgasm, for example, stimulating by hand.
Any sexual contact or experience	This is a wider term and can include just kissing or cuddling, not necessarily leading to genital contact or intercourse.

Source: Erens et al. (2001).

Spelling out exactly what is meant by a term is also important if the questionnaire is translated into another language and there is no equivalent term (Bhopal et al., 2004). For example, a sexual behaviour questionnaire that used the term 'opposite sex' caused confusion when piloted among Eastern European migrants living in London, as it was interpreted to mean deviant behaviour (A. Evans, personal communication, 2008).

We now consider issues relating to a number of specific question themes unique to measuring sexual behaviour: first sexual experiences; sexuality, attraction and identity; sexual partner numbers; sexual partnership characteristics; and condom use.

Asking Questions about First Sexual Experiences

As a 'once in a lifetime' event, first sexual intercourse is likely to be well recalled by most people, even if this occurred several decades ago (Wellings et al., 2001). For some, this first occasion may have been non-consensual or as a result of child sexual abuse, so in order to avoid evoking traumatic memories and causing distress for the participant, it may be advisable to ask whether intercourse has occurred with anybody else since a particular age, for example, age 13, and if so, ask questions about this later occasion. Of course, the choice of age is arbitrary and may mean that some participants may still refer to an occasion of non-consensual sex, while for others, this approach may mean that their first occasion of consensual sex is overlooked.

Although people are likely to have good recall of their age at first intercourse, subjective questions concerning perceptions of their 'first time' are likely to change over time. For example, if asked at the time of first sex, they may give their motivation as 'being in love'; whereas if asked several years or decades later, hindsight may mean that they attribute their first sex to wanting to please their partner (Elo, King and Furstenberg, 1999; Wight et al., 2000; Wellings et al., 2001). For surveys where a large proportion of participants are asked to think back a number of years to their 'first time', then it is important that questions about first sexual experience emphasize the need for participants to think back to that occasion by using such wording as: 'Looking back now to the first time you had sexual intercourse ...' or 'which of these things applied to you *at the time*?' (Erens et al., 2001: 66).

Collecting valid data on the circumstances of first sex is also important for considering the concept of 'sexual competence', that is, the idea that focusing solely on absolute age at first intercourse may not take into account variations in individual development and social norms (Wellings et al., 2001). Assuming that first intercourse should, ideally, be characterized by absence of duress and regret, autonomy of decision, and the use of a reliable method of contraception, including questions on these topics enables a measure of sexual competence to be constructed (Wellings et al., 2001).

Of course, depending on the eligible population, it may be that not all participants have experienced sexual intercourse by the time of the interview. This can be included as an option when wording questions about first sexual intercourse so as not to alienate such participants or make them feel abnormal, for example: 'How old were you when you first had sexual intercourse with someone of the opposite sex, or hasn't this happened yet?' (Erens et al., 2001: 62).

It is also important to take this issue into consideration when estimating the average age at first intercourse (or indeed any other 'first' event). Survival or lifetable analysis should be used so that the resulting estimates can be considered as broadly representative of all people in the birth cohort who have experienced the event by the time of the interview or who will go on to do so.

Asking Questions about Sexuality, Attraction and Identity

As Kinsey wrote in his 1948 manuscript: 'Males do not represent two discrete populations, heterosexual and homosexual. The world is not to be divided into sheep and goats ...' (Kinsey, Pomeroy and Martin, 1948: 639). As such he proposed the now frequently cited 'Kinsey scale' to recognize sexuality as a continuum by using a seven-point scale, from 0 denoting 'exclusively heterosexual' through to 6 'exclusively homosexual' (see Figure 8.1).

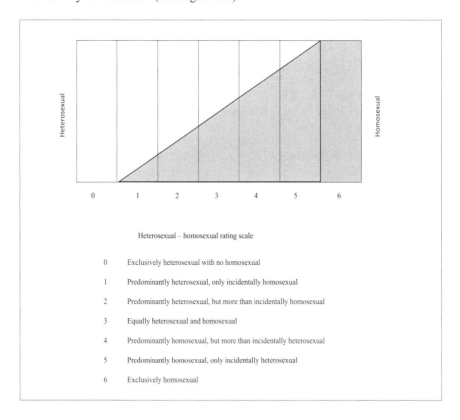

Heterosexual – homosexual rating scale

0	Exclusively heterosexual with no homosexual
1	Predominantly heterosexual, only incidentally homosexual
2	Predominantly heterosexual, but more than incidentally homosexual
3	Equally heterosexual and homosexual
4	Predominantly homosexual, but more than incidentally heterosexual
5	Predominantly homosexual, only incidentally heterosexual
6	Exclusively homosexual

Figure 8.1 The Kinsey scale
Source: Kinsey, Pomeroy and Martin (1948): 638.

The Natsal surveys used an adapted version of the Kinsey scale to ask about sexual attraction. This question was part of the face-to-face interview but involved the participant reading a showcard and reporting a concealed response code (see Figure 8.2).

Now please read this card carefully as it is important that you understand it and are as honest as you can be in your answer. When you've finished reading, tell me which letter represents your answer.

CARD SAYS:*
I have felt sexually attracted ...

(K) Only to females, never to males
(C) More often to females, and at least once to a male
(F) About equally often to females and to males
(L) More often to males, and at least once to a female
(D) Only ever to males, never to females
(N) I have never felt sexually attracted to anyone at all

Figure 8.2 Wording of the question on sexual attraction in the Natsal surveys
Note: * The wording given is for male respondents. References to 'male' and 'female' would be interchanged for female respondents.
Source: Erens et al. (2001).

Unlike the Kinsey scale, the Natsal surveys avoided using the terms 'heterosexual' and 'homosexual', reflecting how people do not always identify with these labels. In addition, a category was included for people who have not experienced sexual attraction, estimated as approximately 1 per cent of the general population (Prause and Graham, 2007).

While popular, it has been argued that Kinsey's scale over-simplifies sexual orientation, and other classifications have been devised, such as the Klein Sexual Orientation Grid (Klein, 1993). The Klein Grid takes account of sexual attraction, behaviour, fantasies, emotional, social and lifestyle preferences, as well as self-identification. Distinguishing between sexual attraction, identity and behaviour is important. For example, in Natsal 2000, one in twenty people who described their sexual attraction as 'only to people of the opposite sex, never to people of the same sex' also reported some kind of sexual experience or sexual contact with someone of the *same* sex. Thus, people's behaviour may differ from their identity and/or their attraction (see Figure 8.3). Consequently, it is important not to confuse sexual attraction with sexual behaviour, for example, by using responses to a question about sexual attraction to filter participants to questions on sexual behaviour with one particular gender.

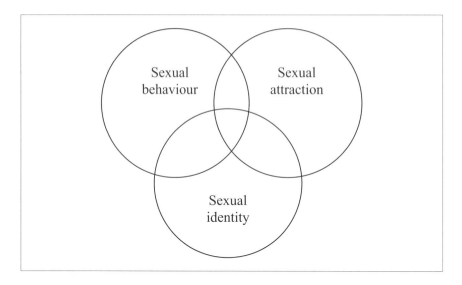

Figure 8.3 Distinguishing between sexual behaviour, sexual attraction and sexual identity

In addition to asking about sexual attraction and behaviour, it is also important to ask about sexual identity. The UK's Office for National Statistics undertook extensive research to develop a question on sexual identity for use in social surveys. This question asks people to classify themselves simply into 'heterosexual/straight', 'gay/lesbian', 'bisexual', or 'other' – that is, using terms familiar and acceptable to most people (Office for National Statistics, 2008).

Asking Questions about Sexual Partner Numbers

As Table 8.1 showed, the Natsal surveys define sexual partners as: 'People who have had sex together – whether just once, or a few times, or as regular partners, or as married partners' (Erens et al., 2001: 78). This emphasizes that sexual partners include *all* people that participants have had sexual intercourse with, regardless of the social relationship between people. Indeed, cognitive testing has revealed that, paradoxically, people may not always include their spouse as a sexual partner even where the relationship is sexually active (Wellings et al., 1994). Adopting this 'all inclusive' approach avoids the subjectivity of differentiating between different types of partnership. Live-in partnerships are usually straightforward to define because of their cohabitation status, but casual partnerships are more difficult to differentiate between because of the lack of an objective measure of their partnership status. It is also worth noting that the status of a partnership can change with time. Thus, while a partnership may not be regular at the time of the interview, it may go on to become regular, and so such partnerships should be interpreted as 'not (yet) regular'.

The number of sexual partners a person has had is one of the best measures of sexual risk and predictors of adverse sexual health outcomes (Fenton et al., 2001; Fenton et al., 2005; Aral and Holmes, 2006). However, to which time-frame should this question refer? Ever? The past five years? The past year? The past three months? The past four weeks? The choice of time-frame will depend on the research question, as one time-frame does not fit (or answer) all research questions. A recent time-frame such as the past year is useful to give a measure of current sexual activity and/or risk exposure. However, since a majority of people have only one sexual partner in a year (Johnson et al., 2001a), this time-frame is not very useful for differentiating people, nor is it informative of cumulative or past risk exposure. Of course, asking people to recall partner numbers for a recent time-period has the advantage that it is easier for the participant and so less likely to result in item non-response or recall error. These are particular challenges for those with many sexual partners, and there is often digit preference or 'heaping' on numbers ending in 0 or 5 (see Figure 8.4).

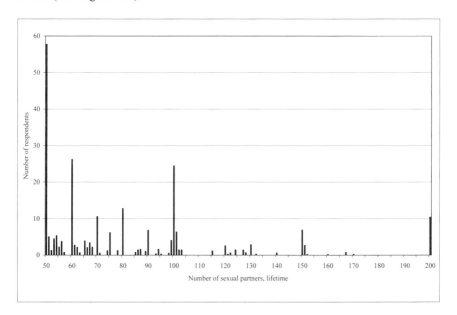

Figure 8.4 Digit preference or 'heaping' on sexual partner numbers among those reporting at least 50 partners in their lifetime

Source: Natsal (2000), unpublished data.

While participants can be asked to choose a categorical response such as 0, 1, 2–4, 5–9, 10+, obtaining continuous data on partner numbers is preferable as it is more versatile for analysis and statistical and mathematical modelling purposes. Another option may be to ask participants the certainty of their report. For example, in the Natsal surveys, participants reporting more than four sexual partners in their lifetime were asked: 'Are you certain of that number or have you had to estimate it?' (Erens et al., 2001: 79).

In Natsal 2000, approximately half of all such participants said that they had reported an estimate of the number of partners they had had, with this proportion correlated with partner numbers, and men being more likely to do so than women. In addition, cognitive testing for Natsal 2000 revealed that men tended to 'round up' their estimate of number of sexual partners while women tended to 'round down' their estimate (Mitchell et al., 2007), reflecting, in part, social desirability bias. (See Wadsworth et al., 1996, and Brown and Sinclair, 1999, for further discussion of the gender difference in reporting sexual partnerships).

Strategies can be employed to help improve recall, such as encouraging participants to use 'anchor points' to assist them, for example, the number of sexual partners they had before leaving home, the number of partners they had before getting married, and so on (Mitchell et al., 2007). Similarly, using dates may clarify the time-frame being asked about. For example: 'How many partners have you had sex with in the past year, that is since September 2007?' Inviting participants to methodically go through their partnership history year-by-year, from their first sexual experience, is another option (National Center for Health Statistics, 2008), but this may not be achievable in the time available for the interview.

Asking Questions about Sexual Partnership Characteristics

The characteristics of sexual partnerships, for example, the partner's age (relative to the participant), the length of time between first meeting and first sex, or questions about sexual risk within a particular partnership, such as whether or not condoms were used at first and most recent sex with the partner, are key variables for modelling population patterns of STI transmission and other projections. In many studies, data on sexual partnerships are sought by asking participants detailed questions about their current or most recent sexual partnership (Anderson et al., 1999; Darroch, Landry and Oslak, 1999; Calazans et al., 2005), and/or their two or three previous partnerships in a specified time frame (Luke, 2005; Kraut-Becher and Aral, 2006; Juarez and Martin, 2006). The extent to which these partnerships are representative at either the individual or population level is unknown, but asking participants about more than their three most recent partnerships can be time-consuming as well as challenging to recall, especially if the partnerships occurred some time ago and/or were casual in nature. In a survey of the general population, however, the majority of people are likely to have had relatively few sexual partners (Johnson et al., 2001a), and of course, the more recent the time-frame of interest, the larger the proportion of participants who will be invited to report detailed data for all their partnerships. Yet even with a relatively recent focus, such as in the past year, there will be some participants who report many partners, for whom detailed data will be collected only for a proportion of all their partnerships. Of course, an individual's most recent sexual encounter(s) at a specified interview date may be atypical for them, and for the population of all their partnerships in the last year. In a sample of partnerships obtained in this way, casual partnerships will be under-represented due to their brevity and episodic nature, reducing their probability of being captured by a survey relative to longer-term partnerships such as marriages and cohabitations. From an epidemiological perspective, this is unfortunate since it is well established that individuals with larger numbers of partners contribute disproportionately to STI transmission in populations (Garnett et al., 1996; Fenton et al., 2005; Turner et al., 2006). In order to address this potential bias, statistical weights can be developed so that partnerships reported in detail can be weighted to account for partnerships lacking such data, although this can be computationally intensive (Copas et al., 2008; Mercer et al., 2009).

By asking participants the dates (that is, month and year) of first and last sex with a particular partner, the length of the partnership can be estimated in order to further categorize partnerships described as 'casual'. Of course, for partnerships of long duration, this may create recall problems, at least as far as the month of first sex is concerned, if not the year of first sex. Again, it may be helpful to encourage participants to use 'anchor points' to assist in their recall (Mitchell et al., 2007). Another problem is for partnerships that may not have been continuous, as this cannot be captured by this method. This is particularly important when the start and end dates of partnerships are used to try and ascertain whether or not partnerships were overlapping or 'concurrent'. For example, a romance that petered out in the teenage years, but which is rekindled at a school reunion a decade later, would appear to have lasted at least ten years, and any other partnerships during this period would appear to overlap, wrongly denoting concurrency. One solution might be to ask the participant whether or not there were any breaks in the partnership, although defining a break is again subjective. It is also difficult to ascertain whether or not partnerships were concurrent if first sex with one partner is reported as the same month and year as last sex with the previous partner. Depending on the target population, it may be possible to ask participants a direct question about concurrency. For example: 'Do you think your partner has had sex with anyone else while in a sexual relationship with you?' However, researchers who have collected data from both participants and their sexual partners have found poor correlation between what people think their partners do and what their partners actually report (Drumright, Gorbach and Holmes, 2004).

Relying on participants to report information about their partners can be problematic even for less sensitive topics such as occupation and education, let alone for casual partnerships or partnerships of shorter duration. However, the proportion reporting 'don't know' to such questions may provide a useful marker of the extent to which people think they know about their sexual partners. In

Natsal 2000, a significantly larger proportion of participants who described their most recent partner as 'not regular' said that they did not know this partner's age, in contrast to those who described this partner as regular.

Asking Questions about Condom Use

If a study is looking at sexual risk, it is essential to include questions on whether or not sexual behaviour was protected from the risk of STIs or unplanned pregnancy, often by the use of condoms. Numerous questions have been devised to ask about condom use (see, for example, Slaymaker, 2004), but as discussed above regarding questions on numbers of sexual partners, one condom use question cannot answer all research questions. Typically, questions on condom use are either partnership-specific or time-period specific. For example, asking: 'Did you always/sometimes/ never use condoms in the past four weeks?' gives no indication of condom use with specific partners. Similarly, asking participants about condom use with their most recent partner is not particularly informative in terms of their use of condoms in a particular time-period, or indeed, about condom use in general with a particular partner.

Clearly, non-use of condoms does not always equate to sexual risk behaviour, for example, if the participant or their partner is, or is trying to become, pregnant, or they are using other more effective and/or long-acting contraceptive methods, especially if protection from STIs is not required due to mutual monogamy. Reasons for not using condoms, and more generally contraception, may therefore need to be established via further questions.

Asking whether or not condoms were used does not establish whether or not condoms were used correctly. Epidemiological studies may need to ask additional questions about the timing of condom application and whether or not the condom slipped or broke during intercourse, in order to get a measure of the extent of STI/HIV risk exposure. Of course, questions on condom use are subject to social desirability bias in that people know that they should use condoms and that condoms should be applied at the start of intercourse to give the maximum protection against infections and pregnancy. Social desirability bias is not limited, however, to condom use, and may affect data collected for questions on a range of topics, especially those concerned with risk behaviours and behaviours that are not considered culturally or socially acceptable (for example, injecting drug use). Consequently, care needs to be taken that data obtained from surveys is regarded and documented as reported behaviour rather than actual behaviour.

Conclusions

In summary, this chapter has discussed some of the key issues that need to be considered when designing a survey to measure sexual behaviour. While conducting surveys on this subject is challenging because of the highly sensitive subject matter, it is possible to reduce bias and increase the accuracy of estimates of sexual behaviour and attitudes using this data collection tool. As emphasized, planning and preparation, and careful training are crucial for the successful execution of such sensitive surveys, and the role of the interviewer cannot be overstated in this respect. Technological advances in social research methods and the use of biological markers are continuing to offer new opportunities, increasing the utility of surveys as rich data sources.

References

Anderson, J.E., Wilson, R., Doll, L., Jones, T.S. and Barker, P. (1999), 'Condom Use and HIV Risk Behaviors Among US Adults: Data from a National Survey', *Family Planning Perspectives* 31, 1: 24–8.

Aral, S.O. and Holmes, K.K. (2006), 'The Epidemiology of STIs and Their Social and Behavioral Determinants: Industrialized and Developing Countries', in K.K. Holmes, F. Sparling, W. Stamm, P. Piot, J. Wasserheit, L. Corey and M. Cohen (eds), *Sexually Transmitted Diseases* (4th edition) (New York: McGraw Hill).

Baker, P. and Harris J.F. (1998), 'Clinton Admits to Lewinsky Relationship, Challenges Starr to End Personal "Prying"', *Washington Post*, 18 August, A01.

Bates, S.M. and Rogstad, K.E. (2000), 'Postal Research: Too Many Problems?' *Sexually Transmitted Infections* 76: 332–4.

Bhopal, R., Vettini, A., Hunt, S., Wiebe, S., Hanna, L. and Amos, A. (2004), 'Review of Prevalence Data in, and Evaluation of Methods for Cross Cultural Adaptation of, UK Surveys on Tobacco and Alcohol in Ethnic Minority Groups', *British Medical Journal* 328: 76, doi:10.1136/bmj.37963.426308.9A.

Brown, N.R. and Sinclair, R.C. (1999), 'Estimating Number of Lifetime Sexual Partners: Men and Women Do It Differently', *The Journal of Sex Research* 36, 3: 292–7.

Calazans, G., Araujo, T.W., Venturi, G. and França, I.J. (2005), 'Factors Associated with Condom Use Among Youth Aged 15–24 Years in Brazil in 2003', *AIDS* 19, supplement 4: S42–S50.

Copas, A.J., Mercer, C.H., Farewell, V.T., Nanchahal, K. and Johnson, A.M. (2008), 'Recent Heterosexual Partnerships and Patterns of Condom Use: A Weighted Analysis', *Epidemiology* 10.1097/EDE.0b013e318187ac81.

Couper, M.P., Baker, R.P., Bethlehem, J., Clark, C.Z.F., Martin, J., Nicholls II, W.L. and O'Reilly, J.M. (eds) (1998), *Computer Assisted Survey Information Collection* (Hoboken, NJ: Wiley).

Craig, R. and Mindell, J. (eds) (2008), *Health Survey for England 2006: Volume 3: Methodology and Documentation* (London: The Information Centre).

Darroch, J.E., Landry, D.J. and Oslak, S. (1999), 'Age Differences Between Sexual Partners in the United States', *Family Planning Perspectives* 31, 4: 160–67.

Dillman D.A. (2000), *Mail and Internet Surveys: The Tailored Design Method* (2nd edition) (Hoboken, NJ: Wiley).

Dodds, J.P., Mercey, D.E., Parry, J.V. and Johnson, A.M. (2004), 'Increasing Risk Behaviour and High Levels of Undiagnosed HIV Infection in a Community Sample of Homosexual Men', *Sexually Transmitted Infections* 80: 236–40.

Dodds, J.P., Mercer, C.H., Mercey, D.E., Copas, A.J. and Johnson, A.M. (2006), 'Men Who Have Sex with Men: A Comparison of a National Probability Sample Survey and a Community Based Study', *Sexually Transmitted Infections* 82: 86–7.

Drumright, L.N., Gorbach, P.M. and Holmes, K.K. (2004), 'Do People Really Know Their Sex Partners?' *Sexually Transmitted Diseases* 31, 7: 437–42.

Edwards, P., Roberts, I., Clarke, M., DiGuiseppi, C., Pratap, S., Wentz, R. and Kwan I. (2002), 'Increasing Response Rates to Postal Questionnaires: Systematic Review', *British Medical Journal* 324: 1183–92.

Elo, I.T., King, R.B. and Furstenberg, F.F. Jr. (1999), 'Adolescent Females: Their Sexual Partners and the Fathers of Their Children', *Journal of Marriage and the Family* 61: 74–84.

Erens, B., McManus, S., Field, J., Korovessis, C., Johnson, A.M. and Fenton, K.A. (2001), *National Survey of Sexual Attitudes and Lifestyles II: Technical Report* (London: National Centre for Social Research).

Evans, A.R., Wiggins, R.D., Mercer, C.H., Bolding, G.J. and Elford, J. (2007), 'Men Who Have Sex with Men in Britain: Comparison of a Self-selected Internet Sample with a National Probability Sample', *Sexually Transmitted Infections* 83: 200–205.

Evans, A.R., Personal communication, October 2008.

Fenton, K.A., Korovessis, C., Johnson, A.M., McCadden, A., McManus, S., Wellings, K., Mercer, C.H., Carder, C., Copas, A.J., Nanchahal, K., Macdowall, W., Ridgway, G., Field, J. and Erens, B. (2001), 'Sexual Behaviour in Britain: Reported Sexually Transmitted Infections and Prevalent Genital *Chlamydia trachomatis* Infection', *Lancet* 358: 1851–4.

Fenton, K.A., Mercer, C.H., Byron, C., McManus, S., Erens, B., Copas, A.J., Nanchahal, K., Macdowall, W., Wellings, K. and Johnson, A.M. (2005), 'Reported Sexually Transmitted Disease Clinic Attendance and Sexually Transmitted Infections in Britain: Prevalence, Risk Factors, and Proportionate Population Burden', *Journal of Infectious Diseases* 191, Supplement 1: S127—S138.

Garnett, G.P., Hughes, J.P., Anderson, R.M., Stoner, B.P., Aral, S.O., Whittington, W.L., Handsfield, H.H. and Holmes, K.K. (1996), 'Sexual Mixing Patterns of Patients Attending Sexually Transmitted Diseases Clinics', *Sexually Transmitted Diseases* 23: 248–57.

Gilbart, V.L., Mercer, C.H., Dougan, S., Copas, A.J., Fenton, K.A., Johnson, A.M. and Evans, B.G. (2006), 'Factors Associated with Heterosexual Transmission of HIV to Individuals without Major Risk Factors within England, Wales and Northern Ireland: A Comparison with National Probability Surveys', *Sexually Transmitted Infections* 82: 15–20.

Groves, R.M., Biemer, P.P., Lyberg, L.E., Massey, J.T., Nicholls, W.L. and Waksbeerg, J. (eds) (1988), *Telephone Survey Methodology* (Hoboken, NJ: Wiley).

Health Protection Agency (2007), *Testing Times: HIV and Other Sexually Transmitted Infections in the United Kingdom: 2007* (London: Health Protection Agency).

Johnson, A.M., Wadsworth, J., Wellings, K. and Field, J. (1994), *Sexual Attitudes and Lifestyles* (Oxford: Blackwell Scientific Publications).

Johnson, A.M., Mercer, C.H., Erens, B., Copas, A.J., McManus, S., Wellings, K., Fenton, K.A., Korovessis, C., Macdowall, W., Nanchahal, K., Purdon, S. and Field, J. (2001a), 'Sexual Behaviour in Britain: Partnerships, Practices, and HIV Risk Behaviours', *Lancet* 358: 1835–42.

Johnson, A.M., Copas, A.J., Erens, B., Mandalia, S., Fenton, K., Korovessis, C., Wellings, K. and Field, J. (2001b), 'Effect of Computer-assisted Self-interviews on Reporting of Sexual HIV Risk Behaviours in a General Population Sample: A Methodological Experiment', *AIDS* 15: 111–15.

Juarez, F. and Martin, C.T. (2006), 'Partnership Dynamics and Sexual Health Risks Among Male Adolescents in the Favelas of Recife, Brazil', *Family Planning Perspectives* 32, 2: 62–70.

Kinsey, A.C., Pomeroy, W.B. and Martin, C.E. (1948), *Sexual Behavior in the Human Male* (Philadelphia: W.B. Saunders).

Kinsey, A.C., Pomeroy, W.B., Martin, C.E. and Gebhard, P.H. (1953), *Sexual Behavior in the Human Female* (Philadelphia: W.B. Saunders).

Klein, F. (1993),*The Bisexual Option* (2nd edition) (Binghamton, NY: The Haworth Press).

Kraut-Becher, J.R. and Aral, S.O. (2006), 'Patterns of Age Mixing and Sexually Transmitted Infections', *International Journal of STD and AIDS* 17: 378–83.

Laumann, E.O., Paik, A. and Rosen, R.C. (1999), 'Sexual Dysfunction in the United States: Prevalence and Predictors', *Journal of the American Medical Association* 281: 537–44.

Luke, N. (2005), 'Confronting the "Sugar Daddy" Stereotype: Age and Economic Asymmetries and Risky Sexual Behaviour in Urban Kenya', *Family Planning Perspectives* 31: 6–14.

Mercer, C.H., Fenton, K.A., Johnson, A.M., Copas, A.J., Macdowall, W., Erens, B. and Wellings, K. (2005), 'Who Reports Sexual Function Problems? Evidence from the 2000 National Survey of Sexual Attitudes and Lifestyles ("Natsal 2000")', *Sexually Transmitted Infections* 81: 394–9.

Mercer, C.H., Copas, A.J., Sonnenberg, P., Johnson, A.M., McManus, S., Erens, B. and Cassell, J.A. (2009), 'Who Has Sex with Whom? Characteristics of Heterosexual Partnerships Reported in the Second National Survey of Sexual Attitudes and Lifestyles', *International Journal of Epidemiology* 38: 206–14.

Mitchell, K., Wellings, K., Elam, G., Erens, B., Fenton, K. and Johnson, A. (2007), 'How Can We Facilitate Reliable Reporting in Surveys of Sexual Behaviour? Evidence from Qualitative Research', *Culture, Health and Sexuality* 9, 5: 519–31.

National Center for Health Statistics, 'National Survey of Family Growth', <http://www.cdc.gov/nchs/NSFG.htm>, accessed 6 December 2008.

Office for National Statistics, 'Sexual Identity Project', <http://www.ons.gov.uk/about-statistics/measuring-equality/sexual-identity-project/index.html>, accessed 4 December 2008.

Prause, N. and Graham, C.A. (2007), 'Asexuality: Classification and Characterization', *Archives of Sexual Behavior* 36: 341–56.

Question Bank, 'ESRC Question Bank', http://surveynet.ac.uk/sqb/>, accessed 1 March 2010.

Slaymaker, E. (2004), 'A Critique of International Indicators of Sexual Risk Behaviour', *Sexually Transmitted Infections* 80, Supplement II: ii13–ii21.

Spencer, L., Faulkner, A. and Keegan, J. (1988), *Talking About Sex: Asking the Public About Sexual Behaviour and Attitudes* (London: Social Community Planning Research).

Turner, C.F., Ku, L., Rogers, S.M., Lindberg, L.D., Pleck, J.H. and Sonenstein, F.L. (1998), 'Adolescent Sexual Behavior, Drug Use, and Violence: Increased Reporting with Computer Survey Technology', *Science* 280: 867–73.

Turner, K.M.E., Adams, E.J., Gay, N., Ghani, A.C., Mercer, C.H. and Edmunds, W.J. (2006), 'Developing a Realistic Sexual Network Model of Chlamydia Transmission in Britain', *Theoretical Biology and Medical Modelling* 3: 3.

Villarroel, M.A., Turner, C.F., Rogers, S.M., Roman, A.M., Cooley, P.C., Steinberg, A.B., Eggleston, E. and Chromy, J.R. (2008), 'T-ACASI Reduces Bias in STD Measurements: The National STD and Behavior Measurement Experiment', *Sexually Transmitted Diseases* 35, 5: 499–506.

Wadsworth, J., Johnson, A.M., Wellings, K. and Field, J. (1996), 'What's in a Mean: An Examination of the Inconsistency Between Men and Women in Reporting Sexual Partnerships', *Journal of the Royal Statistical Society. Series A. Statistics in Society* 159, 1: 111–23.

Wellings, K., Field, J., Johnson, A.M., Wadsworth, J. and Bradshaw, S. (1994), *Sexual Behaviour in Britain* (London: Penguin).

Wellings, K., Nanchahal, K., Macdowall, W., McManus, S., Erens, B., Mercer, C.H., Johnson, A.M., Copas, A.J., Korovessis, C., Fenton, K.A. and Field, J. (2001), 'Sexual Behaviour in Britain: Early Heterosexual Experience', *Lancet* 358: 1843–50.

Wellings, K., Collumbien, M., Slaymaker, E., Singh, S., Hodges, Z., Patel, D. and Bajos, N. (2006), 'Sexual Behaviour in Context: A Global Perspective', *Lancet* 368: 1706–28.

Wight, D., Henderson, M., Raab, G., Abraham, C., Buston, K., Scott, S. and Hart, G. (2000), 'Extent of Regretted Sexual Intercourse Among Young Teenagers in Scotland: A Cross Sectional Survey', *British Medical Journal* 320: 1243–4.

Chapter 9

Measuring Health

Nicola Shelton and Jennifer Mindell

Introduction

Choosing Health, echoing points made in Derek Wanless's report *Securing Good Health for the Whole Population* (Wanless, 2004), highlighted the need for better, more timely surveillance of health and lifestyle (Department of Health, 2004). The subsequent government action plan *Delivering Choosing Health* specifically included an action 'to develop appropriate systems for recording lifestyle measures' (Department of Health, 2005).

The two most commonly used measures to describe health in a population, particularly ill-health and healthy or unhealthy behaviours, are *incidence* and *prevalence*. *Incidence* is the rate at which new cases occur in a specified population during a specified time period. *Prevalence* is the proportion of a specified population that are cases at a point in time. Examples include:

- Weekly incidence of influenza (the number of new cases that occur in a week), as reported by GP 'Spotter practices' to provide early warning of an epidemic
- The prevalence of obesity – what proportion of the population is obese when measured at a particular time

Mortality (death rate) is the incidence of death. For each of these, the *numerator* refers to the number of cases, while the *denominator* refers to the population at risk of being a case.

A *crude* incidence, prevalence, or mortality rate relates to the population taken as a whole, without subdivision or refinement. Crude death rate (CDR) is the number of people dying as a proportion of the population – usually per 1,000 population. Measures of ill-health, such as hospital admission rates or cancer incidence rates, are usually stated as per 100,000 population, while prevalence of obesity or smoking is usually given as a percentage; these general guidelines depend on how common a condition is. *Specific rates* (usually by age and/or sex) allow comparisons between groups; they may be *standardized* to adjust for differences in age, sex or other factors that may obscure the comparisons of interest. For example, SMRs (Standardized Mortality Ratios) adjust for differences in age and sex composition in different areas to allow the mortality in areas with more or fewer older people to be compared with the national average, without this being distorted by the known higher death rates in older people. Infant mortality (IMR) is a particular problem, as the denominator for this rate is live births, with IMR calculated per 1000 births.

Both incidence and prevalence can vary by sub-population: age, gender or ethnic group. Each can be viewed as high or low in relative or absolute senses. Low incidence can lead to high prevalence when diseases are incurable but seldom affect survival, for example, osteoarthritis. A cold is a disease with high incidence in the winter but low prevalence, as it is self-limiting. Lung cancer also has low prevalence, because of its high *case fatality rate*, the proportion of affected people who die as a result of the disease.

Content

This chapter looks at what is carried out in a typical health survey and why. It includes a short history of health surveillance in Britain. The chapter also looks at who uses health surveys and why. The chapter draws contemporary examples from the UK, particularly England, Scotland and London, and also looks at the feasibility of running internationally comparable health surveys. The chapter will cover health surveys as a cross-sectional measurement of the 'state of the nation' as well as socio-economic and regional health inequalities analysis. Some important issues when measuring health, such as confidentiality, data protection and security, consent, and research ethics approval are outwith the scope of this chapter but have recently been reviewed in detail (Tolonen et al., 2008a).

History of Health Surveillance

There is a long history of interest in the health of particular groups and/or places. Prior to the nineteenth century, Bills of Mortality were the main source of mortality statistics, designed to monitor deaths from the plague; they ran from the 1660s to 1830s. They included weekly statistics for the number buried in each parish who died of the plague and those who died of other causes by sex and number christened, with yearly summaries.

In the nineteenth century, the expansion of the disciplines of statistics and demography, the growth of the population of cities, and increasing interest in the public's health combined – and health surveillance exploded. National health surveillance in Britain had its origins in 1801 with the first census of England and Wales, which gave a much more accurate population count from which national mortality rates could be calculated.

From 1837 the General Register Office (GRO) began to publish annual reports of births, deaths (with cause of death) and marriages (Woods and Shelton, 1997). These reports also gave breakdowns by region and for occupation-specific regions (for example, mining). Occupational health and mortality surveillance had a long history: William Farr, in the decennial supplements to the GRO's annual reports, also looked at mortality among miners (Eyler, 1979). The heights and weights of army recruits were collected by the Army Medical Department for over 100 years from 1860–1972 (Rosenbaum, 1988; Rosenbaum and Crowdy, 1992). The 1848 Public Health Act led to the appointment of Medical Officers of Health who carried out local health surveillance and published reports. Several other key reports and enquiries used survey methods. Arguably the most famous were Chadwick's Sanitary Conditions of the Labouring Population in 1842 (Chadwick, 1842, reprinted in Flinn, 1965), Booth's report on London (Booth, 1902: 159–60), and Rowntree's report on York (Rowntree, 1899). In the early twentieth century, the 1911 Census showed fertility by occupational group with a focus on child health outcomes (1911census.co.uk).

In the mid twentieth century, Cochrane and Doll and Hill developed the method now called case-control studies, including that which established the link between smoking and lung cancer (Doll and Hill, 1952). This approach collects data from cases and from controls without the condition and calculates the *odds ratio*, the ratio of the odds of a case having been exposed to a putative risk factor compared with the odds of a control having been so exposed. A more powerful method is the cohort (or panel) study, in which participants are assessed at baseline and followed up over time to assess the *relative risk* of becoming a case or dying for those exposed to a putative risk factor, compared with those not so exposed. This was first carried out in Britain for people born in 1946, and then successive national birth cohorts were carried out in 1958, 1970, 2000 and one is planned for 2012. Although the methods used for analysis and interpretation of a retrospective case-control study or a prospective or retrospective cohort study differ from a cross-sectional survey, the methods to assess health and its determinants at a single time period, that is, the health measurement methods and the tools used, are very similar to those of the national and local surveys described below.

There have been population-based health examination surveys running in England annually since 1991 and in Scotland in 1995, 1998, 2003 and annually from 2008. These are examples of surveys that are both a Health *Interview* Survey (HIS) and Health *Examination* Survey (HES). They are used by government ministers to inform new policies and evaluate existing policy. They are used to determine trends and forecast the future. They are expensive to run compared with smaller scale surveys; they were evaluated and reviewed in 2006 (Scotland) (Scottish Executive, 2008) and 2008 (England) (Information Centre, 2008).

Contemporary Case Study: The Health Survey for England

The Health Survey for England (HSE) is used to collect information on health and related behaviour annually. In most years, around 16,000 adults and 4,000 children in selected households are eligible for inclusion. Data collection is undertaken throughout the entire calendar year to avoid seasonal effects. Each year, a nationally representative sample of addresses is selected from the Postcode Address File in two stages: the primary sampling unit is postcode sectors, stratified by the percentage of non-manual households, with individual addresses selected in a second stage. After sending an advance letter, trained interviewers visit the household to recruit all adults and up to two children (selected at random). Data collection is by face-to-face Computer-Aided Personal Interviewing (CAPI) with some self-completion questionnaires completed during the interviewer visit. This is followed by a nurse visit for collection of health examination measurements and biological samples.

Results in report format are produced by the National Centre for Social Research (Natcen) and University College London (UCL) and are available from the Information Centre (IC) within 12 months of the end of the data collection. Since 2003, data have been weighted for non-response at different stages of the survey. Anonymized datasets from the HSE are available from the UK Data Archive at Essex University (UK Data Archive, 2008) and teaching data sets from the Economic and Social Data Service (ESDS) at Manchester University (ESDS, 2004).

Why Measure Health?

Health is measured in order to:

- Assess the current health status of the population
- Measure the incidence or prevalence of specific conditions
- Predict changes in incidence or prevalence of a condition
- Plan health and social care services
- Monitor or evaluate the impact of interventions or policies

Local and national government, public bodies responsible for health or health care, and other organizations need health and health behaviour data at a population level for planning, targeting and evaluating local services and initiatives aimed at improving health and reducing health inequalities through lifestyle change. Data are needed both at local jurisdiction level and for smaller areas (for example, neighbourhood, ward or GP practice) for:

- Comparison with other local areas
- Within-area comparisons to identify inequalities between population sub-groups differing by age, gender, ethnicity, area of residence
- Analysis of trends over time and progress towards local targets
- Measuring the outcomes and impacts of interventions on the local population, or
- Measuring the outcomes and impacts of services on service users

Contemporary Case Studies: Why Do We Collect the Data We Do?

National Diet and Nutrition Survey

This aims to obtain information about the dietary habits and nutritional status of the UK population. The survey results are used to develop national nutrition policy and to contribute to the evidence base for government advice on healthy eating.

Health Survey for England (HSE)

The first Health Survey for England (HSE), carried out in 1991, was designed to collect information on important aspects of health relevant to cardiovascular disease (CVD) and nutrition. These included combinations of risk factors and their effects, monitoring trends in the nation's health. The survey formed part of a programme including National Psychiatric Morbidity Survey and biennial diet and nutrition surveys. The survey aimed to describe the 'State of the Nation' by providing a cross-sectional snapshot. Two Health of the Nation cardiovascular disease targets were set and the aim was to monitor progress towards targets:

- To reduce mean systolic blood pressure by 5mmHg by 2005 in adults aged 16–64
- To reduce the proportion of adults aged 16–64 who were obese to 6 per cent of men and 8 per cent of women by 2005

Analysis of the HSE data shows the blood pressure target was just met (Shelton, 2008). The target for obesity was not met in 2005 and in the same year HSE data was instead used to forecast obesity to 2010 (Zaninotto et al., 2006) and subsequently to 2012 (Zaninotto et al., 2009).

Who uses HSE data? There are three main user groups: national governmental users including policy makers; local government and public health specialists; and academics. The survey is used to monitor the nation's health for setting targets, monitoring progress towards them, as a driver for action, for intervention evaluation, and planning for the future. The data is used to populate national and international databases (for example, WHO) and to develop and monitor National Service Frameworks (NSFs) for improving health care for specific diseases or age groups. It is also used to answer parliamentary questions. Local users are keen to have more local level data. The Health Survey for England is the fifth most popular data set in the ESRC Data Archive.

Changes in reporting style Over time the reports have become more disease/outcome focused. 'Anthropometry' became 'Anthropometry and Obesity' in HSE 2003; 'Anthropometric measures, overweight, and obesity' in 2004; and 'BMI, overweight and obesity in 2006'; and in Scottish Health Survey 2003 became 'Obesity'. 'Blood Pressure' became 'Hypertension' in HSE 2005.

What Information is Wanted?

To fulfil the objectives of health surveillance, it is important not only to monitor health status but also the factors that affect these, such as lifestyle risk factors and social determinants of health. Lifestyle factors that affect the risk of death, disease and disability include the use of alcohol, tobacco and illicit drugs; diet (both quantity and composition); and physical activity (Department of Health, 2004).

Health varies dramatically across the world, both between and within countries, by income, occupation and education level, as well as by age, sex and ethnicity. The risk of a woman dying during pregnancy and childbirth is one in 17,400 in Sweden but one in eight in Afghanistan. A child born in one Glasgow suburb has a life expectancy 28 years less than another child living only 13km away. In the USA, 886,202 fewer deaths would have occurred between 1991 and 2000 if African Americans had the same mortality rate as whites, five times the lives saved there by medical advances (Marmot, 2008). Biology does not explain these inequalities. They result from the social environment in which people live. Such social *inequities* (unfair inequalities) are important arbiters of inequalities in health and have highlighted the importance of social determinants of health. These include education, housing, transport, relative and absolute poverty and exclusion, occupation and working conditions, unemployment, and social support (Marmot and Wilkinson, 1999; Wilkinson and Marmot, 2003). In addition to improving living conditions and reducing inequitable distribution of resources, the World Health Organization's Commission on Social Determinants of Health's third recommendation was to 'Measure and understand the problem and assess the impact of action'(Marmot, 2008).

What is in a health survey is what the funder (usually local or national government or health body) has decided is important to look at in health terms. Therefore health surveys provide both a valuable window into the concerns and aims of the current administration, as well as a 'picture of health'. The content changes over time and will change again. The content is also mediated by what is practical and affordable. Objective measures, such as physical measurements or analysis of biological specimens, are less subject to reporting and recall bias but are much more expensive to obtain and also suffer from higher non-response rates. However, self-report is subject to *recall* and *reporting bias*, such as *social acceptability bias*, in which participants give what they perceive as socially acceptable answers (such as current smokers describing themselves as ex-smokers, or people overestimating the amount of physical activity they undertake).

Health Surveys in Developing Countries

The Demographic and Health Surveys (DHS) Project

This is the third consecutive worldwide research project initiated by the US Agency for International Development (USAID) to provide data and analysis on the population, health and nutrition of women and children in developing countries. Two hundred surveys have been conducted in 75 countries. Its two predecessors, the World Fertility Survey (1972–82) and the Contraceptive Prevalence Surveys (CPS), paved the way for the DHS project by focusing their research on questions related to fertility, family planning and mortality (Demographic and Health Surveys, 2008).

Potential Sources of Health Data

Measures of Health

Paradoxically, ill-health is more easily, and therefore more often, measured than good health. In high income and many other countries, death registration is a legal requirement and total mortality rates are accurate. Data on cause of death depends on diagnosis, so changes over time in diagnostic coding frames or fashion, knowledge, availability of tests, and decisions between immediate and underlying causes can each affect trends. Hospital admissions data (such as HES Online Hospital Episode Statistics, 2008) are the most frequent measure of *morbidity* (ill-health). Other measures include primary care data, which are less widely available. Self-reported data may enquire about specific diseases or general health. A number of instruments have been developed to measure physical or mental ill-health.

Contemporary Case Study: Measures of Self-reported Health in Health Survey for England and Scottish Health Survey

General Health

Participants are asked the question: 'How is your health in general? Would you say it was 'very good', 'good', 'fair', 'bad', or 'very bad'?'

Limiting Longstanding Illness

Participants are asked the question: 'Do you have any longstanding illness, disability or infirmity? By longstanding, I mean anything that has troubled you over a period of time, or that is likely to affect you over a period of time?' Those who report such an illness are asked what the illness/es is/are and are then asked whether the illness/es or disability/ies limit their activities in any way.

Heart Attack

In some years, participants are asked: 'Have you ever had a heart attack (including myocardial infarction or coronary thrombosis)?' and (if so): 'Were you told by a doctor you had a heart attack (including myocardial infarction or coronary thrombosis)?' (Craig and Mindell, 2008).

Social Determinants of Health and Socio-demographic Data

Not only health but also lifestyle risk factors are closely related to socio-economic circumstances, so individual and area-level data are generally required to examine inequalities and compare health and lifestyle behaviours in specified population sub-groups. Individual and household data can be obtained from interview or self-completion questionnaires. Geo-coded data for individuals can enable linkage to area-level data, such as local unemployment rates, indices of local area deprivation, or census information, useful where individual data are not available (for example, ethnicity for death certificates).

Lifestyle Factors

The following have each been used recently as sources of local-level lifestyle data:

- National surveys
- Synthetic estimates derived from national surveys
- Local surveys, including regional surveys
- NHS primary care data
- Datasets offered by commercial organizations

Physical Measurements

Physical measurements can be collected by trained staff. Anthropometric data are used to assess growth and obesity (height, weight), abdominal obesity (waist and hip circumference), and nutritional status (mid-upper arm circumference). Blood pressure is easily measured, but bone density, lung function or an electrocardiogram (ECG) require more complex equipment.

Biological Markers

Biological samples can be collected for laboratory analysis. These include blood, urine, saliva and hair. A very wide range of analyses can be performed to measure lifestyle behaviours in the population (urinary sodium and creatinine to assess salt intake, salivary cotinine to measure individual's smoking status and exposure to other people's smoke), the prevalence of risk factors (serum cholesterol levels), organ function (serum creatinine to predict kidney function), and disease management (glycated haemoglobin to assess glycaemic control in people with diabetes).

Methods of Data Collection

Routine Data

Routine data have the advantage of being much cheaper because they are collected anyway. However, they may not fulfil the needs of health surveillance because of being designed for administrative purposes. Much measurement of health therefore involves bespoke surveys.

Surveys

Postal surveys are cheaper than interview surveys but generally have lower response rates, even with the use of reminders and incentives. They exclude participants who cannot read or write (as do self-completion questionnaires within interviews). They preclude measurements, except as a second stage.

- *The Welsh Health Survey* used postal surveys in 1995 and 1998, each with an achieved sample size of around 30,000 adults

Telephone surveys are common in the USA but less common in the UK. They exclude those without a landline telephone (which is particularly common among more deprived residents in the UK) and those who are unable to communicate in that language.

Health interview surveys involve a face-to-face interview, more recently almost always using Computer-Aided Personal Interviewing (CAPI). They may also include self-completion questionnaires, especially for more sensitive or complex topics such as smoking, drinking or sexual behaviour. Some surveys also use private CAPI in order to allow answers to be made without the interviewer having sight of them. The interviewers may take some measurements (such as height and weight in the Health Survey for England).

Other approaches may combine features of the above approaches. A new continuous Welsh Health Survey began in autumn 2003, which achieved a sample size of more than 32,000 adults and 7,500 children over a two-year period. Interviewers call at selected households and leave bilingual English and Welsh self-completion questionnaires, returning at a later date to collect them. This approach was taken to enable a much larger sample size to be included: the surveys are designed to provide some data, including smoking prevalence, at local government level within the limited resources available, by aggregating data from the first two years of the survey (Lader, 2007).

Examples of Health Interview Surveys in the General Population

National Diet and Nutrition Survey (Interview Stages)

The new rolling National Diet and Nutrition Survey (NDNS) began in April 2008. Each year, 500 children aged 18 months to 18 years and 500 adults aged 19 or over will be interviewed in their home. Questions include socio-demographic data, questions on smoking and alcohol consumption, physical activity, sun exposure and food preparation. Participants (or their carers) keep a four-day unweighed food diary.
Other examples include:

- Health Education Population Survey
- Survey of Activity and Health

Examples of Health Surveys of a Particular Age Group

Drug Use, Smoking and Drinking among Young People in England

This survey is conducted in secondary schools, using self-completion questionnaires completed under examination conditions, then sealed into envelopes by each participant themselves. Designed to provide national-level prevalence statistics only, it is used to monitor the government's targets for smoking for children aged 11 to 15 years (Fuller, 2008).

Other examples include:
The General Household Survey (GHS) began in 1971. It is conducted by the Office for National Statistics (ONS) and is a continuous survey of around 9,000 households and about 16,000 adults aged 16 and over per year. Data, published annually, cover Great Britain; some regional tabulations are available (General Household Survey, 2008). The government's targets for adult smoking are based on this data.

- Survey of Health and Well-being of Adults
- Survey of the Development and Well-being of Children and Adolescents
- Infant Feeding Survey

Example of Health Survey of People with a Particular Condition

Survey of the Needs and Lifestyles of Visually Impaired Adults

This survey was commissioned by the Royal National Institute for the Blind to provide a picture of the needs and lifestyles of the visually impaired in Great Britain and Northern Ireland in 1998–99 and to update the information collected in a similar survey in 1986. Interviewers also administered a sight test and a practical reading/contrast test. It involved 1,260 adults.

Examples of General Surveys which Include a Large Health-related Component

General Household Survey

ONS Omnibus Survey

These surveys have been conducted 12 times a year since April 2005. Sets of questions are funded by a range of government departments and other public sector or not-for-profit organizations. In 2006, about 2,500 adults aged 16 and over were asked, amongst other topics, about their smoking behaviour and habits, giving up and stopping smoking, perceptions and awareness of issues related to smoking, attitudes related to smoking and smokers' response to their attitudes (Office for National Statistics, 2008).

Other examples include:

- Birth cohort studies, including 1946 cohort study, BCS70, Millennium Cohort Study
- Other cohort studies, such as the English Longitudinal Study of Ageing
- British Social Attitudes Survey
- Scottish Social Attitudes Survey

Contemporary Case Study of a Health Examination Survey

Health Survey for England (Interview Stage)

The interview stage of the HSE includes both core modules, asked each year of all participants, and additional modules, asked in certain years or of a sub-sample of participants, depending on the research focus and budget.

Demographics for example, age, sex, ethnicity, occupation, education, area deprivation
Health and illness for example, mental health, diabetes, cardiovascular disease, fractures

Lifestyle factors for example, smoking, eating habits, drinking, physical activity, knowledge and attitudes to health

Healthcare use for example, GP visit, hospital in/outpatient, medication

Health Survey for England (Nurse Stage)

The nurse stage of the HSE also includes both core modules, asked each year of all eligible participants, and additional modules, asked in certain years or of a sub-sample of participants, depending on the research focus and budget.

Questions

- *Core*: vitamin supplements (all), and immunisations (0–1 year), prescribed medications (all), and since 2006 nicotine replacement therapies
- *Some years*: eating habits: fats, salt (16+), cigarette brand (16+)

Measurements

- *Core*: supine length (6 weeks–2 years), blood pressure (5+), waist/hip circumference (11+)
- *Occasional years*: lung function (7+ years), step test (16–74), ECG (35+), demi-span (65+), balance, grip strength, and walking speed (65+)

Biological samples

- Saliva (4+ years) – for cotinine analysis
- Urine (16+ years) – for Na/K/albumin/creatinine ratios
- Blood (16+ years) – Non fasting and/or fasting blood samples; analytes vary

---

Health Examination Surveys

The above measures are generally collected in health surveys, also called health interview surveys (HIS). For a health *examination* survey (HES), some or all of the above details of a health interview are collected, either at the same time or at a previous visit, but additional physical measurements and collection of biological samples are also undertaken. These are usually carried out by clinically qualified staff:

- Health Survey for England (nurses)
- Adult Dental Health Survey (dentists)
- Dental Health Survey of Children and Young People (School Dental Service)
- UK National Diet and Nutrition Survey (nurses and paediatric phlebotomists)

Geographical Level of Data

Data Collection

National surveys   Over the past decade, a national health examination survey has been conducted in 13 European countries (including the Health Survey for England and Scottish Health Survey); 17 countries have active plans to conduct a health examination survey on adults between 2008 and 2012. The National Health and Nutrition Examination Survey (NHANES) in the USA is the most comprehensive health examination survey: a nationally representative sample (currently 5,000 participants per year) are invited to attend mobile examination centres for a seven-hour visit (Centers for Disease Control, 2008). Other English-speaking countries that run health surveys include Canada (a new health examination survey started in 2008), and New Zealand and Australia (health interview surveys with some examination components). The National Diet and Nutrition Survey (NDNS) covers the UK: to enable analysis at country level, Scotland, Wales and Northern Ireland have each funded a boost sample in their country.

Regional and local surveys   These include both bespoke surveys and local or regional boosts of national surveys. A local boost means oversampling of the national survey at a local level to increase the sample size to generate more robust local results. For example, Scottish Health Survey has boosts for areas with Scottish Index of Multiple Deprivation Scores in the highest 15 per cent in 2008–11 and for Grampian, Fife and Borders Health Boards in 2008 and 2009. Each has boosted their sample size by an additional 200 adults. Boosted interviews will only include core questions. Health Boards will be given further opportunities to boost their samples in each of the following three years of the current survey.

Contemporary Case Studies: Local Boosts of Health Survey for England

London Boost

Usually around 15 per cent of the national annual HSE sample are London residents. A consortium of NHS organizations, local and regional government, and non-statutory organizations commissioned an additional boost sample. Data collection ran from February 2006 until May 2007. The survey was designed to be sufficiently large to generate London-wide and (with more limited precision) primary care trust (PCT) level data, allowing sub-group analyses (for example, by ethnic group, age or social class) for London. An average sample size of around 200 adults and 55 children per each of London's 31 PCTs was planned.

The design used a modified version of the Welsh Health Survey method. The sample was selected as for the national HSE but within each PCT, with oversampling for inner London. It comprised a brief household-level survey, measurement of height and weight, and later collection of self-completion questionnaires. The London boost was similar to the London region response rate in the national survey (the lowest response rate in the national HSE).

Prevalence of long-term illness, limiting long-term illness, current smoking and alcohol consumption did not differ significantly between the national HSE London region and the London boost survey. However, there were a number of statistically significant differences between the estimates for some key measures, which are likely to be due to a combination of mode (for example, portions of fruit and vegetables consumed, physical activity levels, number of cigarettes smoked, number of alcoholic units consumed on the heaviest drinking day) and context (for example, general health and GHQ12 score) (Tipping et al., 2008).

Camden and Islington Boost

In 1999, a local boost survey of residents of the (erstwhile) Camden and Islington Health Authority was conducted alongside the main HSE. The boost sample size was just under 2,000 adults (response rate 60 per cent) and the questionnaire coverage and survey procedures were identical to the main HSE 1999 survey. As part of the 2006 London boost, Camden and Islington PCTs also paid for additional boosts of their local populations.

Merseyside Boost

Merseyside organizations funded an HSE boost using identical methodology to the national survey. A first Merseyside HSE boost covered six local authority areas over the period October 2003 to October 2004. Six hundred and fifty-five households participated, including 1,113 individual interviews with adults, and physical measurements including blood samples from more than half of the participants (Capewell, Lloyd-Williams and Ireland, 2005). A second Merseyside boost, to contribute to the evaluation of five years of the Heart of Mersey programme, is currently being planned.

Data Analysis

National Level

The main constraint on analysis is the number of participants to be considered. Many surveys are designed only for analysis at national level. Larger surveys can also be analysed by sub-group, such as age groups.

Contemporary Case Study: Reporting on the Health Survey for England

Analyses in the Report

Prevalence of conditions, behaviours, knowledge and attitudes are reported by age and sex. Unlike much of social science, epidemiological analysis is almost entirely carried out on men and women separately to reduce effects of clustering within households (but sometimes combining boys and girls if numbers of children are small). The reports also have a health inequality focus. They contain age-standardized analysis by one or more measures of social class. The choice of socio-economic status variable differs by year of survey. In 2007, equivalized household income was used; in 2006, the index of multiple deprivation. The latter is available for everyone in the survey (but 2001 Census data on which it is calculated by 2007 is relatively old). NS-SEC is also collected, but these too have missing data.

Regional Variation

Age-standardized analysis is carried out by region (smaller area geography is difficult due to the cluster sampling design) to allow comparison between regions. Also reported are observed results by regions so that regional service and intervention planning can occur.

Regressions Using Odds Ratios

These are (relatively) easy to understand. For example, a $1kg/m^2$ increase in BMI (Body Mass Index – used to determine overweight and obesity) is associated with an increase in blood pressure of 2mm Hg. More than one factor can be taken into account at the same time. For example, the odds of having diabetes are ten times higher in those aged 75 and over than those aged 35–44 and are three times higher in London than in the northwest of England. The geography has taken age distribution into account and vice versa. Logistic regression is usually used in the report. The results are somewhat more straightforward to interpret than linear multiple regression. For example, the odds of being obese are 1.5 times higher in the lowest income quintile than the highest, but the results are less accurate than linear regression.

International Comparisons

There are now pan-European data collected from a health interview survey (ECHI Project, 2008). There are plans for a pan-European health examination survey (Tolonen et al., 2008b). The World Health Organization's STEPS programme (STEPwise Approach to Surveillance, 2008) is a simple method for collecting, analysing and disseminating small amounts of useful information on a regular and continuing basis. By using standardized questions and protocols, STEPS information can also be used for making comparisons across countries.

Regional Level

The Health Survey for England and the General Household Survey have larger sample sizes or are undertaken on a more frequent basis, accruing sufficient data to provide sub-national statistics, for example, relating to government office regions or strategic health authority areas.

Local Level

By aggregating data over a number of years, analyses at geographical levels below regional level are possible, with two caveats. One is access to data with geo-coding below regional level (which is not archived publicly, for data protection and confidentiality reasons); the other is that the smaller the area, the more years' data are required to enable meaningful local data to be presented, affecting timeliness and the ability to monitor trends over time. Another option would be to increase the sample size to enable data to be analysed for smaller areas. However, the sample size would need to be dramatically larger, posing problems not only of affordability but also of feasibility.

Continuity and Differences

Continuity is important for trend analysis, and surveillance is ongoing. Choices need to be made whether to continue with existing questions or protocols, to obtain comparable data over time for trends, or whether to change the survey instruments to improve their validity or to take account of changes in policies or lifestyle recommendations.

For example, physical activity is difficult to measure. Information is generally wanted on frequency, duration, mode and type of activity, for each activity undertaken: accuracy therefore requires a long questionnaire but this precludes questions on other topics, due to concerns for participant burden.

Continuity and Difference in the Health Survey for England (HSE)

Participants

In some years there is a focus on particular population groups such as children, older people and minority ethnic groups; in these years, the 'core' general population group may be reduced to enable such boosting to be resourced. Boost samples have included:

- 1999 and 2004: minority ethnic groups
- 2002: children and young people
- 2000 and 2005: aged 65+

Content

Additional modules used in some years include:

- 1994, 1998, 2003, 2006: cardiovascular disease
- 2001: respiratory disease and disability and accidents

Measuring physical activity has been undertaken six times in adults between 1998 and 2008. A long CAPI questionnaire was used in 1997, 1998 and 2006; a shorter CAPI questionnaire was used in 1999, 2003 and 2004. For 2008, a revised questionnaire was designed to allow for changes in the recommendations for adults that the 30 minutes of at least moderate activity that should be undertaken most days can be accrued in ten-minute bouts. To enable analysis of trends over time, the long questionnaire was amended (extended) to enable analysis using the previous questionnaire as well as new analyses to match the new recommendations. Additionally, an objective measure of activity (actigraph) and of physical fitness (step test) have been included in sub-samples of participants.

Further Data

Even cross-sectional data can be used prospectively if participants agree either to be contacted again or to have their administrative records 'flagged'.

Follow-up Studies Based on Health Survey for England and Links to National Data Sets

All participants in the HSE are asked if they agree to be contacted for future research. Studies that have used the HSE in this way include EMPIRIC, a study of Ethnic Minority Psychiatric Rates in the Community 1999 (n = 4,281) (Nazroo and Sprosten, 2002) and ELSA, the English Longitudinal Study of Ageing (n = 11,391) (Banks et al., 2008).

Follow-up of HSE areas has also been carried out. Using areas selected from HSE 1994–99, people living in these areas (not necessarily HSE participants) were asked to report on levels of social capital in their area (Stafford et al., 2003). This was then linked to HSE participants' data for those areas.

If participants give written consent, their records from HSE can be flagged for hospital admissions (Hospital Episode Statistics), mortality and cancer registration, effectively allowing the data to be used as cohort data.

Example of Previous Research Using HSE Data

Research using HSE has been very diverse and has focused on whole populations, specific age groups, and other sub-groups. Examples include trends in fractures in adults (Donaldson et al., 2008), distinguishing smokers from non-smokers using an objective measure (salivary cotinine, Jarvis et al., 2008), obesity in English children (Stamatakis et al., 2005), vitamin D concentrations among the elderly (Hirani and Primatesta, 2005), mortality from alcohol consumption (Britton and McPherson, 2001), smoking and blood pressure association (Primatesta et al., 2001), and CVD risk factor intervention in diabetics (Colhoun et al., 1999).

Who is Involved in Conducting the Health Surveys?

The Funders

In England this comprises various government departments and 'arms-length bodies', such as the NHS Information Centre for health and social care, which has commissioned the Health Survey for England since 2005. Until then, it was commissioned by the Department of Health. In Scotland, it is commissioned by the Scottish Executive Health Department. Local public sector bodies may also commission boosts to their area.

The Survey Contractors

The Joint Health Surveys Unit of the National Centres for Social Research (Natcen in England/Scotcen in Scotland) and the Department of Epidemiology and Public

Health, UCL have carried out the Health Survey for England since 1994 and the Scottish Health Survey since 1995, the latter in conjunction with the MRC Epidemiology Glasgow.

The Future of Health Surveys

Response rates have fallen in recent years due to a plethora of reasons, including increased security leading to difficulty in accessing premises, lack of participants' time, and fears about data security. To establish whether, and if so, how, to change the focus of the IC Survey Programme to maximize its strategic fit, there was a public consultation in 2008. This asked which topics were most important and which of geographic coverage/frequency/depth of topic was most important. The outcome of the review determined that there was a need for an HSE in 2009, and that the inequalities agenda remained a key component of the survey. There was a call for a greater focus on health and wellbeing, a push on prevention, a move to local accountability and to a greater focus on outcome measures.

The Need for Local Data

The geographic coverage preferred by those responding to the consultation was evenly split between national, regional and local data. NHS organizations favoured local data, other government departments and 'arms-length bodies' wanted national or regional data, charities were evenly divided, and academics leaned heavily toward national or regional data. Other geographical variables are available, including the index of multiple deprivation, social capital (certain years), social support and some environmental data (such as damp housing, and so on), and since 2007 the ONS area classification at supergroup level. There is also the opportunity to apply for geographic-level data to be attached at Natcen and/or to work in the Natcen data enclave with the small area-level data, or to have data from Natcen with 5 per cent perturbation to provide anonymity. Scotland has moved to collecting data that will allow greater regional analysis but will involve data collection over a longer period.

The Cost of Running a Health Survey

Cardiovascular disease, which is the main focus of the survey, is the major cause of death and over 99 per cent of the £2 billion NHS coronary heart disease (CHD) budget is currently spent on medical interventions, particularly revascularization, with less than 1 per cent spent on the monitoring of CHD.

Designing a New Survey – Comparability of Measures

Elements to consider when setting up any survey include:

- Content (topics, wording of questionnaires, measurements)
- Organizational model
- Sampling and recruitment of participants
- Legal and ethical issues
- Standardized measurement protocols
- Data management, documentation and reporting

To be able to compare findings over time or with different areas or populations, measures need to be standardized. For questions, this is not only the general topic ('How would you describe your health?') but the context ('Considering the last year; three months; fortnight ...') and the answers suggested (open; excellent to poor; very good to very poor).

Sources of Questions

The Question Bank, hosted by the University of Surrey, is a guide to good practice. It provides examples of piloted questions that have been proved in the field. TheSouth East Public Health Observatory (SEPHO, 2008) also hosts an electronic lifestyle survey toolkit. It contains information on how to conduct a health and lifestyle survey, some theory for those with little previous experience, question banks and other resources.

A European Health Examination Survey (EHES)

National HESs in Europe, the USA and Canada have recently been reviewed (Tolonen et al., 2008c) as part of a feasibility study for a pan-European HES, which would produce comparable data at a national but not regional level (FEHES, 2008). This has published recommendations for *standardization* and *quality control* for a standardized EHES (Tolonen et al., 2008b). It supports a flexible model where elements or degrees of complexity can be added on the basis of user needs and available resources, which both vary by country (a modular, stepwise approach, or 'core' and additional list).

Criteria for Topic Selection (Primatesta and Chaudhury, 2008)

Recommendations from ECHI for Developing Health Indicators

- Comprehensive
- Meeting user needs
- Based on earlier work (for example, WHO, OECD)
- Innovative
- Based on the results of the Health Monitoring Programme and Public Health Programme

Recommendations from FEHES for a European HES

- Inclusion in previous national HESs
- Availability of national standards
- Clear interpretation of the results
- Practicality/ease of administration
- Acceptability to the participants
- Ethical acceptability
- Cost

For the HIS components, questions from the European HIS (ECHI) shortlist indicators should be used.

Useful Contacts and Further Information

HSE Reports

- Prior to HSE 2004 available from Department of Health: <http://www.dh.gov.uk/PublicationsAndStatistics/PublishedSurvey/HealthSurveyForEngland/fs/en>
- HSE 2004 onwards available from NHS Information Centre. Also trend tables <http://www.ic.nhs.uk/statistics-and-data-collections/health-and-lifestyles-related-surveys/health-survey-for-england>

Health Surveys Users Groups

- <ScottishHealthSurvey@scotland.gsi.gov.uk>
- <http://www.ccsr.ac.uk/esds/join> (General government surveys)

Archived Data

- Full HSE and SHS data <http://www.data-archive.ac.uk/findingData/hseTitles.asp>

- Teaching data sets <http://www.esds.ac.uk/government/hse>

Survey Contractors

- <http://www.ucl.ac.uk/hssrg/hse.html>
- <http://www.natcen.ac.uk/natcen/pages/or_health.htm#hse>

References

Banks, J., Breeze, E., Lessof, C. and Nazroo, J. (2008), *Living in the 21st Century: Older People in England. The 2006 English Longitudinal Study of Ageing Wave 3* (London: Institute for Fiscal Studies).

Booth, C. (1902), *Life and Labour of the People in London*, Vol. 1 (London: Macmillan).

Britton, A. and McPherson, K. (2001), 'Mortality in England and Wales Attributable to Current Alcohol Consumption', *Journal of Epidemiology and Community Health* 55, 6: 383–8.

Capewell, S., Lloyd-Williams, F. and Ireland, R. (2005), *In Sickness and in Health: 2003 Health Survey for Greater Merseyside* (Liverpool: Heart of Mersey), <www.heartofmersey.org.uk/uploads/documents/nov_06/hom_1163156363_ In_Sickness_and_in_Health_-_20.pdf>.

Centers for Disease Control, 'NHANES' [website] (updated 11 September 2008), <http://www.cdc.gov/nchs/nhanes.htm> (home page), accessed 30 October 2008.

Colhoun, H., Dong, W., Barakat, M.T., Mather, H.M. and Poulter, N.R. (1999), 'The Scope for Cardiovascular Disease Risk Factor Intervention Among People with Diabetes Mellitus in England: A Population-based Analysis from the Health Surveys for England 1991–94', *Diabetic Medicine* 16, 1: 35–40.

Craig, R. and Mindell, J. (2008), *Health Survey for England 2006* (London: Information Centre).

'Demographic and Health Surveys', *US Agency for International Development* [website] <http://www.measuredhs.com/> (home page), accessed 30 October 2008.

Department of Health (2004), *Choosing Health: Making Healthier Choices Easier* (London: TSO).

Department of Health (2005), *Delivering Choosing Health: Making Healthier Choices Easier* (London: Department of Health).

Doll, R. and Hill, B.A. (1952), 'A Study of the Aetiology of Carcinoma of the Lung', *BMJ* II, 1271–86.

Donaldson, L.J., Reckless, I.P., Scholes, S., Mindell, J.S. and Shelton, N.J. (2008), 'The Burden of Fractures in England', *Journal of Epidemiology and Community Health* 62, 2: 174–80.

'ECHI (European Commission Health Indicators) Project' (2008), *European Commission* [website] <http://ec.europa.eu/health/ph_information/dissemination/ echi/echi_en.htm> (home page), accessed 31 October 2008.

ESDS (2004), *SN 5033 – Health Survey for England, 2002: Teaching Dataset*, <http://www.esds.ac.uk/findingData/snDescription.asp?sn=5033> (published online 2004), accessed 30 October 2008.

Eyler, J.M. (1979), *Victorian Social Medicine: The Ideas and Methods of William Farr* (Baltimore/London: The Johns Hopkins University Press).

FEHES [website] (updated 8 September 2008) <www.ktl.fi/fehes/> (home page) accessed 29 October 2008.

Flinn M.W. (ed.) (1965), *Chadwick, Edwin. Report on the Sanitary Condition of the Labouring Population of Great Britain*, 1842 (Edinburgh: Edinburgh University Press).

Fuller, E. (ed.) (2008), 'Smoking, Drinking and Drug Use Among Young People in England in 2007' (Leeds: Information Centre), <http:/www.ic.nhs.uk/pubs/sdd07fullreport> accessed 29 October 2008.

'General Household Survey', *Office for National Statistics* <http://www.statistics.gov.uk/ssd/surveys/general_household_survey.asp>, accessed 30 October 2008.

'Health Survey for England', *Information Centre*, <http://www.ic.nhs.uk/statistics-and-data-collections/health-and-lifestyles-related-surveys/health-survey-for-england>, accessed 31 October 2008.

'HES Online Hospital Episode Statistics', <http://www.hesonline.nhs.uk/> (home page), 2005–2008, Health and Social Care Information Centre. All rights reserved, accessed 29 October 2008.

Hirani, V. and Primatesta, P. (2005), 'Vitamin D Concentrations Among People Aged 65 Years and Over Living in Private Households and Institutions in England: Population Survey', *Age and Ageing* 34, 5: 485–91.

Information Centre (2008), *Review of Population-based Health-related Surveys*, <http://www.ic.nhs.uk/work-with-us/consultations/review-of-population-based-health-related-surveys>, accessed 31 October 2008.

Jarvis, M.J., Fidler, J., Mindell, J., Feyerabend, C. and West, R. (2008), 'Assessing Smoking Status in Children, Adolescents and Adults: Cotinine Cutpoints Revisited', *Addiction* 103, 9: 1553–61.

Lader, D. (2007), *Smoking-related Behaviour and Attitudes, 2006* (London: ONS).

Marmot, M. (ed.) (2008), *Commission on the Social Determinants of Health* (Geneva: World Health Organization).

Marmot, M. and Wilkinson, R.G. (eds) (1999), *Social Determinants of Health* (Oxford: Oxford University Press).

National Statistics (2006), 'Welsh Health Survey 2003/05: Local Authority Report' (Cardiff: National Assembly for Wales), <http://new.wales.gov.uk/topics/statistics/headlines/health-2007/health-2006/hdw20060906/?lang=en> (home page), accessed 31 October 2008.

Nazroo, J. and Sprosten, K. (2002), *Ethnic Minority Psychiatric Illness Rates in the Community (EMPIRIC)* (London: The Stationery Office).

Office for National Statistics (ONS) (2008), 'Omnibus Survey', *National Statistics* [website] (updated 1 April 2008), <http://www.ons.gov.uk/about/who-we-are/our-services/omnibus-survey> (home page), accessed 30 October 2008.

Primatesta, P., Falaschetti, E., Gupta, S., Marmot, M.G. and Poulter, N.R. (2001), 'Association Between Smoking and Blood Pressure: Evidence from the Health Survey for England', *Hypertension* 37, 2: 187–93.

Primatesta, P. and Chaudhury, M. (2008), 'Core Module and Additional Topics', in Tolonen et al. (2008b).

'Question Bank', *University of Surrey* <http://qb.soc.surrey.ac.uk> (home page), accessed 29 October 2008.

Rosenbaum, S. (1988), '100 Years of Heights and Weights', *Journal of the Royal Statistical Society. Series A (Statistics in Society)* 151, 2: 276–309.

Rosenbaum, S. and Crowdy, J.P. (1992), 'British Army Recruits: 100 Years of Heights and Weights', *Journal of the Royal Army Medical Corps* 138, 2: 81–6.

Rowntree, B.S. (1899, 2000), *Poverty. A Study of Town Life. New Edition with an Introduction by Jonathan Bradshaw* (Bristol: The Policy Press).

Scottish Executive (2008), 'Scottish Health Survey', *Scottish Executive Health Department* [website] (updated 16 April 2008) <http://www.scotland.gov.uk/Topics/Statistics/Browse/Health/scottish-health-survey> (home page), accessed 31 October 2008.

Scottish Government (2008), *Scottish Health Survey Consultation* <http://www.scotland.gov.uk/Topics/Statistics/Browse/Health/scottish-health-survey/Consultation2008> (published online 2008), accessed 30 October 2008.

SEPHO, 'Lifestyle Survey Toolkit', *South East Public Health Observatory* [website] <www.lifestylesurvey.org.uk/> (home page), accessed 30 October 2008.

Shelton, N. (2008), *The Production of Ill Health – Examples from the Health Survey for England and Scottish Health Survey*, Conference Presentation at The Royal Geographical Society Annual Conference, London.

Stafford, M., Bartley, M., Sacker, A., Marmot, M., Wilkinson, R., Boreham, R. and Thomas, R. (2003), 'Measuring the Social Environment: Social Cohesion and Material Deprivation in English and Scottish Neighbourhoods', *Environment and Planning A* 35, 8: 1459–75.

Stamatakis, E., Primatesta, P., Chinn, S., Rona, R. and Falascheti, E. (2005), 'Overweight and Obesity Trends from 1974 to 2003 in English Children: What is the Role of Socioeconomic Factors?' *Archives of Diseases in Children* 90: 999–1004.

'STEPwise Approach to Surveillance (STEPS)', *World Health Organization* [website] <http://www.who.int/chp/steps/en/> (home page), accessed 30 October 2008.

Tipping, S., Hope, S., Pickering, K., Mindell, J. and Erens, B. (2008), *An Analysis of Mode Effects Using Data from the Health Survey for England 2006 and the Boost Survey for London* (London: Natcen).

Tolonen, H., Koponen, P., Aromaa, A., Conti, S., Graff-Iversen, S., Grøtvedt, L., Heldal, J., Kanieff, M., Mindell, J., Natunen, S., Primatesta, P., Verschuren, M., Viet, L. and Kuulasmaa, K., for the Feasibility of a European Health Examination Survey (FEHES) Project (eds) (2008a), *Recommendations for Organizing a Standardized European Health Examination Survey* (Helsinki:

KTL, Finnish National Public Health Institute), <http://www.ktl.fi/attachments/suomi/julkaisut/julkaisusarja_b/2008/2008b22.pdf> accessed 28 October 2008.

Tolonen, H., Koponen, P., Aromaa, A., Conti, S., Graff-Iversen, S., Grøtvedt, L., Kanieff, M., Mindell, J., Natunen, S., Primatesta, P., Verschuren, M., Viet, L. and Kuulasmaa, K., for the Feasibility of a European Health Examination Survey (FEHES) Project (eds) (2008b), *Recommendations for the Health Examination Surveys in Europe* (Helsinki: KTL, Finnish National Public Health Institute), <http://www.ktl.fi/attachments/suomi/julkaisut/julkaisusarja_b/2008/2008b21.pdf> accessed 28 October 2008.

Tolonen, H., Koponen, P., Aromaa, A., Conti, S., Graff-Iversen, S., Grøtvedt, L., Kanieff, M., Mindell, J., Natunen, S., Primatesta, P., Verschuren, M., Viet, L. and Kuulasmaa, K., for the Feasibility of a European Health Examination Survey (FEHES) Project (eds) (2008c), *Review of Health Examination Surveys in Europe* (Helsinki: KTL, Finnish National Public Health Institute), <http://www.ktl.fi/attachments/suomi/julkaisut/julkaisusarja_b/2008/2008b18.pdf> accessed 28 October 2008.

'UK Data Archive', *University of Essex* [website] (updated 31 October 2008), <http://www.data-archive.ac.uk/> (home page), accessed 31 October 2008.

Wanless, D. (2004), *Securing Good Health for the Whole Population: Final Report* (London: HM Treasury/Department of Health).

Wilkinson, R.G. and Marmot, M. (2003), *Social Determinants of Health: The Solid Facts* (2nd edition) (Copenhagen: World Health Organization).

Woods, R. and Shelton, N. (1997), *An Atlas of Victorian Mortality* (Liverpool: Liverpool University Press).

Zaninotto, P., Wardle, H., Stamatakis, E., Mindell, J. and Head, J. (2006), *Forecasting Obesity* (London: Department of Health), <http://www.dh.gov.uk/assetRoot/04/13/86/29/04138629.pdf>.

Zaninotto, P., Head, J., Stamatakis, E., Wardle, H. and Mindell, J. (2009), 'Trends in Obesity Among Adults in England from 1993 to 2004 by Age and Social Class and Projections of Prevalence to 2012', *Journal of Epidemiology and Community Health* 63: 140–46.

1911 Census Project <http://www.1911census.co.uk>, accessed 30 October 2008.

Chapter 10

Measuring Social Capital: Formal and Informal Activism, its Socio-demographic Determinants and Socio-political Impacts

Yaojun Li

Abstract

In both academic and policy-making communities, social capital is increasingly regarded as having great potential for tackling many of the socio-economic problems facing our society. Yet how to define and measure social capital remains hotly debated. This chapter seeks to contribute to the debate by using a theoretically informed and methodologically rigorous approach to measuring formal and informal social capital. Drawing on the Home Office Citizenship Survey of 2003, we show that in addition to informal volunteers, formal participants can be further differentiated into civic and political activists. All three groups have different socio-demographic bases and different socio-political orientations. While civic activists have confidence in the institutions, trust their neighbours and believe in their ability to influence decision making at the local and national levels, political activists are critical of political institutions and are keen to make a change. Informal volunteers provide crucial help to people in need but tend to keep a low profile in the political sphere. On the other hand, it is also the case that all three groups are situated in more advantaged socio-economic positions, suggesting that reducing socio-economic inequality is the key to building an inclusive, dynamic and prosperous society.

Key words: Formal and informal social involvement, socio-political
           orientation, socio-economic inequality

Introduction

Most capitalist countries including Britain experienced a downturn from the heyday of socio-economic prosperity immediately following World War II to a depressing 'social malaise' at the turn of the century, as witnessed by persistent or even growing socio-economic inequality, decreasing socio-political trust and declining electoral participation (Blanden and Gibbons, 2006; Goldthorpe and

Mills, 2008; Paxton, 1999; Phelps, 2004). These forces erode the very foundations of our democratic system and have been the major concern for both social scientists and policy makers. In their search for a solution, social scientists have identified social capital as offering great potential for tackling these problems (Putnam, 1993 and 2000). They believe that its diminishing stock is responsible for the socio-economic problems we face, and that its replenishment may provide a way to reinvigorate democracy. And yet, how to define and measure social capital remains a topic of heated debate. This chapter seeks to contribute to the debate by using a theoretically informed approach to measuring social capital using survey instruments.

In this chapter, we shall first give a review of the social capital debate, focusing on the implications of the key traditions for measurement using survey data. We shall then give a brief account of the data and methods to be used for the present analysis, followed by discussion of empirical findings. The chapter will conclude with some discussion of the findings, combining insights from research on social stratification and social capital to show that lying at the heart of social capital deficit is the problem of socio-economic inequality, and that only by tackling the socio-economic inequality faced by the most disadvantaged groups can we hope to provide a fertile soil for an all-inclusive and dynamic social capital to develop and flourish.

Theoretical Review

In the past decade or so, the notion of social capital caught the imagination of the academic and policy-making communities like wild fire. Scholarly publications on this topic have increased exponentially, especially since Putnam's (2000) much-celebrated work, *Bowling Alone* (Halpern, 2005: 5). International and national institutions such as the World Bank and the Office for National Statistics in Britain have set up websites specifically devoted to the topic.[1] Probably more than any other concept in the social sciences, social capital has seen a prolonged and heated debate. Interestingly, in spite of waves of criticism (Portes, 1998; Harper, 2001), the concept has shown remarkable resilience, enjoyed growing popularity and found application far beyond its original remit of sociological and political research to reach economics, public health, management studies, criminology, ethnic studies, and so on (see Putnam, 2007: 138 for a summary in this regard). Most of the criticisms centre round the notion of social capital as enunciated by Putnam. Yet, even though highly influential, Putnam's theory of social capital is just one of the many accounts, and three other influential theories also deserve attention here so that we can gain a fuller appreciation of the strengths and weaknesses in Putnam's

---

1   See, for instance, <http://www.worldbank.org/poverty/socialcapital> and <http://www.statistics.gov.uk/about_ns/social_capital/>.

work. The following review will pay special attention to how the various accounts of social capital can be measured in survey research.

The three other theories that have also had a profound influence on social capital research are developed by Bourdieu (1986), Coleman (1988) and Lin (2000). They are all sociological in orientation. Bourdieu's main interest is in accounting for intergenerational social reproduction and he identifies three mechanisms – cultural, social and economic capital – for that purpose. While the three forms of capital are held to be mutually convertible and rooted in the economic sphere, the greatest importance is attached to cultural capital, with social capital relegated to secondary importance, useful only when middle-class parents have to mobilize their social networks to help their poorly qualified children gain access to more privileged positions (Savage, Li and Tampubolon, 2006). Social capital, as he sees it, consists of 'the aggregate of the actual or potential resources which are linked to possession of a durable network of more or less institutionalised relationships of mutual acquaintance and recognition' (Bourdieu, 1986: 248). This definition is comprehensive in coverage but weak in feasibility. It is hardly possible for social surveys to collect data on all those more or less institutionalized relationships. Thus while Bourdieu's theory on social capital remains influential among theorists and qualitative researchers, it has not been, and can hardly hope to be, adequately validated using survey instruments.

Coleman's theory on social capital has been influential for research in education. For him, social capital 'is defined by its function. It is not a single entity, but a variety of different entities, having two characteristics in common: They all consist of some aspect of a social structure, and they facilitate certain actions of individuals who are within the structure' (Coleman, 1990: 302). This functionalist definition has been rightly criticized as 'tautological' (Lin, 2000: 26), but it does specify mechanisms for the social structure to have an impact on educational attainment, namely, that the closely knit networks among parents, children and teachers engender social support (parents more connected to other parents have better access to information and are better able to establish and reinforce norms with their children) and social control (parents' positive social networks offer collective socialization of children). This serves to reduce isolation and alienation from school authorities, improve cooperative and responsive relationships between parents and teachers, and enhance aspiration and good learning behaviour among children, which is especially important for disadvantaged groups including immigrant communities. Yet, from the perspective of conducting research through national surveys, its weakness is also evident: even among the population of parents, children and schools, it is hard to collect information about how closely parents are connected to their children, other parents and schools, and what measures they individually or jointly take to reinforce moral values to enhance children's learning. Thus whilst Coleman's theory is good for in-depth research including the use of some survey elements within particular locales, its value in national representative sample surveys has been so far untested.

While Coleman is interested in the role of social capital on children's educational attainment, Lin's focus is on the benefits of social networks for getting (good) jobs in the labour market. For Lin, social capital is 'investment of resources with expected returns in the marketplace' (2000: 3). The unique contribution of his work to social capital research using survey data is his development of the 'Position Generator' approach. Basically, the survey instrument (the questionnaire) provides a list of different occupations and asks the respondent whether he or she knows people on the list, the length of time knowing the contacts, the relationship with the contacts, whether the contacts helped the respondents find the (first, second … or) present job or, if not, through whom also on the list the respondent could come to know such a contact (Lin, 2000: 124). As the jobs on the list are usually drawn from the national statistics of occupations, one could, from the information collected, analyse the social stratification in the network construction as well as the potential role of social networks for occupational attainment by looking at the various attributes associated with the contacts, such as the volume (number of contacts), position (the social score of the contact in a stratification system such as the SES in the US or the Cambridge Social Interaction and Stratification Scales (CAMSIS) in Britain), range (the distance between the highest and the lowest scores of contacts), and reachability (the highest score of contacts) (Lin, 2000). One could also explore the social inclusivity or exclusivity in the friendship construction, an important perspective for investigating the trends of social cohesion in society (Pahl and Pevalin, 2005; McPherson, Smith-Lovin and Brashears, 2006). The unique advantage of this approach is that it provides a very economical and efficient way to examine the multiple stratification systems in society and to explore the associations between social position, friendship construction and the labour market. Yet, viewed from a broader perspective of social capital research, it may be said that while the mechanism between social contacts and occupational attainment is clearly specified and the empirical value amply established (Lin and Erickson, 2008), its value in researching the civic tradition of social capital is rather limited. For instance, the volume and social distance of contacts are not found to affect generalized trust (Li, Savage and Warde, 2008: 405).

Having looked at the three sociological accounts of social capital, we now turn to a socio-political account in Putnam's work which has been the focus for most of the debate in the last decade. Here the first thing to note is that, as a political scientist, his main interest is in explaining why democracies are 'in flux' (Putnam, 2002) rather than how social networks enhance children's school performance or help people find jobs. All his major works in recent years concern why dissipating social engagement or loosening social cohesion erodes our confidence in the fellow citizens and the political institutions (Putnam, 1993, 2000 and 2007). His earlier book (1993) seeks to explain why there was better political governance in the northern but not in the southern part of Italy, which he says was a 'by-product of singing groups and soccer clubs' (1993: 176). His most celebrated and controversial book (Putnam, 2000) studies how the civic spirit which had so much fascinated Tocqueville nearly two centuries before was faring in present-day

America. While the earlier book focuses on formal civic engagement alone, thereby attracting much criticism, both formal and informal forms of social engagement are discussed in detail in the later work where he defines social capital as 'social networks and the norms of reciprocity and trustworthiness that arise from them' (Putnam, 2000: 19). This rather loose definition, combining cause (networks) and consequences (norms of trust and reciprocity) in one piece, is a source of much of the controversy and confusion in empirical research. For instance, how can we differentiate and measure an individual's trust as an attitudinal and/or a behavioural attribute? What is the distinction between trustworthiness and gullibility (Putnam, 2004)? Is it plausible at all to use the response to the question on generalized trust as an individual's social capital, or does trust only exist at the aggregate, namely national, level (Newton, 1997)? Leaving aside these issues for the moment, the basic conclusion from this monumental project drawing on dozens of datasets covering several decades and involving millions of respondents is that, since around the 1960s, Americans have been 'dropping out in droves', from not only formal civic organizations such as bowling leagues, but also many other sorts of informal sociable activities such as card games and dinner parties. And all this occurred in spite of the great increase at the societal level of both economic and human capital in the corresponding period. The great strength of this book is, for our present purposes, that the patterns and trends of social capital depicted for the US society are based on solid, national representative, social surveys, thus paving the way for other researchers to test and develop the thesis using other social surveys and similar, or more elaborate, methods.

Summing up, we can say that although the four most influential theorists differ in the domains of application, they all share a basic assumption that social capital resides in the resource-generating social networks. Such networks can be formal as encompassed in participation in civic organizations, or informal as ensuing from sociable activities with friends, colleagues, neighbours, acquaintances or relatives. Indeed, the benefits of such social networking activities may not even accrue to those doing the good deeds but to outsiders, onlookers, the wider community or even the national society. In other words, such a relationship of exchange may, as Putnam (1993: 172) aptly notes, be 'unrequited or imbalanced' at any given time.

Given the basic agreement about the most fundamental aspect of the social capital concept, the next and yet more perplexing issue is one that concerns its measurement. As noted above, Bourdieu's and Coleman's notions of social capital are not readily adaptable to survey instruments, and Lin's is mainly on occupational benefits in the labour market. Given this and the fact that most debates centre on Putnam's work, we shall, in the following, discuss how we can draw inspiration from and develop his work on formal and informal aspects of social capital.

One of the most interesting distinctions that Putnam makes concerns what he calls *machers* and *schmoozers*.[2] The former are those who 'invest lots of time in formal organizations' to 'make things happen in the community' and the latter 'spend many hours in informal conversation and communion'. As compared with *machers*, *schmoozers*' involvement is 'less organized and purposeful, more spontaneous and flexible' (Putnam, 2000: 93–4). The former are 'all-around good citizens of their community' whereas the multifaceted activities of the latter involve the 'flow of the soul'. The two types of social capital are, he believes, largely distinct at an empirical level in that 'many people are active in one sphere but not the other. And many people do neither; they are not involved in community affairs, and they don't spend much time with friends and acquaintances' (Putnam, 2000: 94). One may wonder which type is relatively more important. To this, Putnam's answer is that each is important in its own way. 'When philosophers speak in exalted tones of "civic engagement" and "democratic deliberation",' he says, 'we are inclined to think of community associations and public life as the higher form of social involvement, but in everyday life, friendship and other informal types of sociability provide crucial social support' (Putnam, 2000: 95). From this we may infer that while informal volunteering is useful in everyday life, formal engagement in civic organizations and activities is more important in community building and deliberative governance.

This brings us to a rather unfamiliar territory: are there differences in formal civic engagement? Or do people involved in different formal organizations and activities have the same characteristics and act for the same purposes? Putnam does not say much in this regard, apparently for good reason. His main interest, as we noted earlier, is in providing a broad picture of the patterns and trends of social capital so that he could, and does so quite successfully, forge a possible link between the weakening deliberative governance and the declining social capital. For this thesis to hold, further differentiation within the formal domain would only complicate matters. Moreover, as his empirical work is mainly geared to the general public, he does not present highly sophisticated analyses as usually found in academic writings. However, given his overall interest in the 'civic' tradition of social capital research, one might argue that there are good grounds for making further distinctions between a 'civic-oriented' type of participation and a 'politically orientated' type. While both groups may act on an organizational basis, which may be true more of the former than of the latter, the main difference lies in the purposes of their actions (Sorensen and Torfing, 2003; Li and Marsh, 2008). Civic participants typically act for the social (including instrumental and aesthetical) purposes, while political activists typically act for political

---

2   Another important distinction that Putnam makes is that between bonding and bridging social capital, with the former referring to 'exclusive social networks that are bounded within a given social category' and the latter to 'inclusive social networks that cut across various lines of social cleavage, linking people of different races, ages, classes, and so on'. Owing to the space limit, we do not discuss this distinction further in this chapter (see Li, 2009 for more discussion on this).

change. Civic participants tend to act in groups, but political activists may act individually and spontaneously. For instance, people who take a leading role in political party or trade union activities can be expected to be quite different from those who are routinely engaged in a bird-watching or arts club, or those who join a neighbourhood watch group, or go to church services mainly to chat with friends. Even though both kinds of participant act in a more or less organized way, the former is clearly politically motivated whilst the latter may not have any political agendas at all. Furthermore, formal involvement is characterized more by content than by format, which may be especially true of political engagement. For instance, people who sign a petition, join a public protest, contact their elected representatives, or write to a local or national newspaper rarely do so as a member of a particular organization, for there may be no such organizations for many of the actions. Such actions are formal in manner,[3] but spontaneous in formality. At least, they are not based on an organization in the traditional sense, with a hierarchical structure of the organization and a physical entity of the headquarters. Such actions have become more prevalent in recent years, such as protests and public demonstrations which are increasingly organized via the internet, and the 'organizations' exist only, or mainly, in a virtual or event-specific way.

Given the foregoing discussion, we may expect to find three broad types of participant: civic, political and altruistic. The first two are more or less organized but the last is purely spontaneous. While all three types have purposeful actions, the political agenda for the first type is the most evident. It should also be pointed out at this juncture that the demarcation may not always be clear-cut at the empirical level. An individual member of the society may take different actions for different purposes on different occasions. For instance, a trade union activist may be campaigning against a factory closure in the morning, attending a parent–teacher committee meeting in the afternoon, picking up a child for a neighbour on the way home, and inviting some friends to dinner in the evening. Such instances are, to be sure, atypical. Generally, one may expect that most people in formal civic organizations are rank-and-file members performing fairly routine and mundane activities, and that many people in society may do a lot of small but valuable things for others in need without even thinking that they are doing anything extraordinary.

Having argued our case for a three-tiered structure in social involvement, we need to establish the case at the empirical level. Yet, before that, it is necessary to give a brief account of how existing literature using survey data goes about measuring social capital. Basically, we find three ways:

- To use it as an aggregate measure. This is amply found in Putnam's (2000) own work where he constructs an index of social capital at the state level and then correlates it with various outcomes such as children's educational performance, crime level, health status and so on.

---

3 Writing a letter of complaint to a Congressman in the US or to an MP in Britain is, in general understanding, a much more formal thing to do than writing an email to a friend.

- To count the number of civic memberships and to use it as an outcome variable, as frequently found in earlier research (Hall, 1999; Li et al., 2002; Li, Savage and Pickles, 2003; Li, Pickles and Savage, 2005; Paxton, 1999 and 2007).
- To construct different types of civic engagement such as the distinction between 'isolated' and 'connected' voluntary associations (Paxton, 2007), that between 'expert citizens' and 'everyday makers' (Li and Marsh, 2008), or that between different latent classes (Li, Savage and Warde 2008).

While there has been much refinement in the measurement of social capital, no existing research has, to our knowledge, identified political activism, civic activism and voluntary altruism in the same piece while simultaneously seeking to establish their criterion and construct validity, namely, whether the indicators do appear to map onto the distinctions as theoretically conceived, and whether the distinctions thus constructed do have the predictive values for the socio-political orientations as may ensue from our theoretical understanding of the relationship between social capital and socio-political behaviour. To this we turn in the following.

Data and Methods

To address the research questions outlined above, we use the Home Office Citizenship Survey (HOCS) for 2003.[4] There are currently four HOCS datasets available (2001, 2003, 2005 and 2007). We chose the 2003 dataset as only this contains information on voting which is crucial for testing the hypothesis outlined above, namely, that political activists will be different from civic participants and altruistic volunteers in being more likely to vote.

The survey contains a total of 14,057 respondents (including a large sub-sample of minority ethnic groups, N = 5,244) aged 16 and over and resident in private households in England and Wales at the time of interview. In this analysis, we shall only use data for respondents aged between 18 and 70, as people under 18 are not eligible to vote and for those over 70, no data are collected on their educational qualifications. Even with this constraint and after dropping cases with missing data on the variables used in this analysis, there are still 10,659 respondents, which is the best data source currently available for our purposes. We shall use the term 'Britain' as shorthand in the following discussion, although we do not necessarily mean that the findings reported here can be generalized to Scotland. The data have rich details on, among other things, (1) socio-demographic attributes, (2) numerous indicators of formal and informal social capital from which to construct our variables on political activism, civic participation and voluntary altruism, and (3) trust, efficacy and voting as outcome variables for the three types of social capital.

---

4   The data are available at <http://www.data-archive.ac.uk/findingData/hocsTitles.asp>.

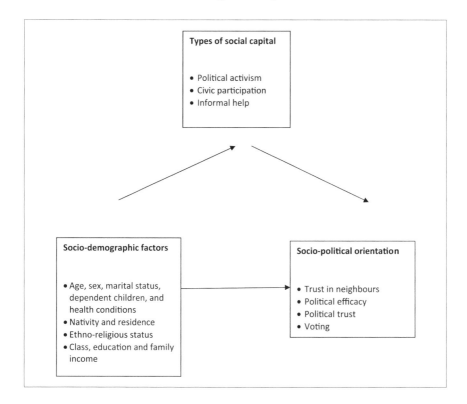

Figure 10.1 Types of social capital, socio-demographic determinants and socio-political orientation

Figure 10.1 shows the relationship between the explanatory and outcome variables used in this analysis. As earlier indicated, our purpose is to explore the determinants of the three types of social capital and their impact on socio-political orientations including trust, efficacy and voting. In the first stage of our analysis the aim is to explore the factors underlying different types of social capital. Here, the independent variables are the ones that previous research has found to be the most important: age, sex, marital and ethno-religious status, class and educational qualifications, and so on. As our main interest in this study is in the measurement of the three types of social capital and their impacts, we need to give more account of these here.

With regard to measuring the three types of social capital, the first thing we wish to point out is that social capital is, in our understanding, a multifaceted phenomenon which is unlikely to be adequately captured in any single-item measurement such as the time spent in voluntary activities (Letki, 2008), or the perception of local area social cohesion (Lawrence and Heath, 2008). We thus use a range of indicators covering 15 types of membership in formal civic organizations, 11 types of formal civic activity and seven types of political 'voice' to tap into the underlying structure of political activism and civic participation; in addition, we use information on 11 types of informal, unpaid and voluntary help provided to non-relatives living outside the respondent's household, to tap the underlying structure of informal volunteering. All these indicators pertain to activities in the last twelve months.[5] Apart from these, we use, as shown in Figure 10.1, a range of outcome variables on socio-political orientations such as trust in neighbours and political institutions (the police, the courts, Parliament and the local council), political efficacy (belief that one can influence decision making at the local and the national level), and voting in the last local and national elections.[6] These indicators on socio-political orientations refer mostly to the respondent's general perceptions and can thus be assumed to be the consequences of social capital.

Our analysis investigates each of these hypothesized relationships as shown in Figure 10.1. We wish to point out that although the figure looks like a path diagram, we shall not conduct a path analysis due to the categorical nature of many of the socio-demographic variables. We shall use what we believe to be the most appropriate method in each case.

We also give a brief description here of the socio-demographic variables used in the analysis. Ethno-religious status is coded following standard practice in British research with eight categories for ethnicity (White, Black Caribbean, Black African, Indian, Pakistani, Bangladeshi, Chinese and Other) and six categories for religion[7] (Christian, Hindu, Sikh, Muslim, Other and None). As around 20 per

---

5   There is only one respondent who scored 0, namely who was not involved in any of the 40-some items of formal and informal activities in our data. Thus whilst Putnam's observation that some people are neither *machers* nor *schmoozers* may be correct at the conceptual level, the number of such 'non-activists' is insignificant and negligible at the empirical level. In light of this, we did not include 'none' as a type.

6   As the question wordings are long, they are not listed here. Interested readers can find political activism and civic participation variables in *Fgroup(F02)* and *Funpd(F03)* on p. 130, *PActUK(C1)* and *Prally(C2)* on p. 123, and informal help variables in *Ihlp(I1)* on p. 133. As for variables on socio-political orientations, trust in neighbours can be found in *STrust(S10)* on p. 118, efficacy in *PActLoc(C5)* and *PActGB(C8)* on pp. 124–5, political trust in *PTPolc(C10)*, *PTCrt(C11)*, *PTParl(C12)* and *PTCncl(C15)* on pp. 127–8, and voting in the last local and general elections in *PVote(C16)* on p. 128 on <http://www.data-archive.ac.uk/doc/5087/mrdoc/pdf/5087userguide.pdf>. The variables were recoded where necessary so that higher scores denote greater involvement in the socio-political domains. The construction of the latent structures was carried out using the item response theory (IRT) models (see Li, Pickles and Savage, 2005; Li and Marsh, 2008, for further discussion on the application of this method to social capital research) and the resulting scores were all standardized for analysis in this study. The indicators for efficacy do not include Wales and London, and those for political trust do not include the Welsh Assembly and the Greater London Assembly.

7   Previous work (Li, 2007a; Li and Marsh, 2008; Lawrence and Heath, 2008) also found significant differences in social capital between ethnic groups. It is worth noting here that Letki does not include ethnicity on the grounds that 'including it significantly worsened the model fit' (2008: 11). With regard to religion, we need to note that there are two sets

cent of Black Africans and a similar proportion of Indians are Muslims, we shall conduct interaction effects (reported in the text or footnotes, but not in tables) where necessary. With regard to class, a three-way Goldthorpe (1987) class schema is used, differentiating the salariat class (professionals, administrators and managers), the intermediate class (petit bourgeois, routine non-manual, and forepersons and lower technicians) and the manual working class (skilled, semi-skilled and unskilled manual workers, including agricultural labourers). As people's family class position is frequently, as in the present research, found to have a greater impact on socio-political orientations than their own class (Pahl and Pevalin, 2005), we use the family head's or the respondent's class, whichever is higher. For educational qualifications, we differentiate tertiary, secondary and primary/no qualifications. Several other variables are included, such as the length of residence in the neighbourhood, whether having dependent children, foreign born and having limiting long-term illness, and family income,[8] which have been shown in existing studies to have considerable impact on social capital (Putnam, 2007; Letki, 2008; Lawrence and Heath, 2008). All analysis was conducted using weighted data.

Analysis

Having discussed the theoretical and methodological issues, we present the findings in this section. Table 10.1 shows that formal and informal activities over the last 12 months have three fairly clear latent structures (factors) as judged from the cross-factor loadings. The first factor, relating to formal memberships/activities in education, sports, health, religion and various other clubs, stands out as formal civic engagement. The second factor, relating partly to organized groups and activities such as political groups, justice and human rights groups, local community and neighbourhood groups, and trade unions and campaigns, and partly to unorganized activities such as contacting councillors, Members of Parliament, officials working in local or central government, attending public meetings, joining public demonstrations or protests, or signing petitions, is clearly political in orientation. The third factor pertains to provision of informal, voluntary and unpaid help to other people who are not relatives of, and who do not live with, the respondent. The voluntary activities range from keeping in touch with people by visits, emails or phone calls, through doing shopping, cooking, decorating, baby-sitting, caring for the sick and the frail, looking after property or pets when someone is away, to filling forms or escorting people to hospital or on an outing, and so on.

---

of such variables in the data: religious upbringing during childhood and current religious practice. The latter is used here, combining whether the respondent currently actively practises a religion and, if yes, which one.

  8   Family income is constructed as the log of the per capita household income, namely, the sum of the midpoint values of the respondent's (and, if in couples, partner's) banded income divided by the number of people in the family.

Table 10.1 Latent scores for items of the types of social capital

	Varimax rotated loadings		
	1	2	3
Civic participation			
Children's education	**0.613**	0.063	0.179
Youth activities	**0.650**	0.027	0.113
Adult education	**0.477**	0.251	0.153
Sports	**0.546**	0.074	0.054
Religion	**0.455**	0.120	0.115
Elderly	**0.437**	0.188	0.212
Health, Disability and Welfare	**0.472**	0.258	0.197
Safety	**0.421**	0.143	0.208
Environment	**0.395**	0.373	0.113
Citizen's groups	**0.429**	0.223	0.072
Hobby, arts and social clubs	**0.464**	0.243	0.115
Raising/handling money	**0.759**	0.189	0.123
Leader/member of a committee	**0.699**	0.382	0.022
Organizing an activity	**0.791**	0.248	0.106
Visiting people	**0.574**	0.225	0.366
Befriending/mentoring	**0.589**	0.202	0.306
Giving advice	**0.610**	0.344	0.266
Secretary/admin/clerical	**0.653**	0.316	0.090
Providing transport	**0.657**	0.086	0.252
Representing	**0.542**	0.443	0.156
Other practical	**0.612**	0.040	0.281
Political activism			
Politics	0.196	**0.631**	0.038
Justice and human rights	0.347	**0.534**	0.168
Local community and neigh groups	0.350	**0.401**	0.147
Trade union	0.243	**0.367**	0.023
Campaigning	0.360	**0.693**	0.107
Contacting local councillor	0.100	**0.628**	0.059
Contacting MP	0.115	**0.691**	0.088
Contacting local govt. official	0.146	**0.552**	0.138
Contacting govt. official	0.087	**0.600**	0.100
Attending public meetings	0.154	**0.723**	0.126
Taking part in public protests	0.078	**0.619**	0.116
Signing a petition	0.230	**0.494**	0.171

Informal help			
Keeping in touch with people	0.215	0.168	**0.575**
Doing shopping etc for others	0.047	0.011	**0.695**
Cooking, cleaning for others	0.065	0.014	**0.621**
Decorating, repairs for others	0.069	0.059	**0.443**
Babysitting for others	0.270	-0.056	**0.445**
Caring for sick and frail	0.092	0.144	**0.592**
Looking after property for someone	0.217	0.129	**0.374**
Giving advice	0.220	0.238	**0.561**
Writing letters for someone	0.207	0.281	**0.586**
Representing or filling forms	0.209	0.425	**0.502**
Transporting or escorting someone	0.245	0.088	**0.584**

Note: All political, civic and informal volunteering refers to unpaid help that took place over the last 12 months, and all informal volunteering to help given to non-relatives.
Source: The Home Office Citizenship Survey of 2003.

That a three-tiered structure in formal and informal social involvement manifests itself clearly, lends support to the criterion validity of our approach. It is also worth noting that even though the overall pattern is clear, there is a small number of cases where the distinction between civic and political orientation is less clear-cut, such as environment groups and representing under 'civic', and justice, local community and trade unions under 'political'. Overall, such instances are rare (five out of 44). Further analysis shows that the correlation between civic and political activism, between civic participation and informal help, and between political activism and informal help is 0.79, 0.68 and 0.63 respectively (all significant at the 0.001 level). Whilst the correlations are fairly strong, as would be expected from a theoretical perspective (Putnam, 2000: 94), they are not too strong as to cause problems of intercollinearity.

Having established the distinctive structure of the different types of participation in the formal and informal domains of socio-civic engagement, we now explore their socio-economic determinants. Table 10.2 shows the regression coefficients on each of the three types of participant by a range of socio-demographic attributes. Looking at the data, we find that people with higher educational qualifications, in higher social classes, and with higher family incomes, are all significantly more likely than their counterparts with poor qualifications, in working-class positions and with lower family incomes, to exhibit higher scores in all three types of social capital, echoing previous research on the social stratification in social civic engagement in Britain (Hall, 1999; Li et al., 2002; Li, Savage and Pickles, 2003; Li, Pickles and Savage, 2005; Li, Savage and Warde, 2008; Li and Marsh, 2008). In addition to socio-economic factors, we also find considerable impacts by cultural attributes, namely, ethnic identities and religious affiliations. In this regard, we find that religious affiliations tend to exert much more influence than ethnic identities, especially in terms of civic participation and informal help. The findings here present a rather interesting contrast to the relationship between ethno-religious identity and labour market experience where it is the ethnic rather than the religious identity that tends to incur direct discrimination (Li, Devine and Heath, 2008). As compared with those not practising any religion, Christians and people of other religious affiliations (Buddhists and Judaists) are most actively engaged in all three types of socio-civic activity and informal volunteering. Ethnic minority groups are, in most cases, less likely – and significantly so – than whites to be engaged, particularly in civic participation. While being partnered is negatively associated with the three types of involvement, having dependent children tends to offset that, most probably because of involvement in parent–teacher associations, children's education and youth activities. People born outside the UK tend to be less active than their British-born peers. Holding constant all other variables in the models, age, gender and length of residence in the neighbourhood do not seem to be prominent factors, although older respondents tend to be more active in politically oriented activities and women tend to provide more informal help than men.

The patterns shown in Table 10.2 are the main effects and do not show how people with joint attributes would behave. For instance, when we find that the two black groups are significantly less likely (-0.137 and -0.195 respectively), and that Christians are significantly more likely (0.575), to be in civic participation, what it means is that the two black groups are less likely than whites, and Christians are more likely than those without religion, to be thus involved. In order to find out the effects of such joint attributes, we conducted interaction effects between ethnic and religious identities, such as Black Caribbean Christian, Black African Christian, Black African Muslim, Indian Hindu, Sikh and Muslim respectively, Pakistani Muslim, and Bangladeshi Muslim. The results show that Black African Christians are significantly less involved in civic participation, that Indian and Bangladeshi Muslims significantly more involved in both civic and political activity (than the white non-religious), and that there were no ethno-religious differences in informal help. Finally in this connection, we may note that most minority ethnic groups except Indians and Chinese were found significantly less likely to be in civic participation, and Pakistanis and Bangladeshis significantly less likely to be informal volunteers. Further analysis shows that for those in higher (salariat) class positions, there were no significant differences between most of these groups and whites in the three types of participation.[9]

9　Only Black African salariat were found to be significantly less politically active than their white peers (b = -0.268, p = .036).

Table 10.2 Regression on socio-capital and informal help by socio-economic attributes

	Civic participation	Political activism	Informal help
Age/10	0.075	0.160*	-0.015
Age/10 sq	-0.005	-0.010	-0.000
Female	0.027	-0.007	0.076**
Partnered	-0.081**	-0.046	-0.159***
Dependent child under 16	0.125***	0.082***	0.084***
Long-term illness	-0.046	0.031	0.083*
Length of residence	0.001	0.000	0.001
Foreign born	-0.196***	-0.120*	-0.096
Household income (ln)	0.056***	0.046**	0.087***
Black Caribbean	-0.137*	-0.133*	-0.085
Black African	-0.195*	-0.149	-0.069
Indian	-0.081	-0.072	-0.097
Pakistani	-0.209*	-0.162	-0.210*
Bangladeshi	-0.266**	-0.103	-0.258*
Chinese	-0.028	-0.107	0.037
Other ethnicity	-0.163**	-0.144*	-0.157**
Christian	0.575***	0.402***	0.329***
Hindu	0.370***	0.151	0.278***
Sikh	0.375***	0.122	0.243*
Muslim	0.363***	0.359***	0.296***
Other religion	0.640***	0.503***	0.503***
Salariat	0.444***	0.343***	0.262***
Intermediate	0.177***	0.137***	0.135***
Tertiary	0.518***	0.484***	0.452***
Secondary	0.352***	0.293***	0.306***
Constant	-1.337***	-1.393***	-1.114***
R^2	0.212	0.147	0.119
N	10,659	10,659	10,659

Notes: The reference categories are male, non-partnered, no long-term limiting illness, UK born, white, no religion, working class, and people with only primary or no formal educational qualifications. 2 * p< .05; ** p< .01; *** p< .001.
Source: The Home Office Citizenship Survey of 2003.

Table 10.3 Regression on political orientations by socio-capital and informal help and socio-economic attributes

	Trust in neighbours	Political efficacy	Trust in institutions	Voting
Civic participation	0.096***	0.066**	0.125***	0.030
Political activism	0.009	0.099***	-0.048*	0.171***
Informal help	-0.031	-0.040*	-0.066***	-0.046**
Age/10	0.165*	0.130	-0.140*	0.485***
Age/10 sq	-0.005	-0.014	0.017*	-0.029***
Female	-0.069**	0.025	0.023	0.020
Partnered	0.130***	-0.036	-0.044	0.122***
Dependent child under 16	0.003	-0.014	0.023	0.014
Long-term illness	-0.176***	-0.139***	-0.171***	0.018
Length of residence	0.003***	-0.003**	-0.001	0.006***
Foreign born	-0.100	0.008	0.245***	-0.276***
Household income (ln)	0.000	0.005	-0.014	0.010
Black Caribbean	-0.363***	0.082	-0.431***	-0.011
Black African	-0.425***	0.144	0.009	-0.040
Indian	-0.236***	0.115	-0.033	0.293***
Pakistani	-0.215*	0.183	0.025	0.542***
Bangladeshi	-0.314**	0.126	0.094	0.687***
Chinese	-0.149	-0.035	0.131	-0.212*
Other ethnicity	-0.352***	0.094	0.057	-0.127*
Christian	-0.008	0.072*	0.095**	0.084**
Hindu	-0.002	0.153	0.399***	0.369***
Sikh	-0.035	0.354**	0.233*	0.162
Muslim	0.174*	0.157	0.314***	0.161*
Other religion	-0.254**	-0.109	-0.041	-0.082
Salariat	0.206***	0.069	0.143***	0.138***
Intermediate	0.080*	-0.009	0.001	0.031
Tertiary	0.194***	0.168***	0.170***	0.221***
Secondary	0.098**	0.070*	0.078*	0.108***
Constant	-0.693***	-0.414*	0.149	-1.944***
R²	0.051	0.052	0.053	0.235
N	10,659	10,659	10,659	10,659

Notes: The reference categories are male, non-partnered, no long-term limiting illness, UK born, white, no religion, working class, and people with only primary or no formal educational qualifications. 2 * p< .05; ** p< .01; *** p< .001.
Source: The Home Office Citizenship Survey of 2003.

Having looked at the socio-economic and cultural factors underpinning socio-civic involvement, we now turn to their joint effects on socio-political orientation – trust in neighbours, political efficacy, trust in institutions and voting.[10] The same socio-demographic variables as used in Table 10.2 are included here as control variables. The three social capital variables are our main interest in this regard.

The data in Table 10.3 show that, other things being equal, people who take an active part in civic organizations and activities are significantly more likely than others to trust their neighbours and political institutions, and are as likely as the political activists to believe that they can influence decision making at the local and the national levels.[11] Political activists, while being highly efficacious, are characterized by their mistrust of political institutions and their simultaneous enthusiasm to vote at both local and national elections. The informal volunteers, or *schmoozers* as Putnam (2000) calls them, are conspicuously invisible in the socio-political domains: they do not believe that they have any influence over the decision-making process at the local or the national level, they do not trust the political institutions, and they do not vote. In sum, civic participants come closest to Putnam's notion of 'good-citizens' making their community work; political activists come closest to Norris's (1999) notion of 'critical citizens' who are knowledgeable about the government decision-making processes, critical of the drawbacks of the various political institutions, and active in performing their citizen duties in voting. In contrast, the voluntary helpers keep a rather low profile in all these domains of socio-political trust and action.[12] They are happy as *schmoozers*.

Turning to the socio-economic and cultural factors, we find much weaker effects as compared with the patterns in Table 10.2. This is to be expected as some of the effects are now filtered through the social capital variables controlled for in the models. Thus, the class and education effects are roughly half the sizes as they were in Table 10.2, although still generally significant (with the exception of the salariat class in political efficacy). The intermediate class are now generally similar to the working class. More notably, as the religious effects that were seen to hold

---

10   'Trust in neighbours' was coded $0 = $ None, $1 = $ A few, $2 = $ Some and $3 = $ Many. Voting was coded $1 = $ Neither local nor general, $2 = $ Either local or general, and $3 = $ Both local and general. The scores were then standardized for use in Table 10.3. We also conducted analysis using ordinal logit regressions for the two variables. The patterns were very similar to those reported in Table 10.3 (results are not presented here but are available on request). The scores for efficacy and trust in political institutions were constructed using IRT models.

11   Further analysis shows that the slightly higher score by political activists over civic participants in institutional trust (0.033) is not significant ($F = 0.72$; $p > 0.396$).

12   Constructing interaction terms for the three types of social capital, we find that, with all other variables controlled for in the models, there are non-significant effects for these terms, suggesting that those respondents who have high scores in informal help *and* high scores in civic or political activism are no less efficacious and trusting, and are no less likely to vote in elections.

prominent for civic participation are now exerting their impact mainly through the direct route of civic participation, the effects are now largely insignificant in both social trust and political efficacy, although they are still quite significant in institutional trust and voting. Also notable is the fact that all minority ethnic groups are shown to be less likely to trust their neighbours and that the Chinese are less likely to vote (-0.212). This is probably due to 'weaker roots' in the neighbourhood. After all, immigration in Britain was a rather recent phenomenon which occurred mainly in the past few decades (Cheung and Heath, 2007: 512). The Chinese in Britain are known for their economic niche employment in restaurants and take-aways, entailing the frequent need for geographic mobility for their business (Li, 2007b). As Putnam says: 'For people as for plants, frequent repotting disrupts root systems' (2000: 205). One might ask whether it is the minority status per se or their shorter residence in the neighbourhood that led to their lower trust in neighbours? Further analysis of the interaction between minority ethnic status and the length of residence in the neighbourhood shows that *none* of the minority ethnic groups are less trustful of their neighbours if they have lived in the neighbourhood for the same length of time as the whites, and that the Chinese with the same length of residence in the neighbourhood as whites are actually more likely to vote (b = 0.019, p < 0.047). Class may also be an important factor, as existing research (Li, Devine and Heath, 2008) shows that many of the minority groups suffer an 'ethnic penalty' in not getting the same returns on their human capital (educational qualifications) as do whites. Further analysis shows that those minority ethnic members who do gain access to the advantaged salariat positions are no less trusting than their white peers (data not presented but available on request). Finally in this regard, we find that the middle aged and the partnered are more likely to trust their neighbours and to vote, but less likely to trust political institutions.

Discussion and Conclusion

Social capital has been the pearl in the crown for the social science and policy-making communities in the last decade. Amidst the flurry of debates and publications, one gets the feeling that the research may lose focus unless we have a clear idea of what we mean by, and what we do with, the term. Conceptual clarity and methodological rigour therefore lie at the heart of furthering social capital research. For this purpose, we revisited the four most influential accounts of social capital by Bourdieu, Coleman, Lin and Putnam, with a special view to their research value using the survey instrument. Although Lin's theory of social capital was also found suitable for use in large-scale social surveys, only Putnam's notion is used here as it offers a broader perspective for our present purposes.

    We also sought to develop Putnam's thesis on formal and informal social capital in a conceptually refined and methodologically rigorous way. One of the most interesting ideas in Putnam's (2000) book is his distinction between *machers* and *schmoozers*. He devotes several pages to the distinction in a quite 'exalted tone', but does not go deeper, giving the impression that all those in formal civic organizations are *machers* and all those not acting in an organized way are *schmoozers*. In this research, we went beyond that and placed greater attachment to the purpose of action. We attempted a three-tiered structure and wished to show both the criterion and the construct validity as our data permit.

Using the most authoritative data source currently available for our research purposes in this study, namely the Home Office Citizenship Survey of 2003, we showed that there are indeed clear signs of a three-tiered structure in socio-civic participation, as we would expect from the theoretical understanding. This establishes the criterion validity of our approach. We further showed, as confirming the construct validity of our approach, that the three types of participant have distinct patterns of socio-political orientations. Civic participants are 'good citizens', as characterized by their trust in their neighbours and in political institutions, as well as their confidence in their ability to influence decision making at the local and national levels. Political activists also have confidence in their abilities to influence decision making, but are mistrustful of political institutions and take a very active part in local and the national elections, presumably to effect some changes in the democratic processes. Informal volunteers are keen to provide help to people in need but tend to keep a very low profile in the socio-political domain.

Underlying the differential socio-political engagement is, however, a problem of social stratification. People in more disadvantaged socio-economic positions, be they lower social classes, poorer educational qualifications and lower family incomes, are consistently found to lag behind in civic participation, political activity and voluntary help. Yet the ostensibly weaker levels of socio-political involvement, trust and action by the minority ethnic groups were shown at various points to be traceable to their socio-economic disadvantage. This reinforces previous findings in social capital research in Britain and elsewhere with regard to the socio-structural influences on social capital. Interestingly, we also found that religious rather than ethnic identity played a notable role in civic, political and voluntary domains of activity, while the reverse was true in the socio-political orientations. As immigrants tend to have a relatively shorter history of settlement in the country, further analysis revealed that those with the same residence status as whites did not show any less propensity for constructing good neighbourly ties. In this regard, we wish to point out that even though the disruptive effects of (im)migration on social trust between and within ethnic groups (the 'hunkering down' thesis in Putnam, 2007) may find their expression in some particular locales, such effects may be less enduring in Britain as increasing length of residence in the neighbourhood tends to foster greater understanding between ethnic groups, hence better neighbourly relations.

In sum, our analysis of social capital in contemporary Britain shows three main findings:

1. Three main types of social participants – civic, political and informal – are readily observable, each with different socio-demographic attributes and different socio-political orientations
2. While membership in formal civic organizations may be in decline, a new social force – that of political activists who may be semi-organized but are mainly acting spontaneously and for political agendas – appears to be on the rise
3. While it is important to examine patterns and trends of social capital and its impact on socio-political life, it is equally, and arguably more, important to look beneath the surface and focus our gaze at the most disadvantaged groups, for it is people who are poorly qualified, in poor or no jobs, and frequently from minority ethnic origins, that are most often found to lag behind various kinds of active participation in the socio-political life of our society.

This leads to our conclusion that only by reducing socio-economic inequality can we hope to build a dynamic, inclusive and prosperous democracy. We are, at the moment, far from reaching this goal (Cabinet Office, 2008).

References

Blanden, J. and Gibbons, S. (2006), *The Persistence of Poverty across Generations: A View from Two British Cohorts* (York: Joseph Rowntree Foundation).
Bourdieu, P. (1986), 'The Forms of Capital', in J.G. Richardson (ed.), *Handbook of Theory and Research for the Sociology of Education* (New York: Greenwood), 241–58.
Cabinet Office (2008), *Getting On, Getting Ahead. A Discussion Paper: Analyzing the Trends and Drivers of Social Mobility* (London: The Strategy Unit).
Cheung, S. and Heath, A. (2007), 'Nice Work If You Can Get It: Ethnic Penalties in Great Britain', in A. Heath and S. Cheung (eds), *Unequal Chances*: *Ethnic Minorities in Western Labour Markets* (Oxford: Oxford University Press), 505–48.
Coleman, J. (1988), 'Social Capital in the Creation of Human Capital', *American Journal of Sociology* 94: S95–120.
Coleman, J.S. (1990), *Foundations of Social Theory* (Cambridge, MA: Harvard University Press).
Goldthorpe, J. with Llewellyn, C. and Payne, C. (1987), *Social Mobility and Class Structure in Modern Britain* (Oxford: Clarendon Press).
Goldthorpe, J. and Mills, C. (2008), 'Trends in Intergenerational Class Mobility in Modern Britain: Evidence from National Surveys', *National Institute Economic Review* 205: 83–100.
Hall, P. (1999), 'Social Capital in Britain', *British Journal of Political Science* 29: 417–61.

Halpern, D. (2005), *Social Capital* (Cambridge: Polity).

Harper, R. (2001), 'Social Capital: A Review of the Literature', *Social Analysis and Reporting Division* (London: Office for National Statistics).

Lawrence, J. and Heath, A. (2008), *Predictors of Community Cohesion: Multilevel Modeling of the 2005 Citizenship Survey*, <http://www.communities.gov.uk/documents/communities/pdf/681539>.

Letki, N. (2008), 'Does Diversity Erode Social Cohesion? Social Capital and Race in British Neighbourhoods', *Political Studies* 56: 99–126.

Li, Y. (2007a), 'Social Capital, Social Exclusion and Wellbeing', in A. Scriven and S. Garman (eds), *Public Health: Social Context and Action* (London: Sage), 60–75.

Li, Y. (2007b), 'Assessing Data Needs and Gaps for Researching Ethnic Minority Entrepreneurship', research report for the ESRC/DTI/CRE/EMDA, <http://www.berr.gov.uk/files/file41029.doc>.

Li, Y. (2009), 'Unravelling a Mystery: Why More Room at the Top Has Not Led to More Social Capital in Britain?', mimeo, Institute for Social Change, Manchester University.

Li, Y., Devine, F. and Heath, A. (2008), *Equality Group Inequalities in Education, Employment and Earnings: A Research Review and Analysis of Trends Over Time* (Manchester: The Equality and Human Rights Commission).

Li, Y. and Marsh, D. (2008), 'New Forms of Political Participation: Searching for Expert Citizens and Everyday Makers', *British Journal of Political Science* 38, 2: 247–72.

Li, Y., Pickles, A. and Savage, M. (2005), 'Social Capital and Social Trust in Britain', *European Sociological Review* 21, 2: 109–23.

Li, Y., Savage, M. and Pickles, A. (2003), 'Social Capital and Social Exclusion in England and Wales (1972–1999)', *British Journal of Sociology* 54, 4: 497–526.

Li, Y., Savage, M., Tampubolon, G., Warde, A. and Tomlinson, M. (2002), 'Dynamics of Social Capital: Trends and Turnover in Associational Membership in England and Wales: 1972–1999', *Sociological Research Online* 7, 3.

Li, Y., Savage, M. and Warde, A. (2008), 'Social Mobility and Social Capital in Contemporary Britain', *British Journal of Sociology* 59, 3: 391–411.

Lin, N. (2000), *Social Capital* (Cambridge: Cambridge University Press).

Lin, N. and Erickson, B. (eds) (2008), *Social Capital: An International Research Program* (Oxford: Oxford University Press).

McPherson, M., Smith-Lovin, L. and Brashears, M. (2006), 'Social Isolation in America: Changes in Core Discussion Networks Over Two Decades', *American Sociological Review* 71, 3: 353–75.

Newton, K. (1997), 'Social Capital and Democracy', *American Behavioural Scientist* 40, 5: 575–86.

Norris, P. (ed.) (1999), *Critical Citizens: Global Support for Democratic Government* (Oxford: Oxford University Press).

Pahl, R. and Pevalin, D. (2005), 'Between Family and Friends: A Longitudinal Study of Friendship Choices', *British Journal of Sociology* 56, 3: 433–50.

Paxton, P. (1999), 'Is Social Capital Declining in the United States? A Multiple Indicator Assessment', *American Journal of Sociology* 105: 88–127.

Paxton, P. (2007), 'Association Memberships and Generalized Trust: A Model of Generalized Trust in Thirty-One Countries', *Social Forces* 86, 1: 47–76.

Phelps, E. (2004), 'Young Citizens and Changing Electoral Turnout, 1964–2001', *Political Quarterly* 75, 3: 238–49.

Portes, A. (1998), 'Social Capital: Its Origins and Applications in Modern Sociology', *Annual Review of Sociology* 24: 1–24.

Putnam, R. (1993), *Making Democracy Work: Civic Traditions in Modern Italy* (Princeton, NJ: Princeton University Press).

Putnam, R. (2000), *Bowling Alone: The Collapse and Revival of American Community* (New York: Simon & Schuster).

Putnam, R. (ed.) (2002), *Democracies in Flux: The Evolution of Social Capital in Contemporary Society* (Oxford: Oxford University Press).

Putnam, R. (2004), 'Commentary: "Health by Association": Some Comments', *International Journal of Epidemiology* 33, 4: 667–71.

Putnam, R. (2007), '*E Pluribus Unum*: Diversity and Community in the Twenty-first Century, The 2006 Johan Skytte Prize Lecture', *Scandinavian Political Studies* 33, 2: 137–74.

Savage, M., Li, Y. and Tampubolon, G. (2006), 'Rethinking the Politics of Social Capital: Challenging Tocquevillian Perspectives', in R. Edwards, J. Franklin and J. Holland (eds), *Assessing Social Capital: Concepts, Policy and Practice* (Newcastle: Cambridge Scholars Press), 70–94.

Sorensen, E. and Torfing, J. (2003), 'Network Politics, Political Capital and Democracy', *International Journal of Public Administration* 26, 6: 609–34.

Chapter 11

Measuring Social Attitudes

Caroline Roberts

Introduction

The measurement of attitudes is common practice in most major academic surveys, and several important large-scale studies are devoted entirely to the exercise, including the British Social Attitudes (BSA) survey, fielded annually since 1983, the US General Social Survey (GSS), biennially, since 1972, and the German 'Allbus', also biennial, since 1980. In addition to these long-standing national studies, several large-scale cross-national studies, including the European Commission's Eurobarometer surveys, the International Social Survey Programme (ISSP) and, most recently, the European Social Survey (ESS), have regularly collected data about social attitudes Europe- and world-wide for many years. The aim of each of these studies is to describe the way people think and feel about the various features of the world around them, and to make comparisons across different groups in society. The data are used extensively by students and academics across all the social sciences. Outside of academic research, politicians, civil servants, journalists, market researchers and advertising executives frequently use surveys to gauge public reactions to social policies, electoral candidates, political issues, new products and innovations, and these measurements play a critical role in decision making both in governance and business development alike.

Public attitudes are as much a part of social reality as are a society's demographic characteristics or behaviour patterns. Unlike demographic characteristics and behaviour patterns, however, attitudes are not immediately accessible to the researcher interested in measuring them. Because they cannot be observed directly, survey researchers typically rely on respondents' self-reports, which can be notoriously unstable, fluctuating from one measurement attempt to the next. In this chapter, I describe the most common methods used to elicit self-reports of attitudes and discuss the main sources of error that contribute to the instability of measurements. Errors in attitude measurements can distort sample estimates of marginal distributions and expected relationships between attitudes and other variables, leading to inaccurate conclusions about the state of public opinion. Throughout the chapter, I consider how researchers can minimize this error, to enhance the precision of their measurements. To understand some of the challenges involved in measuring attitudes, it is important to have a shared understanding of what attitudes are, so in the next section I provide some definitions.

What Are Attitudes?

The term 'attitude' has become so ubiquitous in our society as to hardly merit a formal definition. Yet though widely used and understood in everyday discourse, the concept is relatively technical and specific to the discipline of social psychology from which it emerged. Like any theoretical construct, attitudes have been conceptualized and researched in many different ways throughout their history. Current thinking in the field, however, generally agrees on the idea that attitudes are cognitive representations of a person's positive or negative evaluations of different 'objects' (for example, Eagly and Chaiken, 1993). People make evaluations about all kinds of things, including actual physical objects, consumer products, other people or groups of people, events, behaviours, political issues and policies, and it is this positive or negative judgment that scholars generally refer to as an attitude, and which is the focus of most measurement attempts. This focus on the evaluative component of attitudes is relatively recent, however. Earlier contributors to the field (for example, Allport, 1935; Katz and Stotland, 1959) conceived of attitudes more broadly, incorporating affective (the emotional reactions a person has towards the attitude object), behavioural (how they act in relationship to it) and cognitive (what they think about it) components into the attitude construct. In more recent definitions of attitudes, however, scholars have sought to distinguish the evaluative judgment implicit in attitudinal response from these other components, which are perhaps best viewed as different types of information on which the attitude is based (Fabrigar, Krosnick and MacDougall, 2005). In fact their relation is more interactive, as each one may influence the formation and transformation of the attitude, which in turn may have a reciprocal influence on people's emotional, behavioural and cognitive responses to the attitude object (Albaracin et al., 2005).

As far as the measurement of attitudes is concerned, perhaps the most significant defining feature of attitudes is that as psychological constructs, they cannot be observed directly. We cannot know exactly what an attitude 'looks like' in the mind of the attitude holder, and our measurements can only ever approximate what we are trying to describe – they are not the same thing as the attitudes themselves (Krosnick, Judd and Wittenbrink, 2005). This characteristic of attitudes has led to disagreement about the cognitive processes that underpin the expression of attitudes. In particular, disagreement exists among scholars about whether attitudes are better described as 'memories' or 'judgments' (Albarracin et al., 2005: 4). While some prefer to think of attitudes as relatively stable structures stored in a person's long-term memory (for example, Fazio, 1990) and capable of being retrieved and reported on request, a substantial body of evidence suggests that this is not the case for all kinds of attitudes (for example, Zaller and Feldman, 1992). In many situations, people do not have a ready-made single evaluation about a specific object, and instead they must construct one on the spot that summarizes whatever considerations were brought to mind when they were asked to report their attitude (Krosnick, Judd and Wittenbrink, 2005; Zaller and Feldman, 1992). As we shall see, different considerations may be brought to mind in different contexts (some negative, some positive), so the judgment made, and consequently the attitude reported, can vary substantially over time and across situations. To complicate matters, characteristics of the context in which the attitude must be reported (including methods used by researchers to measure the attitude) may influence whether positive or negative considerations are brought to mind. In the next section, I describe some of the methods commonly used for measuring attitudes.

Ways of Measuring Attitudes

Given that attitudes cannot be observed directly, investigators have to make inferences about how positively or negatively a person feels about an object, based on the different kinds of information that they can observe. Psychologists have used various sources of observable information to find out about people's attitudes, including their physiological reactions to the attitude object (for example, Mueller, 1977; Rankin and Campbell, 1955; Hess, 1965), their behaviour in relation to the attitude object (for example, Lapiere, 1934; Milgram, Mann and Harter, 1965) and their psychological reactions to it (for example, Dovidio and Fazio, 1992; Greenwald, McGhee and Schwartz, 1998). The problem with each of these sources of information about attitudes is that they are not very practical to work with. They can be difficult to gain access to, hard to interpret and their relation to a person's underlying evaluation is not always as clear cut as it might be presumed to be (Fabrigar, Krosnick and MacDougall, 2005). These methods are also less helpful when the aim is to describe the attitudes of society as a whole. For these reasons, by far the most popular source of information that researchers use to draw inferences about attitudes are people's own descriptions of how they think and feel about a particular object. Asking people directly to report their attitudes provides a relatively quick, easy and cost-efficient way of gathering information about attitudes from a large group of people. In the context of a sample survey, using direct attitude measures allows researchers not only to draw inferences about the nature of respondents' attitudes at the individual level, but also to describe the distribution of attitudes towards a particular object in the population as a whole. For the remainder of the chapter, therefore, I focus primarily on issues surrounding the use of this type of attitude measure.

Researchers face a number of choices when designing questionnaires to elicit respondents' own descriptions of their underlying attitudes. Many of these decisions are guided by resource considerations. For example, one preliminary decision includes whether to use 'open' or 'closed' questions. Compared with open-ended questions, in which respondents' answers to questions are recorded verbatim, closed questions, in which respondents are asked to select their answer from a set of predefined alternatives, are considerably more practical for researchers to work with and usually quicker and easier for respondents to answer (Lazarsfeld, 1944). Closed questions allow large quantities of data to be collected more efficiently from large numbers of people and, as a result, they are used far more frequently by researchers nowadays. However, resource considerations are not the only guiding factor in the design of attitude measures. Concerns about costs must be weighed up against the need to collect data that provide the most accurate description possible of the underlying attitude. Research (for example, by Schuman and Presser, 1981) has shown that open questions tend to produce more diverse answers compared with closed questions and that this can affect the relationship observed between attitudes and respondents' background characteristics. If researchers want to be confident in their conclusions about the attitudes of particular groups in society, therefore, they must be careful to use the methods that will most accurately reflect the real differences present in the population.

Another decision that researchers face is whether to use one or more questions to measure a single attitude. Most direct closed-ended self-report methods used today are based on techniques developed by some of the earliest contributors to the field, including Thurstone's (1928) 'Equal Appearing Intervals' method, Likert's (1932) method of Summated Ratings, and Osgood, Suci and Tannenbaum's (1957) Semantic Differential (Krosnick, Judd and Wittenbrink, 2005). These approaches provide different ways of measuring attitudes using multiple items designed to work together to measure a specific attitude object. In Thurstone's approach, a set of statements is selected to represent the full range of possible attitudes to a given object (from extremely negative to extremely positive). These are then rated by a panel of judges using scores ranging (typically) from 0 to 11, and the two items best representing each point on the scale are then selected to construct the final measure to be administered to respondents. Respondents must indicate whether they agree or disagree with each statement in the final scale and their score on the scale is the mean of the scores that the judges gave to each statement that the respondent agreed with. In Likert's approach, positive and negative statements about the object are selected and respondents must report the extent of their agreement or disagreement with each one using five-point response scales. For each rating they obtain a score ranging from 1 (representing an extremely negative attitude toward the object) to 5 (representing an extremely positive attitude), so that a total score for all items can be computed (as the sum or mean of scores on each item). Correlations between specific items and the overall scale score are then examined, so that items with low correlations (perhaps because they are measuring something other than the attitude of interest) can be removed from the scale and the total score is recalculated. Both techniques have been proven to be effective at obtaining accurate descriptions of attitudes, but in general, researchers have found Likert's procedure to be less labour-intensive (Edwards and Kenney, 1946), which is why Likert scales are among the most widely used methods of attitude measurement today. Nevertheless, both procedures require considerable preparatory work, which is why the less laborious 'semantic differential' technique has proved to be a popular alternative (Osgood, Suci and Tannenbaum, 1957). This involves asking respondents to rate the object of interest on a relatively small number of seven-point response scales, anchored at either end by opposing adjectives (such as good and bad, positive and negative), which Osgood and his colleagues' previous research showed capture the key features of the evaluative dimension of an object's meaning.

Given the high costs involved in collecting data on attitudes in social surveys, and pressures to keep questionnaire length to a minimum, it can be difficult to justify including large numbers of items to measure a single attitude. For this reason, most researchers nowadays tend to use just a few closed questions to assess attitudes in each domain of interest, and frequently just a single item. While this has advantages in terms of cost efficiency, it means that researchers have less information on which to base their descriptions of people's attitudes. This can be problematic because attitude measurements – like any other type of measurement – contain a certain amount of error. A person's score on a given measure consists not only of their 'true score' on the underlying construct of interest, but also of error associated with the method of measurement. Two kinds of error can affect the quality of the measurements obtained: random error, the effects of which are evenly distributed across the data collected; and systematic error, the effect of which is to bias results in a specific direction. Researchers use formal criteria to determine the precision of questions designed to measure attitudes directly, and the extent to which they contain different types of error. These criteria include whether the question measures what it is intended to measure, that is, the construct of interest, and not some source of systematic error (Krosnick, Judd and Wittenbrink, 2005); and whether the same measurement would be obtained using the same question on repeated occasions. The first of these criteria is referred to as the 'validity' of the measure and the second is referred to as its 'reliability' (see Bohrnstedt, 1977 for an introduction to measurement theory). To a certain extent, the greater the validity of a measure, the more likely it is to produce the same answers on repeated occasions. However, because attitudes cannot be observed directly, it is especially difficult for researchers to be sure that they are measuring the construct of interest, and this can lead them to obtain highly variable results from one measurement attempt to the next. To complicate matters, variability in responses to direct attitude measures may not always result from errors associated with the method of measurement, but also from the way in which people respond to direct attitude measures. These sources of variability in attitude measurements are the focus of the remainder of the chapter. I begin by looking at how the cognitive processes involved in responding to direct measures of attitudes can influence the results obtained.

Sources of Variability in Attitude Measurements

Cognitive Processes in Reporting Attitudes

Traditional approaches to the study of attitudes view them as relatively enduring, pre-existing constructs stored in long-term memory (see, for example, Fazio et al., 1986; Fazio, 1990). However, a substantial body of research suggests that it is inappropriate to view attitudes in this way, in particular because measurements of attitudes have been shown to be highly unstable across different measurement attempts. One explanation for this suggests that shifts in responses to attitude measures are essentially random, and occur because people do not hold pre-existing attitudes at all on certain topics and lack the political sophistication required to link complex issues and ideas to form consistent attitudes (Converse, 1964). To avoid admitting that they are insufficiently informed about an issue to have formed an opinion about it, respondents pick one of the response alternatives seemingly at random or at least to concoct a response 'on the spot, based on little or no information' (Fabrigar, Krosnick and MacDougall, 2005: 25). Because these attitude reports do not reflect pre-existing attitudes towards an issue, and lack coherence (meaning they do not relate in expected ways with other variables measured in the same survey) they have been referred to as 'nonattitudes' (Converse, 1970).

Evidence for the existence of nonattitudes comes from studies that have tested the effect of offering versus omitting a 'Don't Know' response alternative in an attitude measure (for example, Krosnick et al., 2002). When the 'Don't Know' option is included, a significantly larger number of respondents will report that they do not know their attitudes than when the option is omitted. This finding suggests that when the 'Don't Know' is not legitimated as an explicit response category, people who are uncertain of their attitude prefer to select a substantive answer than admit to not knowing. This finding is supported by a number of studies that have deliberately asked respondents about *fictitious* issues, to see whether they are still willing to avoid admitting that they do not know their attitude, even when they cannot hold a pre-existing view about the object in question (see, for example, Bishop et al., 1980; Schuman and Presser, 1980). These studies find that large proportions of respondents are willing to report attitudes on topics they know nothing about, so by extension it seems likely that they will report nonattitudes in other contexts too (see Smith, 1985 for a review).

Not only can attitude reports vary randomly across different surveys, but even over the course of a single survey interview can people's attitudes appear to change quite dramatically, depending on different features of the context in which they are measured (Tourangeau and Galesic, 2008). One feature that contributes to this measurement context includes the order in which questions about attitudes are presented in the questionnaire. 'Context effects' occur when respondents modify their responses to survey questions either to make them appear more consistent with responses given earlier in the questionnaire, as in assimilation or 'carryover' effects, or when they interpret later questions as requesting new information that may appear logically inconsistent with earlier reports, as in contrast or 'backfire' effects (Tourangeau and Rasinski, 1988). The presence of context effects in survey data further challenges the idea that respondents in attitude surveys simply report a pre-existing attitude retrieved from their long-term memory (Tourangeau and Galesic, 2008), though the nature of such effects suggests that they are not simply picking answers randomly either. Rather, they show how sensitive attitude reports are to salient features of the measurement setting, lending support to the conclusion that attitudes are online judgments constructed on the basis of considerations brought to mind during questionnaire completion. It is the constructive process of producing an attitude report that explains variability observed in attitude reports.

Tourangeau, Rips and Rasinski (2000) have developed a model for understanding the processes involved in formulating responses to attitude questions in surveys, which is helpful for understanding how context effects and other types of errors arise in survey data. According to the model, answering a survey question involves four components of processing: the first component in the model is *comprehension*: in order to answer a survey question, a respondent must first understand what the question is asking; the second component is *retrieval*: having established the goal of the measurement attempt, the respondent must search his/her memory for any information relevant to the question that will help them to answer it. This process might involve retrieving an existing stored evaluation, or alternatively, if there is no pre-existing attitude, it might involve retrieving various stored 'considerations' associated with that object (including, for example, relevant beliefs, feelings and memories). The third component of the response process involves *judgment* – a process of generating a summary evaluation based on the considerations brought to mind during retrieval; and lastly, in the fourth component of processing, *response*, the respondent must decide how to report their answer by mapping the judgment onto one of the available response alternatives. Each component involves multiple cognitive processes, making formulating a response to a survey question a surprisingly demanding procedure. Furthermore, each component is prone to error, which can affect the accuracy of the reported attitude (Tourangeau and Rasinski, 1988; Tourangeau, Rips and Rasinski, 2000), although it is the retrieval and judgment phases in particular that provide the key to understanding inconsistencies often observed in attitude measurements (Tourangeau and Galesic, 2008).

People typically store in memory a large number of both positive and negative associations with different attitude objects. Even if they have never had to integrate those associations into a single summary evaluation of the object, they will still have a mix of different considerations that can be brought to mind on different occasions and from which they can construct an attitude (Zaller and Feldman, 1992). Because the pool of considerations from which respondents to attitude surveys can draw is typically mixed, the information retrieved at any one time can lead to very different judgments from one occasion to the next. According to Zaller and Feldman's model, 'individuals answer survey questions by averaging across the considerations that happen to be salient at the moment of response' (1992: 586). When confronted with an attitude measure, respondents draw a sample of considerations based on how accessible they are in memory and base the judgment they report on the composition of that sample. Samples containing more positive considerations will lead to more positive evaluations, whereas samples containing more negative considerations will lead to more negative evaluations. Thus, it is the process of retrieval, by which a sample of accessible considerations is drawn (typically including salient features of the questionnaire and data collection context), that determines the valence of the reported judgment.

Response instability in attitude measurement has been found to be more common among respondents with little prior knowledge about or involvement in the attitude issue. This may be because people who have not thought much about the attitude object have a smaller pool of considerations from which to sample, and possibly only one consideration that is immediately accessible when the attitude must be reported (Zaller and Feldman, 1992). Another explanation is that the degree to which a person is involved in an attitude object influences the amount of effort they are willing and able to expend in generating answers to attitude measures (for example, Petty and Cacioppo, 1986). Given that random error in attitude reports can affect conclusions about the distribution of attitudes in the population, as well as the relationships between attitudes and other constructs, it is important to be able to distinguish people with more 'crystallized' attitudes from others. Crystallized attitudes have been shown to be more resistant to persuasion, and therefore less labile over time (Petty and Krosnick, 1995). This highlights the value of gathering information about the strength of reported attitudes at the same time as measuring the attitude itself (such as the certainty with which it is held, the importance and centrality of the attitude to respondents, how much knowledge respondents have about the object and how interested they are in it – see Krosnick and Petty, 1995), so that researchers have additional data on which to judge the accuracy of their measurements (Krosnick, Judd and Wittenbrink, 2005).

The Design of the Questionnaire

To minimize the amount of error in attitude reports, it is important for researchers to be aware of how certain types of biases can arise as a result of decisions about how to design attitude questionnaires. Such decisions include how to word attitude measures; how long response scales should be; how to label the response scale; the order in which response categories should be presented; whether to include middle or 'Don't Know' alternatives in the response scale; as well as how to order items in the questionnaire. An accumulated body of research using split-ballot experiments, in which different versions of the same question are administered to a random sub-sample of the total survey sample (see, for example, Rugg and Cantril, 1944; Kalton, Collins and Brook, 1978; Bishop, 1987; Schuman and Presser, 1981) has shown that the outcome of these choices can have important implications for the quality of the data collected, because the answers people give to questions asking about their attitudes vary depending on how the questions are asked. It is beyond the scope of this chapter to extensively review findings from this research, and excellent summaries of what is currently known about best practice in questionnaire design are available elsewhere (see Krosnick, Judd and Wittenbrink, 2005; Fabrigar, Krosnick and MacDougall, 2005; Fabrigar and Krosnick, 1995; see also Krosnick and Fabrigar, forthcoming, for a detailed treatment of this literature). However, given the impact that they can have on the accuracy of our conclusions about the nature of social attitudes, it is helpful to provide some illustrations of how decisions about the design of attitude measures can affect the quality of the data collected.

Media opinion polls often attempt to describe public attitudes using data from just a single item, sometimes in ways that can misrepresent the true distribution of attitudes in the population. The difficulty for analysts (and policy makers) is deciding what the true distribution of attitudes is, based on data collected from different attitude measures. For example, Rugg and Cantril (1944) presented data from studies in which they manipulated the wording of opinion poll questions about US 'interventionism' during World War II to see how the changes affected respondents' answers. They found wide variation in support for intervention depending on how the question was worded, ranging from just 8 per cent answering 'Yes' to the question 'Should the US go into the war now and send an army to Europe?', to 76 per cent saying 'Yes' when the question was worded as: 'Some people say that if the US goes on helping England, Germany may start a war against our country. Do you think we should continue to help England, even if we run this risk?' Kalton and his colleagues (1978) reported similar fluctuations in response depending on whether one or both sides of an issue were presented in a question. Furthermore, in both studies, not only was the comparability of marginal distributions affected across different forms of the same question, but so too were the correlations between related variables. For this reason, many scholars urge caution when drawing conclusions about the state of public opinion based on single-item attitude measures. Other pitfalls to avoid in the wording of attitude measures include unbalanced question formats (Schaeffer et al., 2005), questions containing persuasive arguments (Bishop, Oldendick and Tuchfarber, 1982) and ambiguities in wording, such as so-called 'double-barreled' statements, where it may be unclear which part of the question the respondent should answer (see Oppenheim, 1992: 128) for a list of similar 'rules' for writing attitude measures).

Deciding on the best wording represents just one half of the challenge involved in constructing effective attitude measures. Having written an appropriate question, researchers must decide how respondents should report their answer. Extensive research into questions such as how many points to include on a response scale (see, for example, Jacoby and Matell, 1971; Lehmann and Hulbert, 1972; Masters, 1974; Cox, 1980; Alwin, 1997; Krosnick and Fabrigar, 1997) and how to label scale points (for example, Hakel, 1968; Chase, 1969; Bradburn and Miles, 1979) have revealed significant differences in reliability and validity resulting from the decisions researchers make. Social surveys still vary in terms of the types of response scales they use. For example, while the BSA, in common with other studies, includes many items with five-point, Likert-type response scales (fully labeled from 'Disagree strongly', 'Disagree', 'Neither agree nor disagree', 'Agree', and 'Agree strongly'), both the GSS and the American National Election Studies (ANES) still ask respondents to report liking and disliking of some objects (for example, different groups; electoral candidates) on so-called 'feeling thermometers'

(101-point scales). In contrast, experiments conducted in the context of the ESS have found that in a cross-national context, 11-point semantic differential scales produce higher reliability and validity coefficients than other response formats (for example, Saris, van der Veld and Gallhofer, 2004). Meanwhile, a consensus based on numerous empirical studies has emerged regarding best practice in national[1] studies, agreeing that the optimal length for a response scale is between five- and seven-point depending on whether the construct being rated is unipolar or bipolar (Krosnick and Fabrigar, forthcoming). For bipolar constructs like attitudes, seven-point scales have been found to produce maximal reliability and validity and to be easier to administer (Krosnick and Fabrigar, 1997), particularly where a 'branching' method is used (Malhotra, Krosnick and Thomas, 2009), in which respondents are first asked to indicate the direction they lean in (negative, neutral or positive) and then asked in a follow-up question to indicate the intensity of their leaning (strongly, moderately or slightly negative or positive). Furthermore, providing verbal labels for all scale points 'that have relatively precise meanings for respondents that reflect equal intervals along the continuum of interest' has been shown to enhance both reliability and validity (Krosnick and Fabrigar, 1997: 152).

In the psychometric literature, it has long been recognized that the form of a question can produce particular patterns of answers irrespective of question content, referred to as 'response sets' (Cronbach, 1946). A classic example of a response set associated with questions offering a simple choice between a positive and negative response (such as yes/no, true/false, agree/disagree) is 'acquiescence': the tendency to over-prefer the positive option (see Cronbach, 1946 for other examples). Response sets have been distinguished in the literature from 'response styles' (Rorer, 1965; Fabrigar and Krosnick, 1995), patterns of responding attributed both to respondent personality traits and motivation to respond in biased ways (for example, deliberately guessing in a multiple choice task). As we shall see in the next section, however, this distinction is unhelpful given the complex mix of influences that can lead to the various 'response effects', or errors, often observed in attitude data.

Factors Affecting the Response Process

So far in this chapter I have described two principal sources of variability in attitude measurements: (1) the cognitive processes by which respondents generate their evaluations of objects; and (2) the design of attitude measures themselves. In this section, I consider a third source of error in attitude measurements: factors that affect the response behaviour of survey respondents. Completing each of the processes described in Tourangeau and his colleagues' (2000) model of the response process might be thought of as the 'optimal' way of constructing an attitude report in response to a survey question (Krosnick, 1991). Even with

---

1	These conclusions are based on research findings from surveys conducted in the US.

measures developed using best practice principles of questionnaire design, there are no guarantees that the measurements that researchers obtain will be accurate descriptions of the respondents' underlying attitudes. For the response process to be executed in an optimal way, two conditions must be met. First, respondents need to be both willing and able to exert the necessary effort to generate an attitude report that describes their underlying evaluation in a meaningful way and that can be mapped onto the available response alternatives. Second, respondents must be both willing and able to report their attitudes to researchers truthfully. Meeting these two conditions depends not only on the design of the questions themselves, but also on characteristics of the respondents and characteristics of the measurement setting. When these conditions are not met, response effects can result, lowering the overall quality of the measurements obtained. In this section, I consider the types of response effects that can arise as a result of different factors influencing how respondents execute the survey response process.

Factors Affecting Processing Effort

The process of generating an answer to an attitude measure can place considerable cognitive demands on survey respondents. Even if the respondents' attitudes on a particular topic are relatively crystallized, simply comprehending the task of the measurement exercise, retrieving the relevant evaluation from memory and mapping it onto the most appropriate response category can present a challenge in itself. However, the demands of the exercise increase when the focus of the question is on an attitude object relatively unfamiliar to respondents, because they must first decide what their attitude is, and then decide how (and whether) to report it. To execute each of these processes systematically, respondents need to be both willing and able to devote the time and effort needed to do so. When motivation and ability are low, some respondents may be tempted to take shortcuts in the necessary processing to arrive at an, if not optimal, then adequate response to a question in a shorter amount of time. This shortcutting process has been called 'questionnaire satisficing' (Krosnick, 1991). Satisficing either takes the form of completing each stage of the response process less thoroughly than needed (called 'weak satisficing') or skipping stages altogether (called 'strong satisficing'). Krosnick (1991) classifies different kinds of response effects often observed in attitude measurements according to this typology. Examples of weak satisficing include acquiescence (for example, Knowles and Condon, 1999), in which respondents agree with assertions made by the interviewer (because this requires less cognitive effort than generating reasons to disagree with the statement) and response order effects (Krosnick and Alwin, 1987), in which respondents select the most accessible satisfactory response alternative from the list provided. Examples of strong satisficing include over-endorsement of the 'Don't Know' option, and 'non-differentiation', in which respondents rate a battery of attitude statements using the same point on the response scale. In both cases, answers are selected based on little or no thought.

The likelihood that a respondent will adopt a satisficing response strategy is determined by variables influencing motivation and ability to process and the difficulty of the response task. Motivation and ability to expend the effort to process both vary by individual. Some people enjoy thinking and problem-solving more than others (Cacioppo and Petty, 1982), and natural cognitive abilities, level of education and knowledge of the survey topic are all important determinants of the ability to systematically complete the different stages of the response process. Consistent with this, satisficing effects have been found to be more common among respondents with low levels of education (for example, Narayan and Krosnick, 1996). The previous section considered how the difficulty of the response task varies with the design of the attitude measure and this, in turn, can influence the cognitive demands of generating an answer. For example, ambiguous question wording, sub-optimal scale length, or vaguely labeled response alternatives can all affect the ease with which respondents comprehend what the question is asking and map their attitude judgment onto available response alternatives. However, other factors present in the measurement setting can also influence the difficulty of the response task, including the mode of data collection. Survey interviews conducted by telephone appear to place considerably greater burden on the respondent's processing capacity because they tend to be conducted at a faster pace, and the respondent must attempt to hold both the question and available response alternatives in working memory whilst thinking about their answer. By contrast, in face-to-face interviews and self-completion surveys, respondents can make use of visual cues to aid comprehension and take their time over formulating a response. Consistent with this, response effects associated with satisficing have been shown to be more common in telephone data (Holbrook, Green and Krosnick, 2003).

Factors Affecting Willingness to Report Attitudes Truthfully

One of the most difficult challenges associated with asking people directly to report their attitudes is that they may not always be willing to reveal their true preferences to the researcher. In these situations, respondents are assumed to adapt their answer to the attitude measure to avoid embarrassment (Tourangeau and Smith, 1998), to portray themselves in an otherwise more favourable light, or to give answers that they think the researcher will want to hear (Sudman and Bradburn, 1974; Bradburn et al., 1978). This tendency is referred to as 'social desirability bias' and it can manifest itself in different ways, such as the over-reporting of socially desirable behaviours and the under-reporting of socially undesirable ones. The problem is especially pernicious in the context of attitude measurement, however, because unlike with behavioural measures, which can sometimes be cross-validated against external records, it is particularly difficult to determine to what extent measures of attitudes are affected by the bias. Nevertheless, many different kinds of studies have documented the presence of the bias in attitudinal reports, including 'randomized response' studies, in which interviewers are unaware which of the randomly assigned questions respondents are answering (Warner, 1965), and 'bogus pipeline' studies, where respondents are led to believe that the researcher can discover their true response using a device akin to a lie detector (see Roese and Jamieson, 1993 for a review). Perhaps the most researched and best understood example of how social desirability bias affects attitude measurement and, consequently, the conclusions that researchers draw from surveys about the nature of social attitudes, comes from research into white racial attitudes (for example, Schuman and Converse, 1971; Krysan, 1998). Both the GSS and the ANES have been measuring white attitudes towards different racial groups in the US for several decades. Using data from these surveys, analysts have concluded that white respondents' evaluations of African Americans have become increasingly tolerant over time. However, data from alternative measures of racial prejudice do not support this conclusion, which suggests that rather than the attitudes themselves, it is the social norms surrounding the public expression of those attitudes that have changed during this period. Whereas white respondents participating in these surveys 30 years ago seemed comfortable endorsing negative stereotypes about blacks, it has become increasingly unacceptable for them to do so in more recent years.

Researchers understand well the factors that influence the likelihood of respondents answering attitude measures truthfully, and methods of reducing the risk of social desirability bias are routinely used in social surveys. As with questionnaire satisficing, the propensity to modify attitude reports in line with social desirability concerns appears to be influenced by a mix of respondent characteristics, the design of survey questions, and characteristics of the reporting situation. Some personalities high in 'need for social approval' may be more inclined towards socially desirable responding than others and, indeed, scales have often been included in personality and clinical inventories to control for the bias (Crowne and Marlowe, 1960). Insofar as attitude topics vary by how sensitive they are, different attitude measures will vary in the extent to which they elicit social desirability bias, though there is some disagreement about whether this is a function of the social norms governing the acceptability of certain types of attitudes, or shared values among different groups about what is desirable (DeMaio, 1984). By far the most important factor influencing respondent willingness to report attitudes truthfully is the extent to which the data collection method provides adequate privacy. The more anonymous the respondent perceives their answers to be, the more likely they are to answer honestly (Tourangeau, Rips and Rasinski, 2000). This has been demonstrated in several studies comparing responses given by respondents assigned to different modes of data collection, where modes providing greater anonymity obtained more accurate reports of sensitive behaviours (Weisberg, 2005). Thus, self-administered modes including paper questionnaires, web surveys and computer-assisted self-interviewing, either with an audio component (ACASI) or without (CASI), have been shown to be more effective at reducing social desirability bias than interviewer-administered modes (for example, Sudman and Bradburn, 1974; Tourangeau, Rips and Rasinski, 2000).

Enhancing the privacy of the reporting situation can help to minimize errors associated with direct attitude measures arising from respondents' social desirability concerns, but it may not eliminate it altogether (Tourangeau and Smith, 1998). To tackle the problem, scientists have developed a variety of alternative procedures that aim to measure attitudes indirectly, while respondents remain unaware of the true goal of the measurement exercise. Perhaps the most promising of these, and most amenable to being used in sample surveys, are methods that measure so-called 'implicit' attitudes (for example, Wittenbrink, Judd and Park, 1997). Implicit attitudes are the automatic evaluative responses people have to attitude objects, which they may not even be conscious of (Dovidio and Fazio, 1992). These methods involve presenting research participants with a stimulus and assessing the extent of attitude activation by measuring how long it takes participants to respond to the stimulus. One of the most widely tested examples of such a method is the Implicit Association Test (IAT) (Greenwald, McGhee and Schwartz, 1998), which is designed to test the relative strength of associations between pairs of objects (for example, Senator McCain and Senator Obama) and positive and negative evaluations (good, bad). Faster reaction times when pairing objects with evaluations are said to indicate stronger associations in memory, and hence the extent of attitude activation. Despite their increasing popularity, there has been some scepticism about the validity and reliability of such techniques (for example, Cunningham, Preacher and Banaji, 2001), not helped by the fact that until relatively recently they had only been tested on volunteer samples. However, thanks to advances in data collection methodology, it is now possible to incorporate implicit measures of attitudes in major sample surveys (for example, the 2008 ANES used both the IAT and the Affect Misattribution Procedure (Payne et al., 2005) to assess implicit racial attitudes and candidate liking during the 2008 presidential campaign), expanding the range of methods available to researchers seeking to minimize errors in attitude measurements caused by social desirability bias.

Summary

In this chapter I described the methods most commonly used to measure social attitudes. Because attitudes cannot be observed directly, survey researchers mostly rely on respondents' own descriptions of how they think and feel about different features of the world around them. The aim of measurement is to simplify the complexity of these thoughts and feelings and to describe the underlying attitudes precisely using rigorous methods (Fabrigar, Krosnick and MacDougall, 2005). Measurements of attitudes inevitably contain a certain amount of error affecting the extent to which they accurately capture the construct of interest and their replicability over time. To describe the distribution of attitudes in the population as accurately as possible, it is essential that researchers attempt to minimize the amount of error in their measurements. Several sources of error were described here, including errors arising from the cognitive processes involved in generating attitude judgments in response to survey questions; errors arising from the design of the questionnaire; and errors arising from factors influencing response behaviour. Distinguishing between these different sources of error in this way suggests a somewhat artificial distinction between related influences on respondents' answers. In reality, the quality of attitude measurements, and the conclusions that researchers draw from them about the nature of social attitudes, depend on a complex interaction between characteristics of the respondent, the questionnaire and the data collection context. A wealth of evidence about the impact of these combined influences has led to the development of best practice guidelines about how to enhance the accuracy of attitude measurements. The responsibility now lies with researchers involved in designing attitude measures for social surveys not only to follow these guidelines, but also to exploit opportunities to advance and refine them.

References

Albarracín, D., Johnson, B.T., Zanna, M.P. and Tarcan Kumkale, G. (2005), 'Attitudes: Introduction and Scope', in D. Albarracín, B.T. Johnson and M.P. Zanna (eds), *The Handbook of Attitudes* (Mahwah, NJ: Lawrence Erlbaum Associates), 3–19.

Allport, G.W. (1935), 'Attitudes', in C. Murchison (ed.), *Handbook of Social Psychology* (Worcester, MA: Clark University Press), 798–884.

Alwin, D.F. (1997), 'Feeling Thermometers Versus 7-point Scales: Which Are Better?' *Sociological Methods and Research* 24, 3: 318–40.

Bishop, G.F. (1987), 'Experiments with the Middle Response Alternative in Survey Questions', *Public Opinion Quarterly* 51, 2: 220–32.

Bishop, G.F., Oldendick, R.W. and Tuchfarber, A.J. (1982), 'Effects of Presenting One Versus Two Sides of an Issue in Survey Questions', *Public Opinion Quarterly* 46, 1: 69–85.

Bishop, G.F., Oldendick, R.W., Tuchfarber, A.J. and Bennett, S.E. (1980), 'Pseudo-opinions on Public Affairs', *Public Opinion Quarterly* 44, 2: 198–209.

Bohrnstedt, G.W. (1977), 'Reliability and Validity Assessment in Attitude Measurement', in G.F. Summers (ed.), *Attitude Measurement* (London: Kershaw Publishing Company), 80–99.

Bradburn, N.M. and Miles, C. (1979), 'Vague Quantifiers', *Public Opinion Quarterly* 43, 1: 92–101.

Bradburn, N.M., Sudman, S., Blair, E. and Stocking, C. (1978), 'Question Threat and Response Bias', *Public Opinion Quarterly* 42, 2,: 221–34.

Cacioppo, J.T. and Petty, R.E. (1982), 'The Need for Cognition', *Journal of Personality and Social Psychology* 42, 1: 116–31.

Chase, C.I. (1969), 'Often Is Where You Find It', *American Psychologist* 24: 1043.

Converse, P. (1964), 'The Nature of Belief Systems in Mass Publics', in D.E. Apter (ed.), *Ideology and Discontent* (New York: Free Press).

Converse, P. (1970), 'Attitudes and Non-attitudes: Continuation of a Dialogue', in E.R. Tufte (ed.), *The Quantitative Analysis of Social Problems* (Boston: Addison-Wesley).

Cox II, E.P. (1980), 'The Optimal Number of Response Alternatives for a Scale: A Review', *Journal of Marketing Research* XVII: 407–22.

Cronbach, L.J. (1946), 'Response Sets and Test Validity', *Educational and Psychological Measurement* 6: 475–94.

Crowne, D.P. and Marlowe, D. (1960), 'A New Scale of Social Desirability Independent of Psychopathology', *Journal of Consulting Psychology* 24: 349–54.

Cunningham, W.A., Preacher, K.J. and Banaji, M.R. (2001), 'Implicit Attitude Measures: Consistency, Stability and Convergent Validity', *Psychological Science* 12, 2: 163–70.

DeMaio, T.J. (1984), 'Social Desirability and Survey Measurement: A Review', in C.F. Turner and E. Martin (eds), *Surveying Subjective Phenomena*, Vol. 2 (New York: Russell Sage Foundation), 257–82.

Dovidio, J.F. and Fazio, R.H. (1992), 'New Technologies for the Direct and Indirect Assessment of Attitudes', in J. Tanur (ed.), *Questions About Questions: Inquiries into the Cognitive Bases of Surveys* (New York: Russell Sage Foundation), 204–37.

Eagly, A.H. and Chaiken, S. (1993), *The Psychology of Attitudes* (Orlando, FL: Harcourt Brace Jovanovich).

Edwards, A.L. and Kenney, K.C. (1946), 'A Comparison of the Thurstone and Likert Techniques of Attitude Scale Construction', *Journal of Applied Psychology* 30: 72–83.

Fabrigar, L.R. and Krosnick, J.A. (1995), 'Attitude Meaurement and Questionnaire Design', in A.S.R. Manstead and M. Hewstone (eds), *Blackwell Encyclopedia of Social Psychology* (Oxford: Blackwell Publishers).

Fabrigar, L.R., Krosnick, J.A. and MacDougall, B.L. (2005), 'Attitude Measurement: Techniques for Measuring the Unobservable', in T.C. Brock and M.C. Green (eds), *Persuasion: Psychological Insights and Perspectives* (2nd edition) (Thousand Oaks, CA: Sage), 17–40.

Fazio, R., Sanbonmatsu, D., Powell, M. and Kardes, F. (1986), 'On the Automatic Activation of Attitudes', *Journal of Personality and Social Psychology* 37: 229–38.

Fazio, R.H. (1990), 'Multiple Processes By Which Attitudes Guide Behaviour: The MODE Model as an Integrative Framework', in M. Zanna (ed.), *Advances in Experimental Social Psychology*, Vol. 23 ed. (San Diego: Academic Press), 75–109.

Fishbein, M. (1967), 'A Consideration of Beliefs, and Their Role in Attitude', in M. Fishbein (ed.), *Readings in Attitude Theory and Measurement* (New York: John Wiley & Sons), 257–66.

Fishbein, M. and Ajzen, I. (1975), *Belief, Attitude, Intention and Behaviour: An Introduction to Theory and Research* (Reading, MA: Addison-Wesley).

Greenwald, A.G., McGhee, D.E. and Schwartz, J.L.K. (1998), 'Measuring Individual Differences in Implicit Cognition: The Implicit Association Test', *Journal of Personality and Social Psychology* 74, 6: 1464–80.

Hakel, M.D. (1968), 'How Often is Often?' *American Psychologist* 23: 533–4.

Hess, E.H. (1965), 'Attitude and Pupil Size', *Scientific American* 212: 46–54.

Holbrook, A.L., Green, M.C. and Krosnick, J.A. (2003), 'Telephone vs. Face-to-face Interviewing of National Probability Samples with Long Questionnaires: Comparisons of Respondent Satisficing and Social Desirability Response Bias', *Public Opinion Quarterly* 67: 79–125.

Jacoby, J. and Matell, M.S. (1971), 'Three-point Likert Scales Are Good Enough', *Journal of Marketing Research* VIII: 495–500.

Kalton, G., Collins, M. and Brook, L. (1978), 'Experiments in Wording Opinion Questions', *Applied Statistics* 27, 2: 23–50.

Katz, D. and Stotland, E. (1959), 'A Preliminary Statement to a Theory of Attitude Structure and Change', in S. Koch (ed.), *Psychology: A Study of a Science* (New York: McGraw-Hill), 423–75.

Knowles, E.S. and Condon, C.A. (1999), 'Why People Say "Yes": A Dual-process Theory of Acquiescence', *Journal of Personality and Applied Psychology* 77, 2: 379–86.

Krosnick, J.A. (1991), 'Response Strategies for Coping with the Demands of Attitude Measures in Surveys', *Applied Cognitive Psychology* 5: 214–36.

Krosnick, J.A. and Alwin, D.F. (1987), 'An Evaluation of a Cognitive Theory of Response Order Effects in Survey Measurement', *Public Opinion Quarterly* 51: 201–19.

Krosnick, J.A. and Fabrigar, L.R. (1997), 'Designing Rating Scales for Effective Measurement in Surveys', in L. Lyberg, P. Biemer, M. Collins, E. de Leeuw, C. Dippo, N. Schwarz and D. Trewin (eds), *Survey Measurement and Process Quality* (New York: John Wiley), 141–64.

Krosnick, J.A. and Fabrigar, L.R. (Forthcoming), *The Handbook of Questionnaire Design* (New York: Oxford University Press).

Krosnick, J.A., Holbrook, A.L., Berent, M.K., Carson, R.T., Hanemann, W.M., Kopp, R.J., Mitchell, R.C., Presser, S., Ruud, P.A., Smith, V.K., Moody, W.R., Green, M.C. and Conaway, M. (2002), 'The Impact of "No Opinion" Response Options on Data Quality: Non-attitude Reduction or an Invitation to Satisfice? *Public Opinion Quarterly* 66: 371–403.

Krosnick, J.A., Judd, C.M. and Wittenbrink, B. (2005), 'The Measurement of Attitudes', in D. Albarracín, B.T. Johnson and M.P. Zanna (eds), *The Handbook of Attitudes* (Mahwah, NJ: Lawrence Erlbaum Associates), 21–78.

Krosnick, J.A. and Petty, R.E. (1995), 'Attitude Strength: An Overview', in R.E. Petty and J.A. Krosnick (eds), *Attitude Strength: Antecedents and Consequences* (Hillsdale, NJ: Lawrence Erlbaum Associates).

Krysan, M. (1998), 'Privacy and the Expression of White Racial Attitudes: A Comparison Across Three Contexts', *Public Opinion Quarterly* 62, 4: 506–44.

Lapiere, R.T. (1934), 'Attitudes vs. Actions', *Social Forces* 13: 230–37.

Lazarsfeld, P.F. (1944), 'The Controversy Over Detailed Interviews – An Offer for Negotiation', *Public Opinion Quarterly* 8: 38–60.

Lehmann, D.R. and Hulbert, J. (1972), 'Are Three-point Scales Always Good Enough?' *Journal of Marketing Research* IX: 444–6.

Likert, R. (1932), 'A Technique for the Measurement of Attitudes', *Archives of Psychology* 140: 1–55.

Maio, G.R. and Olson, J.M. (2000), *Why We Evaluate: Functions of Attitudes* (Mahwah, NJ: Lawrence Erlbaum Associates).

Malhotra, N., Krosnick, J.A. and Thomas, R.K. (2009), 'Optimal Design of Branching Questions to Measure Bipolar Constructs', *Public Opinion Quarterly* 73: 303–24.

Masters, J.R. (1974), 'The Relationship Between Number of Response Categories and Reliability in Likert-type Questionnaires', *Journal of Educational Measurement* 11, 1: 49–53.

Milgram, S., Mann, L. and Harter, S. (1965), 'The Lost-letter Technique: A Tool for Social Research', *Public Opinion Quarterly* 29, 3: 437–8.

Mueller, D.J. (1977), 'Physiological Techniques of Attitude Measurement', in G.F. Summers (ed.), *Attitude Measurement* (London: Kershaw), 534–52.

Narayan, S. and Krosnick, J. (1996), 'Education Moderates Some Response Effects in Attitude Measurement', *Public Opinion Quarterly* 60: 58–88.

Oppenheim, A.N. (1992), *Questionnaire Design, Interviewing and Attitude Measurement* (2nd edition) (London: Continuum International Publishing).

Osgood, C.E., Suci, G.J. and Tannenbaum, P.H. (1957), *The Measurement of Meaning* (Urbana, IL: University of Illinois Press).

Payne, B.K., Cheng, C.M., Govorun, O. and Stewart, B.D. (2005), 'An Inkblot for Attitudes: Affect Misattribution as Implicit Measurement', *Journal of Personality and Social Psychology* 89, 3: 277–93.

Petty, R.E. and Cacioppo, J.T. (1986), *Communication and Persuasion: Central and Peripheral Routes to Attitude Change* (New York: Springer-Verlag).

Petty, R.E. and Krosnick, J.A. (1995), *Attitude Strength: Antecedents and Consequences* (Mahwah, NJ: Lawrence Erlbaum Associates).

Rankin, R.E. and Campbell, D.T. (1955), 'Galvanic Skin Response to Negro and White Experimenters', *Journal of Abnormal and Social Psychology* 51: 30–33.

Roese, N.J. and Jamieson, D.W. (1993), 'Twenty Years of Bogus Pipeline Research: A Critical Review and Meta-analysis', *Psychological Bulletin* 114, 2: 363–75.

Rorer, L.G. (1965), 'The Great Response-style Myth', *Psychological Bulletin* 63, 3: 129–56.

Rugg, D. and Cantril, H. (1944), 'The Wording of Questions', in H. Cantril (ed.), *Gauging Public Opinion* (Princeton, NJ: Princeton University Press).

Saris, W.E., van der Veld, W. and Gallhofer, I. (2004), 'Development and Improvement of Questionnaires Using Predictions of Reliability and Validity', in S. Presser, J.M. Rothgeb, M.P. Couper, J.T. Lessler, E. Martin, J. Martin and E. Singer (eds), *Methods for Testing and Evaluating Survey Questionnaires* (Hoboken, NJ: Wiley-Interscience), 275–99.

Schaeffer, E.M., Krosnick, J.A., Langer, G.E. and Merkle, D.M. (2005), 'Comparing the Quality of Data Obtained by Minimally Balanced and Fully Balanced Attitude Questions', *Public Opinion Quarterly* 69: 417–28.

Schuman, H. and Converse, J.M. (1971), 'The Effects of Black and White Interviewers on Black Responses in 1968', *Public Opinion Quarterly* 35, 1: 44–68.

Schuman, H. and Presser, S. (1980), 'Public Opinion and Public Ignorance: The Fine Line Between Attitudes and Nonattitudes', *American Journal of Sociology* 44, 2: 198–209.

Schuman, H. and Presser, S. (1981), *Questions and Answers in Attitude Surveys: Experiments on Question Form, Wording and Context* (New York: Academic Press).

Smith, T.W. (1985), 'Nonattitudes: A Review and Evaluation', in C.F. Turner and E. Martin (eds), *Surveying Subjective Phenomena* (New York: Russell Sage).

Sudman, S. and Bradburn, N.M. (1974), *Response Effects in Surveys: A Review and Synthesis* (Chicago: Aldine Publishing).

Thurstone, L.L. (1928), 'Attitudes Can Be Measured', *The Amercian Journal of Sociology* XXXIII, 4: 529–54.

Tourangeau, R. and Galesic, M. (2008), 'Conceptions of Attitudes and Opinions', in W. Donsbach and M.W. Traugott (eds), *The Sage Handbook of Public Opinion Research* (London: Sage Publications).

Tourangeau, R. and Rasinski, K.A. (1988), 'Cognitive Processes Underlying Context Effects in Attitude Measurement', *Psychological Bulletin* 103, 3: 299–314.

Tourangeau, R., Rips, L.J. and Rasinski, K.A. (2000), *The Psychology of Survey Response* (Cambridge: Cambridge University Press).

Tourangeau, R. and Smith, T.W. (1998), 'Collecting Sensitive Information with Different Modes of Data Collection', in M.P. Couper, R.P. Baker, J. Bethlehem, C.Z.F. Clark, J. Martin, W.L. Nicholls II and J.M. O'Reilly (eds), *Computer-assisted Survey Information Collection* (New York: John Wiley & Sons, Inc).

Warner, S.L. (1965), 'Randomized Response: A Survey Technique for Eliminating Evasive Answer Bias', *Journal of the American Statistical Association* 60, 309: 63–9.

Weisberg, H.F. (2005), *The Total Survey Error Approach: A Guide to the New Science of Survey Research* (Chicago: University of Chicago Press).

Wilson, T.D. and Hodges, S. (1992), 'Attitudes as Temporary Constructions', in L. Martin and A. Tesser (eds), *The Construction of Social Judgments* (New York: Springer-Verlag), 37–66.

Wittenbrink, B., Judd, C.M. and Park, B. (1997), 'Evidence for Racial Prejudice at the Implicit Level and its Relationship with Questionnaire Measures', *Journal of Personality and Social Psychology* 74, 6: 1464–80.

Zaller, J. and Feldman, S. (1992', 'A Simple Theory of the Survey Response: Answering Questions Versus Revealing Preferences', *American Journal of Political Science* 36, 3: 579–616.

Chapter 12

Challenges for Social Measurement

Martin Bulmer

Measurement

Measurement was defined in Chapter 1. One of the most influential twentieth-century statements of the classical approach to measurement was that of psycho-physicist S.S. Stevens, who proposed four scales or degrees of measurement: nominal, ordinal, interval and ratio measurement (1946, 1975). Nominal and ordinal measurement are non-metric; interval and ratio measurement are metric. These theoretical standards are translated in measurement standards in the physical world through organizations such as the United States National Bureau of Standards (NBS). The NBS provides state, county and local officials with technical and operational guides that set out measurement specifications, standard tolerances and model laws designed to support the physical measurement system (Hunter, 1980: 869). The primary standards are those of the International System of Units (SI units) and are seven: length (meter, m), mass (kilogram, kg); time (second, s); electric current (ampere, A); temperature (kelvin, k); luminous intensity (candela, cd); and amount of substance (mole, mol) (Zebrowski, 1979).

This scientific paradigm of physical measurement provides a model that the social sciences, or some social scientists, seek to emulate. The quotation from scientist Lord Kelvin carved on Chicago's Social Science Research Building reflects that aspiration: 'When you cannot measure * your knowledge is * meager* and * unsatisfactory.' The poet e.e. cummings's scepticism reflects doubts as to whether the aspiration is worthwhile in the first place: 'who cares if some one-eyed son of a bitch / invents an instrument to measure spring with'. The place of measurement in social science research is a contentious issue; this tension runs through social science disciplines such as sociology and political science. It is reflected in the ambivalence with which many social scientists look upon research methods such as social survey research. The aim of this final chapter is to consider some of the hindrances to improved measurement of the social, and ways of circumventing these hindrances. There has been a notable failure to agree on standards for social measurement (as distinct from psychological or economic measurement), whether in terms of social indicators and conceptual unification, or at the practical level of operationalizing variables. A certain amount of this ambivalence is reflected in this book.

What Is Involved in Measurement?

Social scientists take up differing positions in relation to the value of what is involved in social measurement. Some part of this may be due to resistance to, or ambivalence about, the place of numbers in the realm of knowledge, coupled with inability to appreciate the role that number may play (cf. Paulos, 1988). But the issue cannot be reduced, in T.D. Weldon's phrase, to making judgments about matters 'like a taste for ice cream'. The merits of measurement in social science, and the obstacles to measurement, need to be set out and debated. In this way, some of the passions which the subject inflames may be restrained and cooled.

Relatively few of those who have approached thoughtfully the issue of social measurement subscribe to classical measurement theory as outlined at the beginning of this chapter. A great deal of social measurement is non-metric, and uses the assignment of numbers to qualities of an object of study as a way to label characteristics or make statements of more or less. A common definition of the properties of social measurement is the following:

> Whenever we classify a number of units we shall talk of measurement. This is a rather broad use of the term, but it leads to no difficulty; if we classify a set of units by a quantitative variate (variable) we have the special case of conventional measurement (Lazarsfeld, 1970: 61).

In terms of Stevens's four levels of measurement (1946), much social measurement is of a nominal or ordinal kind, lacking the properties of interval and ratio measurement. But this creates difficulties. How one characterizes the state of the health of a population, or the level of crime in a particular area, is by no means a straightforward matter, given the wide variety of measures of each that are available.

Operationism and Measurement by Fiat

Recognition of the complexity and provisional character of much social measurement comes from a variety of positions that in other respects may not share much in common. For a time, definitional operationism was in vogue, particularly as put forward by the physicist Bridgman (1927). Donald Campbell, however, criticized this as failing to do justice to the complexity of social constructs, and argued instead for a multiple operationism:

> One of the great weaknesses in definitional operationism as a description of best scientific practice was that it allowed no formal way of expressing the scientist's preponent awareness of the imperfection of his measuring instruments and his prototypic activity for improving them … In the social sciences, a great many of the laws which impinge upon any given measurement situation are as yet

undiscovered. In addition, we use a given instrument (such as the door-to-door interview, or peer-ratings, or newspaper content analysis, or multiple-item attitude tests) to measure a large number of theoretically independent variables. In this situation, where two measures are drawn from the same instrument, it is probable that part of their observed relationship is a function of the shared vehicle, of the shared irrelevancies. Co-symptoms of interview rapport, acquiescence, social desirability response sets, halo-effects in ratings, censorship and attention biases in content analysis, correlates of data quality in ethnographies, are examples (Campbell, 1988: 33–4).

A.V. Cicourel, in a generally critical analysis of social measurement, drew attention to the problems created by what he termed 'measurement by fiat', which failed to do justice to the complexity and theoretical importance of sociological concepts.

Measurement by fiat is not a substitute for examining and re-examining the structure of our theories so that our observations, descriptions and measures of the properties of social objects and events have a literal correspondence with what we believe to be the structure of social reality (1964: 33).

Otis Dudley Duncan, in a series of historical and critical notes on social measurement, is quite clear about the limitations of much social measurement:

With the possible and, in any event, limited exception of economics, we have in social science no system of measurements that can be coherently described in terms of a small number of dimensions. Like physical scientists, we have thousands of 'instruments,' but these instruments purport to yield measurements of thousands of variables. That is, we have no system of units (much less standards for them) that, at least in principle, relates all of the variables to a common set of logically primitive qualities. There are no counterparts of mass, length and time in social science … To the physical dimensions, economics adds money … The fact that social science (beyond economics) does not have such a system of measurements is, perhaps, another way of saying that theory in our field is fragmentary and undeveloped, and that our knowledge is largely correlational rather than theoretical (1984: 162).

Social Measurement *vis-à-vis* Other Types of Measurement

One of the endemic difficulties of social measurement is the lack of agreed standards against which to measure social phenomena. Social measurement presents problems that are not encountered in quite the same form in relation to physical, biological or economic measurement. In the social world, we lack many of the precise measuring instruments of the physical, biological or economic worlds. Although this difference is perhaps one of degree rather than kind, the absence of formal agreed tools of measurement such as length, weight, distance or monetary value is a serious problem for many areas of social life.

This is evident in the history of social research. Paul Lazarsfeld traced the origins of the quantification of the social in the tradition of political arithmetic, and through the rise of Quételet and Le Play, and the French followers of these researchers. 'Some time at the end of the nineteenth century,' he observed, 'quantification in sociology takes on its modern function: to translate ideas into empirical operations and to look for regular relations between variables so created' (Lazarsfeld, 1961: 202–3). The early practitioners of quantitative social research at the University of Chicago between the wars, to take another example, were drawn from political science and psychology, as well as from sociology. Sociologists busied themselves assembling census tract data and producing Local Community Fact Books. Political scientists sought to survey phenomena such as non-voting by using primitive survey methods. Psychologist L.L. Thurstone devoted several years to attitude measurement, publishing articles with titles such as 'Attitudes Can Be Measured' (1928). Jean Converse traced the subsequent early history of attitude measurement and its close association with social survey research and polling (1987: 54–86).

These developments were part of a move in several social science disciplines to make those disciplines more scientific. In economics, political science and sociology, scholars such as Wesley C. Mitchell, Charles E. Merriam and William Fielding Oburn sought greater precision through social measurement, and encouraged their students and younger colleagues to undertake more quantitative studies. Dorothy Ross (1991: 390–470) terms this development 'scientism', and argues that it represented in part a turn away from politics toward the understanding and certainty that rigorous knowledge provided. Objectivity, too, was more certain if evidence and propositions were more rigorously grounded (cf Bannister, 1987; Porter, 1995).

Lack of Measuring Instruments in Social and Political Surveys

Anthony Heath and Jean Martin (1997) provide some thoughtful observations on the matter in their paper, 'Why Are There So Few Formal Measuring Instruments in Social and Political Research?' They contrast psychometric measurement with much social measurement, point out that much social measurement relies upon single items, while there are strong theoretical arguments for preferring a multi-item measure. One issue is theoretical; sociology and political science do not have large numbers of formal concepts embedded in abstract theories. This is the issue which Giovanni Sartori attempted to address in political science, with mixed results (cf Sartori, 1984; Collier and Gerring, 2009).

Sociology and political science rely to a considerable extent on the secondary analysis of large-scale representative social surveys carried out by others (cf Bulmer, Sturgis and Allum, 2009), so as a result most social researchers cannot directly influence the content of these surveys and the measures used in them. A possible exception to this generalization in the UK is the work during the last decade upon the measurement of social class. Unlike the disciplines of psychology or education, moreover, they are less focused upon the individual and action to assist the individual, more interested in relationships between variables, for example, in studying political behaviour or social mobility. Therefore less resources can be justified for devoting to any one instrument, and considerably less effort is made compared to psychometric measurement in developing multi-item scales.

Validity is an important consideration in social science research, and distinctions are usually drawn between face, criterion, predictive and construct validity. In practice, in the social and political sciences, there are few opportunities for rigorous validation, and 'face' validity is the most common type of validity examined. Heath and Martin observe that relatively weak criteria of validity are usually applied to social and political variables, and that there is a series of practical reasons why much political and social measurement fails to develop rigorous measures and cumulate (1997: 82–4).

Heath and Martin compare measurement in social and political research with its equivalent in education and psychology, particularly in relation to test measures in education and attitude scales in psychology, the latter also touched on by Roberts in Chapter 11. Unlike education and psychology, social research rarely involves taking decisions about individuals (for example, progress of a child through the educational system) but looks at broader relationships between variables; consequently fewer resources can be devoted to developing any one instrument. There are, moreover, few opportunities for rigorous validation of the kind employed with educational tests.

They also point to the limitations of social and political research on the conceptual and theoretical front. Sociology and political science are not disciplines with large numbers of abstract concepts embedded in formal theories. In the social sciences, only economics approximates to this state of affairs, and economists do not tend to use surveys as their primary type of data collection. Individual survey items are taken to be of interest in their own right. The problems are compounded by the gulf between theory and empirical observation, which means that there is not a tight relationship between theorists and those engaged in empirical research. Many books about concepts in sociology deal primarily with the theoretical analysis of the concept, with no reference to its operationalization and measurement. Conversely, practising survey researchers in organizations in the UK like the Office for National Statistics (ONS) or the National Centre for Social Research (Natcen) devise questions for surveys in ways that work, without necessarily having a grounded theoretical rationale. There are exceptions to this, discussed shortly, such as social class; but for many variables, a kind of pragmatic criterion of utility flourishes, which at times can verge on what Bridgman called 'operationism'.

Question 'Harmonizaton'

An interesting case in point of this kind of approach to social measurement is provided in recent years in the UK by a systematic effort to harmonize questions in major UK government social surveys, in order to foster comparability between different surveys (Roberts, 1987; Government Statistical Service, 1995). The UK government, through ONS, mounts a considerable number of large continuous surveys such as the Labour Force Survey, the Expenditure and Food Survey, the General Household Survey, and so on. More recently, ONS has attempted to run the Integrated Household Survey (see URL: <http://www.esds.ac.uk/Government/cps/>). This is a very ambitious plan to bring together five continuous surveys with a sample size of 270,000, which is enormous for a sample survey. The plan is to have a core of integrated questions which will be the same for each of the five components of this survey.

The interest here is the rationale of the underlying harmonization of the questions common to each component. The ONS harmonization documents emphasize that the design of the questions is based on technical expertise in the conduct of social surveys, without any presumption that the variables being characterized are defined in theoretical terms. Indeed, many of the variables are justified purely in pragmatic terms, on the basis of common sense or common identification, and the definitions offered, to the extent that they are, are what Bridgman termed 'operational definitions': the variables are defined in terms of the actual wording employed in their use. This is no doubt how professional survey researchers in government operate, and historically there are distinguished examples of how official categorizations can be developed on the basis of pragmatic operational procedures rather than any element of a priori theorizing. The Registrar General's Social Class classification is a case in point. But such an approach is not theoretically robust, and needs to be underpinned by more theory.

Heath and Martin also suggest that there are trade-offs of different kinds between testing of items and choice and length of scales. For example, Heath, Evans and Martin (1994) have explored different types of scale used to explore core beliefs and values in political surveys. Political scientists tend to use short scales such as the postmaterialism and party identification measures, despite much criticism. Inglehart's longer index can be shown to be much superior in terms of test–retest reliability and construct validity than the shorter scales favoured for pragmatic reasons.

> We would suggest that the decisions which social scientists routinely make about these trade-offs should be scrutinized. It may well be that too much weight is conventionally given to easily quantifiable criteria such as Cronbach's alpha and to procedures that are internal to the survey (eg correlations between survey variables to establish construct validity) (Heath and Martin, 1997: 84).

Integrating Conceptualization and Measurement

There remains the practical problem in the social domain of achieving the degree of theoretical integration between concepts and their measurement in empirical data that has been characteristic for economics. In that discipline:

> [w]herever an economic argument is being made, or an inference is derived from comparing statistics of different economic activities, the matter of the accuracy of these data arises. This may involve questions of comparability on grounds of definitions and concepts used. It may concern numerical operations of various kinds ... A study of the entire complex of the accuracy of existing statistics or observation is not only helpful but indispensable in designing programs for the collection of new improved data ... In many offices in which statistics are being gathered, special efforts are being made to improve the quality of the data; nevertheless, a systematic approach is frequently lacking (Morgenstern, 1963: 6).

If it has been frequently lacking in economics, how much more so is this true in other disciplines, such as sociology and social policy. The problems of achieving the degree of integration between conceptualization and measurement characteristic of economics continue to defy solution in the other social sciences. Until these problems are seriously tackled – and there are some signs that they are being tackled piecemeal if not systemically – the prospects for theoretically informed harmonization are slight. Previous discussions of these issues have confirmed the challenge which exists (for example, Bulmer and Burgess, 1986) and the task of achieving a greater degree of harmony in social measurement remains.

The Italian-American political scientist Giovanni Sartori devoted great efforts, particularly through the Committee on Conceptual and Terminological Analysis (COCTA) which he and Fred W Riggs set up within the International Political Science Association in 1970, to advance the theoretical standardization of concepts. Later, the group was joined by members from the International Sociological Association. The results of their work appeared in Sartori (1984). There is a tinge of imperialism to these kinds of efforts. Sociologists and political scientists are less embedded in tight webs of theory than economists, and less inclined to unite over a single approach to measurement of particular concepts. For the organization of sociologists and political scientists, a description like herding cats comes to mind. The point is that attempts to achieve conceptual unification are extremely problematical, and not likely to achieve fruition via either harmonization or unification.

Sociology and Economics

Resolving the definitional and conceptual problems is not enough. The social researcher has to operationalize the concept or classification scheme being used, and embody it in actual research practice. From the point of view of the history of economic and social measurement, it would be instructive to contrast the different courses of economic and social measurement in central government since 1940. Government is important in this context because of the massive resources that it commands, and the lead role that it takes in basic social statistical data collection through the census and large continuous surveys, such as the Current Population Survey in the United States and the Labour Force Survey in the United Kingdom. One of the arguments of this chapter is that the two paths have been divergent, and that it has proved much more difficult to integrate theoretical ideas with practical measurement in the social as compared to the economic spheres.

One explanation of this difference may be sought in the respective roles of expertise in the two areas. The expertise of the economist is both theoretical and empirical, seeking to offer conceptual organization and theoretical propositions, together with the presentation of empirical evidence. That of the social researcher is often purely operational in social survey terms, without embedding the instrument in any theoretical frame. There are also a few examples of the extension of social measurement with at least a latent theoretical idea underpinning it, even though this is not clearly stated.

The Example of Social Class and Socio-economic Classification

The most interesting example in the UK is the Registrar General's Social Class classification, evolved for the analysis of fertility differentials in the 1911 Census out of the occupational classification that the Registrar General's office used for the analysis of mortality differentials in the latter part of the nineteenth century. Social class measurement is discussed by Eric Harrison in Chapter 6. Though imbued with sociological significance, there are good arguments for the view that the official classification produced under the auspices of the Registrar General, at least until World War II, developed independently from any theoretical input from social scientists and was essentially a pragmatic stratification of occupations intended to reflect the grouping of occupations into social strata as officials of the General Register Office (GRO) perceived them (cf. Leete and Fox, 1977; Szreter, 1984 and 1996).

The question then arises of how to validate the classification derived in this way on the pragmatic grounds that it works or appears to work. Usually the route is through cross-checking the results of analyses using this classification with that derived from other sources using alternative classifications. This strategy was employed in the review by the Royal Statistical Society of the measurement of the extent and incidence of unemployment (Royal Statistical Society, 1995). The report (by four leading figures in UK statistics) undertook a careful comparison of the results of the 'Claimant Count' derived from administrative records (and which had been subject to a large number of changes in the previous 15 years due to adjustments in the rules of inclusion and exclusion), and figures derived from the Labour Force Survey (LFS), which provided estimates of the numbers and proportions in the labor force who are unemployed. The report was generally welcomed as an excellent exemplary study of a difficult issue of social statistical measurement, but what its consequences are in practice remain to be seen. For the time being, the Claimant Count remains the headline figure that is released to the press to reflect changes in unemployment levels from month to month. In this case, the harmonization issue lies in the relationship between data from an administrative source and data from a survey source that has been developed as an alternative, and one that many think provides superior data to the administrative source.

The issue is perhaps different from that faced in much social statistical measurement in that the measurement of unemployment has very high political salience, which has contributed both to political interference in the measurement standards used for the Claimant Count, and public concern about what has been produced as a result, leading in turn to the high-level Royal Statistical Society (RSS) review. Much social measurement has, of course, a small 'p' political aspect, but even in contested areas such as the measurement of poverty, it is usually secondary to conceptual, technical and operational issues about the best way to proceed.

How to Promote Better Social Measurement

As this chapter, and the collection to which it provides a coda, comes to an end, the question arises of how any progress can be made at improving social and socio-economic measurement. Two design strategies commend themselves as ways of trying to gain some leverage on more precise social measurement.

One is greater use of replication. This is frequently recommended as a way in which social science can progress, by confirming the results achieved by earlier scholars by repeating the measures which they have used. It is often observed that such exercises do not command very high scholarly prestige, but there is no doubt that they contribute to cumulation in social inquiry. King (1995) has put forward a sustained argument in favour of the practice, and has suggested ways in which it could be made more attractive to scholars at various levels of seniority.

A second strategic approach may be to put more emphasis on longitudinal or panel designs, through which the quality of measurement may be improved, and the quality of causal inference strengthened.

> The accelerated pace at which panel studies are emerging attests to the prevailing belief that panel data are amply suited to the analytical problems that surround the kinds of observational (i.e. non-randomized) data that are common in social research. The fundamental structure of panel data provides the analytical leverage for rigorously achieving the central aim of quantitative research: the estimation of causal effects. ... The problem of causal inference is fundamentally one of

unobservables, and unobservables are at the heart of the contribution of panel data to solving problems of casual inference (Halaby, 2004).

Heath and Martin champion the value of 'greater diversity and competition between measures and research strategies so that the consequences of different trade-offs become apparent. Vigorous competition rather than settled orthodoxy is more likely to promote scientific development' (Heath and Martin, 1997: 84). We agree. Fostering such competition across the UK survey world, divided as it is between those based in universities and those engaged in professional social research in survey agencies, is not easy and will require ingenuity to overcome. This volume shows that the gap between different types of practitioner and different sectors can be bridged, and the struggle will continue, recognizing the important role which social surveys play in many aspects of contemporary British society.

References

Alonso, W. and Starr, P. (eds) (1987), *The Politics of Numbers* (New York: Russell Sage Foundation) [For the National Committee for Research on the 1980 Census].

Bannister, R. (1987), *Sociology and Scientism: The American Quest for Objectivity, 1880–1949* (Chapel Hill, NC: University of North Carolina Press).

Bridgman, P.W. (1927), *The Logic of Modern Physics* (New York: Macmillan).

Bulmer, M. and Burgess, R.G. (1986), 'Do Concepts, Variables and Indicators Interrelate?' in Burgess (ed.), 246–55.

Bulmer, M., Sturgis, P. and Allum, N. (eds) (2009), *Secondary Analysis of Survey Data*, Sage Benchmarks in Social Research Methods, four volumes (London: Sage Publications).

Burgess, R.G. (ed.) (1986), *Key Variables in Social Investigation* (London: Routledge).

Campbell, D.T. (1988), 'Definitional Versus Multiple Operationism', in Donald T Campbell, *Methodology and Epistemology for the Social Sciences: Selected Papers*, E.S. Overman (ed.) (Chicago: University of Chicago Press), 31–6.

Cicourel, A.V. (1964), *Method and Measurement in Sociology* (Glencoe, IL: The Free Press).

Collier, D. and Gerring, J. (eds) (2009), *Concept and Method in Social Science: The Tradition of Giovanni Sartori* (London: Routledge).

Converse, J.M. (1987), *Survey Research in the United States: Roots and Emergence, 1890–1960* (Berkeley: University of California Press).

Duncan, O.D. (1984), *Notes On Social Measurement: Historical and Critical* (New York: Russell Sage Foundation).

Gittus, E. (ed.) (1972), *Key Variables in Social Research*, Vol. 1: Religion, Housing, Locality (London: Heinemann Educational Books).

Government Statistical Service (1995), *Harmonised Questions for Government Social Surveys* (London: HMSO).

Halaby, C.N. (2004), 'Panel Models in Sociological Research: Theory into Practice', *Annual Review of Sociology* 30: 507–44; reprinted in Bulmer, Sturgis and Allum (eds) (2009), Vol. 4, 477–521.

Heath, A., Evans, G.A. and Martin, J. (1994), 'The Measurement of Core Beliefs and Values', *British Journal of Political Science* 24: 115–32.

Heath, A. and Martin, J. (1997), 'Why Are There So Few Formal Measuring Instruments in Social and Political Research?' in Lyberg et al. (eds), 71–86.

Hox, J.J. (1997), 'From Theoretical Concept to Survey Question', in Lyberg et al. (eds), 47–69.

Hunter, J.S. (1980), 'The National System of Scientific Measurement', *Science* 210 (21 November): 869–74.

King, G.S. (1995), 'Replication, Replication', *PS: Political Science and Politics* 28, 3: 444–52; reprinted in Bulmer, Sturgis and Allum (eds) (2009), Vol. 1, 309–28.

Kruskal, W. (1981), 'Statistics in Society: Problems Unsolved and Unformulated', *Journal of the American Statistical Association* 76: 505–15.

Lazarsfeld, P.F. (1961), 'Notes on the History of Quantification in Sociology – Trends, Sources, and Problems', in Woolf (ed.), 147–203.

Lazarsfeld, P.F. (1970), 'Sociology', in *Main Trends of Research in the Social and Human Sciences* (The Hague: Mouton/UNESCO), 61–5.

Leete, R. and Fox, J. (1977), 'Registrar General's Social Classes: Origins And Uses', *Population Trends* 8: 1–7.

Lieberson, S. (1985), *Making It Count: The Improvement of Social Research and Theory* (Berkeley: University of California Press).

Lyberg, L., Biemer, P., Collins, M., de Leeuw, E., Dippo, C., Schwarz, N. and Trewin, D. (eds) (1997), *Survey Measurement and Process Quality* (New York: Wiley).

Moore, P.G. (1995), 'Editorial', *Journal Of The Royal Statistical Society*, Series A, 158, 3: 359–431.

Morgenstern, O. (1963), *On the Accuracy of Economic Observations* (2nd edition) (Princeton: Princeton University Press).

Office for National Statistics (1996), *Ethnicity in the 1991 Census*, Vol. 1: 'Demographic Characteristics', D.C. Coleman and J. Salt (eds), Vol. 2: 'Profiles of the Main Ethnic Groups' C. Peach (ed.), Vol. 3: 'Social Geography' P. Ratcliff (ed.), Vol. 4: 'Education, Employment and Housing' V. Karn (ed.) (London: HMSO).

Paulos, J.A. (1988), *Innumeracy: Mathematical Illiteracy and Its Consequences* (New York: Hill and Wang).

Petersen, W. (1987), 'Politics and the Measurement of Ethnicity', in Alonso and Starr (eds), 187–233.

Porter, T.M. (1995), *Trust in Numbers: The Pursuit of Objectivity in Science and Public Life* (Princeton: Princeton University Press).

Ragin, C.C. (1994), *Constructing Social Research: The Unity and Diversity of Method* (Thousand Oaks, CA: Pine Forge Press).

Roberts, D. (1987), 'Editorial: Harmonization of Statistical Definitions', *Journal of the Royal Statistical Society*, Series A, 160, 1: 14.

Rose, D. (1995), *A Report on Phase I of the ESRC Review of OPCS Social Classifications* (Swindon: Economic and Social Research Council), available at <http://www.iser.essex.ac.uk/staff/phase-1/frame.htm>.

Rose, D. and O'Reilly, K. (eds) (1997), *Constructing Classes: Towards a New Social Classification for the UK* (Swindon: Economic and Social Research Council [with the Office for National Statistics]).

Ross, D. (1991), *The Origins of American Social Science* (Cambridge: Cambridge University Press).

Royal Statistical Society (1995), 'The Measurement of Unemployment in the UK (With Discussion)' (Report of the Working Party on the Measurement of Unemployment in the UK), *Journal of the Royal Statistical Society*, Series A, 158, 3: 363–417.

Sartori, G. (1984), 'Foreword', in G. Sartori (ed.), *Social Science Concepts: A Systematic Analysis* (Beverly Hills: Sage), 9–12.

Stacey, M. (ed.) (1969), *Comparability in Social Research* (London: Heinemann Educational Books).

Starr, P. (1987), 'The Sociology of Official Statistics', in Alonso and Starr (eds).

Stevens, S.S. (1946), 'On the Theory of Scales of Measurement', *Science* 10, 5 (June): 677–80.

Stevens, S.S. (1975), *Psychophysics* (New York: Wiley).

Stone, R. (1973), 'A System of Social Matrices', *Review of Income and Wealth*, Series 19: 143–66.

Szreter, S. (1984), 'The Genesis of the Registrar General's Social Classification of Occupations', *British Journal of Sociology* 35: 522–46.

Szreter, S. (1996), *Fertility, Class and Gender in Britain, 1860–1940* (Cambridge: Cambridge University Press).

Thurstone, L.L. (1928), 'Attitudes Can Be Measured', American Journal of Sociology 33: 529–54; reprinted with seven other papers from 1928–31 in L.L. Thurstone (1959), *The Measurement of Values* (Chicago: University of Chicago Press).

Woolf, H. (ed.) (1961), *Quantification: A History of the Meaning of Measurement in the Natural and Social Sciences* (Indianapolis: Bobbs-Merrill).

Zebrowski Jr., E. (1979), *Fundamentals of Physical Measurement* (North Scituate, MA: Duxbury Press).

Index